Focusing on the Underserved

Focusing on the Underserved

Immigrant, Refugee, and Indigenous Asian American and Pacific Islanders in Higher Education

edited by

Sam D. Museus
Indiana University

Amefil Agbayani
University of Hawai'i at Mānoa

Doris M. Ching
University of Hawai'i

INFORMATION AGE PUBLISHING, INC.
Charlotte, NC • www.infoagepub.com

Library of Congress Cataloging-in-Publication Data

A CIP record for this book is available from the Library of Congress
http://www.loc.gov

ISBN: 978-1-68123-616-2 (Paperback)
        978-1-68123-617-9 (Hardcover)
        978-1-68123-618-6 (ebook)

CONTENTS

PART I

RACISM, RACIAL POLITICS, AND RACE CONSCIOUSNESS

PART II

ADVANCING RACIALLY CONSCIOUS POLICY AND PRACTICE

PART III

VOICES AT THE MARGINS OF THE COMMUNITY

FOREWORD

Moving the Course of History

Mitchell J. Chang

Nearly 15 years have passed since Frank Wu's groundbreaking book *Yellow* (2002) charged that Asian Americans and Pacific Islanders have historically been largely absent in major civil rights deliberations such as those involving the application of affirmative action in college and university admissions. According to Wu, excluding AAPI from consideration of such deliberations and "relegating us to the role of bystanders suggest(s) that we are neither American nor minorities" (pp. 139–140), putting AAPIs at risk of being "inserted cynically" into civil rights debates (p. 140). Even worse, by not staking out a clear position in those debates, we increase our risk of becoming victimized by racial hysteria incited by those who fear that our academic overachievement—and Asia's ascendency as a region of global power—are undermining normative patterns, values, and practices.

Since *Yellow* was published, many organizations have stepped up more publicly to engage in civil rights issues affecting education on behalf of AAPIs. As Wesley Yang's (2011) provocative *New York Times Magazine* article urged, "... we will need more people with the same kind of defiance, willing to push themselves into the spotlight and to make some noise ... " (p. 11). Given this call, this volume is thus timely and will do more than help make some noise—it can guide this kind of sociopolitical *defiance* by providing an

Focusing on the Underserved, pages ix–xii
Copyright © 2017 by Information Age Publishing

intellectual platform to push Asian Pacific Americans' concerns into the spotlight.

The chapters in this volume illuminate the experiences of those who are often ignored or overlooked in our nation's educational settings, even when a critical mass of AAPIs exists in those settings. Through different empirical approaches of collecting and analyzing data, we come to understand and appreciate better those experiences and issues. Together, the chapters uncover historical, sociological, economic, cultural, and political patterns that shape the circumstances for those populations. Applying a wide range of theoretical frameworks, including Bourdieu's social capital, critical race theory, and TibalCrit, the authors help us interpret those patterns and anticipate their trajectory and future impact. By offering this new knowledge, the chapters provide a very different view of AAPI landscapes, ones that challenge dominant narratives about academic achievement and institutional overrepresentation. More importantly, these chapters show that the multiple interests and issues documented are complex and diverse, yet should not prevent us from taking action through key insights for intervention.

Turning recommendations into political action is where those organizations that have embraced Wu's clarion call for a core place for AAPIs can move this scholarship forward. However, some race-based organizations that seek to adjust imbalances of power actually pursue their agenda strictly as political projects rather than intellectual ones. In the long run, those that fail to engage with the growing empirical knowledge base extended by this volume actually undermine their own organizational mission.

For example, I have been receiving e-mails from an organization called *80-20* after I enthusiastically subscribed as soon as they began a mailing list. The 80-20 website (http://www.80-20initiative.net/about/mission.asp) states that this "Political Action Committee" has the central interest of developing a "SWING bloc" vote in favor of political candidates "who better represent the interests of all Asian Pacific Americans." In the past two years, they have sent numerous e-mails to encourage subscribers to take action *against* race-conscious admissions. The 80-20 organization views such practices as discriminatory and a violation of the civil rights of AAPI applicants. Ultimately, I found their position on this issue to be poorly informed and misguided.

I have conducted numerous studies to inform the legal deliberations of those admissions practices, including one (Chang, Witt, Jones, & Hakuta, 2003) cited by former U.S. Supreme Court Justice Sandra Day O'Conner in the Court's majority opinion upholding the University of Michigan Law School's affirmative action admission policy. I have also written extensively about the potential stakes associated with those policies for Asian Americans (e.g., Chang, 2011, 2015). Accordingly, I find internal conflict in

80-20's civil rights advocacy, which potentially undermines the interests of significant proportions of the AAPI population. Indeed, to address the vestiges of racism, the chapters in this book compel us to foster greater and more varied race consciousness—not less—as a matter of political action and policy intervention.

My point here is not to scrutinize any one group's agenda but to encourage race-based organizations to pursue their agendas as both a political and intellectual project. Ideally, political action emerges from a thoughtful analysis of deeper patterns informed by scholarly research, which then shape the problems and issues that require intervention. Those examinations that empirically test such theoretically informed assumptions increase the chances that the immediate ground-level problems and issues will be addressed at their root causes rather than just on the surface. Race-based organizations guided by political interests alone offer neither a cohesive nor comprehensive agenda for dismantling the root causes of inequality and injustice for AAPIs. Focusing only on political interests may even unintentionally undermine that core mission.

Occasionally, we need to step back from the political fray and more seriously examine the deeply rooted patterns that shape the conditions of the most vulnerable AAPI populations. Certainly, a serious intellectual examination should not simply be a thought experiment, but instead lead to meaningful and sustained actions. The excellent collection of chapters in this volume reinforces the value of carefully conducted scholarship in crafting sensible interventions and helps us move forward. How we move forward, however, still requires more serious attention.

In practice, the pursuit of justice for AAPIs as both an intellectual and political project seems to be a delicate balancing act for race-based organizations. They constantly have to reconcile those two sides as forces pressuring one side may impinge on commitments to the other side. For example, take this balancing act concerning an organization's life source, its financial health. Needless to say, well-funded race-based organizations will have greater capacity, especially when it comes to influencing decision makers at the highest level. In order to have this kind of impact, a high priority for those organizations is to increase the size of their wallet. Subsequently, an organization's political action agenda must appeal to those who can potentially contribute to its financial health. This very practical yet important issue of organizational survival may come at the expense of the intellectual side, as some pressing issues raised through scholarship may lack broader funding traction.

Likewise, consider the delicate balance needed to account for the *particular* as much as the *general* when addressing the diverse needs of AAPIs. On the intellectual side, the recommendations made throughout this volume call for targeting particular ethnic groups, often with even sharper focus on those who reside in specific geographic regions or institutions. Yet, those organizations that tend to have the most capacity and influence also tend to work on a more general level with an eye toward the *collective interests* of Asian Pacific Americans. As such, the more narrowly targeted priorities examined by this intellectual project might not be a high priority for our political counterparts.

Perhaps I have overemphasized here the importance of funding and major organizational support in moving forward academic scholarship, and maybe this scale and scope of action are actually overrated. During Fall 2015, college and university campuses across the nation showed us that grassroots student activism conducted at the local level—even with few resources—can draw meaningful national attention. It remains to be seen, however, if those efforts can be sustained over time in ways that reach more deeply into institutions and more widely across the nation. In any case, we will need to figure out how to apply the important knowledge documented in this volume toward making lasting and meaningful difference for the most overlooked Asian Pacific American populations. While this volume provides us with a deeper understanding of the patterns that make political action necessary in the first place, its long term value will rest not only on whether it contributes to the knowledge base but whether it helps to move the course of history for Asian Americans and Pacific Islanders.

REFERENCES

Chang, M. J. (2011, May 23). Is Harvard worth all the fuss? *Huffington Post.* Retrieved from http://www.huffingtonpost.com/mitchell-j-chang/is-harvard-worth-all-the-_b_865774.html

Chang, M. J. (2015). Amplifying Asian American presence: Contending with dominant racial narratives in *Fisher*. In U. M. Jayakumar & L. M. Garces (Eds.), *Affirmative action and racial equity: Considering the Fisher case to forge the path ahead* (pp. 130–149). New York, NY: Routledge.

Chang, M. J., Witt, D., Jones, J., & Hakuta, K. (Eds.). (2003). *Compelling interest: Examining the evidence on racial dynamics in colleges and universities.* Stanford, CA: Stanford University Press.

Wu, F. H. (2002). *Yellow: Race in America beyond Black and White.* New York, NY: Basic Books.

Yang, W. (May 2011). Paper tigers. *New York Magazine.* Retrieved from http://nymag.com/news/features/asian-americans-2011-5/

TAKING STOCK OF RESEARCH ON ASIAN AMERICANS AND PACIFIC ISLANDERS

The Model Minority Myth, Other Racial Realities, and Future Directions for Research to Advance Racial Equity

Samuel D. Museus

Over the last two decades, scholarship on Asian Americans and Pacific Islanders in higher education has come a long way. Before 2000, there were a handful of articles and book chapters examining specific issues faced by these communities (e.g., Nakanishi, 1995; Osajima, 1995). By and large, however, a body of literature on this population had not developed. Since that time, a small but rapidly growing number of books on Asian Americans and Pacific Islanders in higher education have emerged (e.g., Ching & Agbayani, 2012; McEwen, Kodama, Alvarez, Lee, & Liang, 2002; Museus, 2009, 2013b; Museus, Maramba, & Teranishi, 2013; Teranishi, 2010). In addition, several authored and edited volumes more broadly framed around issues of

Focusing on the Underserved, pages xiii–xxviii
Copyright © 2017 by Information Age Publishing
All rights of reproduction in any form reserved.

race and culture, diversity and equity, and student success in higher education have included works on Asian American and Pacific Islander groups (e.g., Mitchell, 2014; Museus & Jayakumar, 2012; Museus, Ledesma, & Parker, 2015; Sasso & DeVitis, 2015). Journal articles on this population continue to multiply, shedding light on both Asian American and Pacific Islander communities more broadly and ethnic subgroups within these communities more specifically (e.g., Chhuon & Hudley, 2008; Lee, 2006; Maramba, 2008; Museus, 2008a, 2008b, 2009, 2011, 2013c; Museus & Maramba, 2011; Museus & Park, 2015; Museus & Truong, 2013; Museus & Vue, 2013; Park, 2008, 2012; Teranishi & Nguyen, 2012). Larger racial theory and discourse have begun to include the voices and interests of Asian Americans and Pacific Islanders (e.g., McCoy & Rodricks, 2015; Museus & Jayakumar, 2012; Museus, et al., 2015). And, the voices of these communities have informed theoretical frameworks focused on larger issues of inclusion and equity in postsecondary education systems (e.g., Museus, 2014).

In this introduction, I discuss existing literature on Asian Americans and Pacific Islanders. In doing so, I highlight some of the ways in which the racial context within which Asian American and Pacific Islander scholars live and work has shaped our realities as researchers and our scholarship. Then, I utilize this reflection to suggest some ideas regarding what could be fruitful pathways to simultaneously enhancing scholarship on this population and advancing a larger racial equity agenda in higher education. In doing so, I highlight how the contributions within the current book can constitute one piece of a larger and more holistic understanding of Asian American realities in postsecondary education and one element of our efforts to advance the aforementioned larger racial equity agenda.

RACE AND SCHOLARSHIP ON ASIAN AMERICANS AND PACIFIC ISLANDERS

Much of the literature on Asian Americans in education has been a response to dominant hegemonic racial narratives that frame this population as relative model minorities. Although generalizations of Asian Americans as superior minorities arguably predate the mid-1900s, the model minority stereotype that all Asian Americans achieve universal and unparalleled academic and occupational success rose to prominence in the 1960s (Suzuki, 1977). In fact, the rise of the model minority myth as a dominant narrative can be traced back to the 1965 Watts riots. In 1965, when racial tensions between police and the Black community were high, California highway patrolmen pulled over a Black man in Watts, California due to a suspicion that he was driving while intoxicated. Black bystanders perceived the incident as yet another case of police violence being committed toward the Black community, and tensions erupted into a five-day riot that resulted in over 30 deaths and $40 million dollars in property damage. Shortly after these riots, then secretary of labor Moynihan (1965) released a report on the state of race relations in the nation. This report recognized the continuing influence of racism on the Black community, but it also contrasted Black female-headed households and Black male unemployment with what were characterized as the strong family ties and productive cultures of Asian American communities. As a result, the vast majority of U.S. society interpreted the report as suggesting that racial inequalities were largely a result of what society perceived as the dysfunction of Black families in the United States (Fultz & Brown, 2008).

In many ways, the public response to the Moynihan Report crystalized the model minority myth in the public eye and psyche, as it positioned Asian Americans as better than Blacks but not quite as good as Whites in national discourse (Kim, 1999; Wu, 1995). In doing so, the report solidified this honorary White status for Asian Americans and the role of the myth in discounting progressive arguments that racism was a major cause of racial inequalities and significant social problem that must be rectified. As a result, the myth bolstered White supremacy, reinforced notions of meritocracy and deficit perceptions of Black communities, and blamed Black people for existing racial challenges. Not surprisingly, scholars have noted that the utilization of the model minority myth to reinforce racism toward other groups of color can also function to pit Asian Americans against these other communities (Matsuda, 1996; Yu, 2006).

As the model minority myth has evolved over the years, it has been deployed to reinforce systems of racial oppression in multiple ways. In addition to turning Asian Americans into a tool to discount systemic racism that shapes experiences *across* racially minoritized populations, the stereotype has masked the vast diversity and inequalities that exist *within* Asian American communities (e.g., Chew, 1994; Lee, 2006 ; Museus & Kiang, 2009; Ngo, 2006). As a result of the assumption that Asian Americans do not face racial challenges, they are often overlooked in race discourse and their needs are all too often ignored (Museus & Chang, 2009; Museus & Kiang, 2009). Due to these factors, the model minority myth, it could be argued, has been a powerful and pervasive racial force shaping both Asian American experiences within education, as well as their responses to this dominant hegemonic racial narrative.

While few would argue that the model minority myth has had a profound influence on Asian American experiences since the 1960s, the degree to which this stereotype is relevant to Pacific Islanders is debatable. It could be argued that Asian Americans and Pacific Islanders have little in common. Certainly, Asian Americans and Pacific Islanders have distinct histories, cultures, and realities, and we discuss some of these differences in greater detail in Chapter 1.

Nevertheless, the U.S. Census Bureau lumped these two groups into the same racial category until the late 1990s. In doing so, the Census Bureau relied on aggregate statistics that showed relatively high rates of educational and occupational success among Asian Americans and Pacific Islanders, thereby reinforcing misconceptions that these groups are a singular population of model minorities. It was not until 1997 that the U.S. government's Office of Management and Budget acknowledged the distinct realities of these two groups, officially split this category into two separate races, and underscored the importance of disaggregating data from these two communities. The 2000 U.S. Census reflected these changes and recognized Asian Americans and Pacific Islanders as two different racial groups for the first time.

Yet, federal agencies continue to lump these two groups together in certain contexts. For example, some data collected by governmental agencies, such as the NCES enrollment trends over time and projections mentioned above, lump Asian American and Pacific Islanders into the same category and cannot be fully disaggregated. In addition, the qualifying criteria to become an Asian American Native American and Pacific Islander Serving Institutions (AANAPISI), the most recently created federally recognized category of minority-serving institutions, are partly based on the representation of both Asian American and Pacific Islander students among the undergraduate student body within an institution. These examples demonstrate the ways in which dominant forces continue to reinforce the problematic notion that Asian Americans and Pacific Islanders are one overachieving racial group.

A substantial body of literature has emerged deconstructing model minority misperceptions by demonstrating the diversity and complexity that characterize Asian American and Pacific Islander communities. Higher education researchers, for example, have disaggregated national data to highlight inequalities and demonstrate differential experiences within and across Asian American and Pacific Islander communities (e.g., Ching & Agbayani, 2012; Museus, 2013a, 2013b). Scholars have also excavated the voices of Asian Americans and Pacific Islanders to offer critical narratives that challenge the dominant model minority discourse (e.g., Buenavista & Chen, 2013; Kiang, 2002, 2009; Museus & Park, 2015; Vue, 2013). And, these researchers have begun to amass a body of literature that humanizes Asian Americans and Pacific Islanders by revealing their real struggles, sources of strength, and overall lived realities. Such humanization has also functioned to challenge the problematic racial fallacy that they overcome racial barriers and succeed, in ways that other communities of color do not, simply because of their perseverance and hard work.

Asian Americans and Pacific Islanders are racialized in ways that deviate from the model minority myth as well. For example, the perpetual foreigner and yellow peril stereotypes characterize Asian Americans as inassimilable outsiders in their own country and frame them as a threat to Western ways of life (Espiritu, 2008; Kim, 1999; Lowe, 1996). Researchers have posited that these vestiges of nativistic racism and xenophobia of foreigners lead to racist discourse about Asians invading and taking over Western universities (Museus, 2013b). And, they have also linked such racist perceptions to efforts to exclude Asian Americans from selective universities. However, research that examines the ways in which this trope shapes contemporary experiences in higher education is more difficult to find.

Systemic racial oppression also intersects with sexism, classism, and other systems of oppression to racialize subgroups of Asian Americans and Pacific Islanders in distinct ways. In local contexts, for example, many Southeast Asian Americans and Pacific Islanders from under-resourced communities are racialized as deviant or inferior minorities who are disproportionately dropouts, welfare sponges, and gang members (Lee, 1994; Museus & Iftikar, 2013; Ngo & Lee, 2007). Scholars have also underscored the ways in which sexualized racial stereotypes shape the realities of Asian Americans and Pacific Islanders. They have demonstrated how the sexualized racialization of Asian American women shapes the ways that they experience sexual harassment and assault in higher education (Cho, 2003; Museus & Saelua, 2014; Museus & Truong, 2013). They have shed light on how the racial emasculation of Asian American men can influence their experiences and behavior in college by creating systemic pressures to overcompensate and prove their masculinity through harmful behavior such as peer-on-peer violence (Tran & Chang, 2013). Again, however, research that sheds light on the ways in which these sexualized racial stereotypes shape the experiences of Asian American and Pacific Islanders is sparse.

It is important to note that the racial stereotypes discussed above are not simply an object of inquiry for Asian American and Pacific Islander scholars in education. These stereotypes—especially the model minority myth—also shape the ways in which Asian Americans and Pacific Islanders engage in research. As Peter Kiang and I wrote several years ago, focusing on the model minority myth "is not a profound or passionate interest for either of us, but it represents an unavoidable contextual constraint that continually frustrates our own research pursuits" (Museus & Kiang, 2009, p. 11). And, over the years, I have spoken with many Asian American and Pacific Islanders scholars who share this sentiment. Unfortunately, many academic journal reviewers, policymakers, college and university leaders, and the general public often continue to view these communities through a model minority lens. As a result, these contextual realities have necessitated scholarly research that debunks the myth and combats model minority overgeneralizations by cultivating a more complex and authentic narrative of these populations. Therefore, while it is important that Asian American and Pacific Islander scholars go beyond deconstructing the myth, completing ignoring the sterotype could lead to problematically disregarding one of the most powerful racial realities shaping the experiences of these communities today.

EMERGING DIRECTIONS IN SCHOLARSHIP ON ASIAN AMERICANS AND PACIFIC ISLANDERS

Over the last two decades, we have done more than deconstruct simplistic majoritarian racial narratives.[1] First, we have begun to develop a more holistic picture of the realities of these communities within higher education. We have outlined a wide array of systemic challenges faced by Asian Americans and Pacific Islanders in postsecondary education, including glass ceilings, invisibility, sexual objectification, masculinities, and racial tension and hostility (Buenavista & Chen, 2013; Chou & Feagin, 2008; Museus, 2013b; Museus & Park, 2015; Museus & Truong, 2013). We have employed anti-deficit lenses to excavate the ways in which Asian American and Pacific Islander cultures, communities, and families provide sources of strength and facilitate their persistence through college (Chhuon & Hudley, 2008; Kiang, 2002, 2009; Museus, 2008b, 2013c; Museus, Lam, Huang, Kem, & Tan, 2012; Museus & Maramba, 2011; Vue, 2013). Many of us have also underscored the ways in which culturally relevant and responsive campus environments can help Asian American and Pacific Islander students thrive in college (Kiang, 2002, 2009; Museus, Shiroma, & Dizon, 2016).

Second, we have begun highlighting the realities of populations that are often marginalized *within* these communities in higher education, such as transracial Asian American adoptees, undocumented Asian Americans and Pacific Islanders, South Asian Americans, Southeast Asian Americans, and Pacific Islanders (Buenavista & Chen, 2013; Chhuon & Hudley, 2008; Hoffman & Peña, 2013; Kiang, 2002, 2009; Museus, 2013c; Museus, Maramba, Palmer, Reyes, & Bresonis, 2013; Museus et al., 2016; Takeuchi et al., 2008). And, several authors of the current volume build on this earlier work by centering the voices of populations that are often overlooked in discourse on Asian American and Pacific Islander communities. As noted in Chapter 1, however, there is a need for more scholarship on the experiences of these and several other subgroups within this larger population.

Third, we have generated new theoretical frameworks that help explain Asian American and Pacific Islander experiences from a more critical lens and advance larger conversations about racism and racial equity in postsecondary education. For example, we generated the first explicit Asian critical theory (AsianCrit) framework to delineate a set of critical race tenets that provide a conceptual lens for understanding and analyzing the ways in which racism and other systems of oppression mutually shape the experiences of Asian Americans in the United States (Museus & Iftikar, 2014). Similarly, the first Kanaka critical theory (KanakaCrit) framework has outlined a set of propositions that centers Hawaiʻian knowledge in the examination and understanding of Native Hawaiʻian realities (Reyes, 2014). The emergence of these perspectives is a significant development, but such frameworks must be utilized and analyzed for them to help advance larger conversations about racism, colonization, oppression, and equity.

Finally, we have engaged the voices of Asian Americans and Pacific Islanders, as well as other groups of color, to create new frameworks aimed at advancing larger conversations about racial equity (e.g., Museus, 2014). And, some of our colleagues have utilized the voices of Asian Americans and Pacific Islanders to inform programming designed to facilitate success among all underserved students in STEM fields (e.g., Fullilove & Treisman, 1992). Despite these advances, however, the voices of Asian Americans and Pacific Islanders remain relatively marginalized in discourse about racial diversity, inclusion, and equity in postsecondary education.

MOVING FORWARD: FUTURE DIRECTIONS FOR SCHOLARSHIP ON ASIAN AMERICAN AND PACIFIC ISLANDERS IN HIGHER EDUCATION

Although completely letting go of the model minority myth might be problematic, the shifting landscape of the field could suggest that "calling for disaggregated data and debunking the model minority myth may no longer need to be the primary points of our publications" (Chang & Kiang, 2009, x). To be clear, this is not to suggest that research on the model minority myth should be devalued or discontinued, or that scholars should cease clarifying the problematic nature of the myth to contextualize their research. On the contrary, given that the myth is alive and well in education arenas across the nation (Museus & Kiang, 2009), many would argue that it is important to continue disaggregating data and conducting research that challenges this dominant hegemonic narrative. At the same time, Asian Americans and Pacific Islander scholarship "must transcend such analyses to develop diverse lines of inquiry and significant bodies of research that illuminate the realities of [their] experiences" (Chapter 1, p. 3).

Chapter 1 provides an overview of the critical contexts (i.e., environments) and subpopulations that should be explored through future empirical research on Asian American and Pacific Islander populations. Chapter 1 also delineates the elements of a research agenda that would help forge a stronger nexus between scholarly research and the arenas of policy and practice to ensure that our scholarship has an impact. But, what might be some of the most important *aims* of future research on these populations? In the remainder of this section, I highlight three key objectives that might inform future scholarship on Asian Americans and Pacific Islanders. This is not intended to be an exhaustive or definitive list of research priorities, and it could certainly be argued that these efforts are already under way. Nevertheless, this section is aimed at stimulating dialogue about how we might continue to conduct research that is most effective at moving the needle of racial justice forward in postsecondary education.

Unpack the Role of Context

Early waves of Asian American immigrants migrated to the United States to seek a better life (Takaki, 1989). In contrast, more recent Southeast Asian American refugee communities largely migrated to the United States as a result of American imperialism in Asia and war. These Southeast Asian American refugee populations experienced traumatic experiences (e.g., separation from family, political persecution, rape, murder, genocide) that heavily influence the experiences of their communities today (Boehnlein & Kinzie, 1997). Pacific Islander communities have historically also been heavily influenced by U.S. imperialism and militarization of the Pacific (Halualani, 2002; Kanahele, 2005). And, a unique history of colonization shapes the experience of indigenous Native Hawai'ian communities in profound ways (Wright & Balutski, 2013). Yet, research and discourse on the ways in which these historical contexts shape the experiences of Asian Americans and Pacific Islanders within higher education specifically is sparse. Shedding light on this context is critical to advancing knowledge that improves the well-being of Asian Americans and Pacific Islander populations.

Center Voices at the Margins

Those of us who have studied Asian Americans and Pacific Islanders in higher education have worked to center the voices of these communities in research and discourse for some time. However, some might argue that we have privileged certain Asian American and Pacific Islanders voices in these efforts, while marginalizing others. For example, some might argue that the voices of East Asian American populations (e.g., Chinese, Japanese, and Korean Americans) have historically been privileged within the discourse on Asian Americans and Pacific Islanders. While other populations (e.g., Southeast Asian Americans and Pacific Islanders) are often engaged to reinforce the notion that these communities face challenges and warrant attention in higher education, they are not often centered in research efforts themselves. We need more scholarship that examines the populations that have been silenced within the discourse on Asian Americans and Pacific Islanders. Centering such voices, through expanding knowledge of the diverse experiences and perspectives in these communities, also challenges the aforementioned problematic hegemonic racial discourses. As mentioned, Chapter 1 provides a more detailed overview of these critical populations, and the remaining chapters of this book represent one effort to center often marginalized voices within higher education research and discourse.

Conduct More Systemic Analyses

Moving forward, one way that we might advance knowledge on Asian Americans and Pacific Islanders in higher education is through the analysis of systemic realities shaping their experiences within postsecondary education. Although we have cultivated some understanding of the ways in which systemic factors influence the experiences of Asian Americans and Pacific Islanders (Museus, 2013b; Wright & Balutski, 2013), much remains to be learned about these systemic contexts. For example, many articles have discussed the salience of the model minority myth and argued that it leads to the dismissal of Asian American needs (e.g., Museus & Kiang, 2009; Suzuki, 2002), but empirical analyses of the ways in which the myth shapes administrator perceptions and decisions, such as whether to invest in Asian American studies programs or making efforts to hire more Asian American faculty and staff, are difficult to find. This is just one example of gaps in our knowledge about how systemic realities shape Asian American and Pacific Islander realities in higher education.

Engage Larger Equity Conversations

Finally, it would behoove us to consider the ways in which work on our communities can inform larger conversations about diversity, inclusion, and equity. Oftentimes, our work becomes an isolated project—one in which we utilize work on our own communities to contextualize our research, generate findings that illuminate the realities of our communities, and make recommendations that are specific to our population. While this work is certainly valuable in and of itself, we also need to consider viewing our destinies as interconnected with those of other racial communities. The emergence of the model minority myth, discussed in the beginning of this chapter, offers one example of how the fortunes of different racial groups are inherently, systemically, and inextricably intertwined. It behooves us to acknowledge and sometimes center that interconnectedness in our work, so that we can shed light on how the knowledge of Black, Latino, Native American, and multiracial communities might inform our understandings of our own conditions, as well as how we can inform a global agenda to advance racial justice.

THE CURRENT VOLUME

The chapters in the current volume advance each of the three goals outlined in the previous section. They center voices that are often at the margins within the Asian American and Pacific Islander community in higher education, offer critical analyses of systemic racial contexts and their impact on these populations, and discuss the realities of Asian Americans in relation to other racial groups. Chapter 1 is the updated version of an analysis of literature that was conducted by Samuel D. Museus, Anthony Lising Antonio, and Peter Nien-chu Kiang (江念祖) in 2012 and helped frame the inaugural summit of the Asian American and Pacific Islander Research Coalition (ARC). The review identifies the major themes and gaps in existing research on Asian Americans and Pacific Islanders in the field of education, and provides context for the remainder of the volume.

Chapters 2–4 focus on racism, racial politics, and racial consciousness among Asian Americans and Pacific Islanders. In Chapter 2, Sumun Pendakur and Vijay Pendakur discuss the ways in which Asian American students negotiate racial and ethnic identities, and call for policies that actively engage Asian American students in co-curricular programs that focus on the politics of race and racial justice. In Chapter 3, Christin DePouw examines how institutionalized racism shapes the experiences of Hmong students and the ways in which Hmong Studies can provide the space for these students to develop a race consciousness and the tools to advocate for racial justice on their campuses. In Chapter 4, Angela Kong analyzes the experiences of Asian American and Pacific Islander students on a predominantly White campus that experienced racial tension in the climate and in the context of the protests that emerged in response to that unrest.

The next six chapters focus on efforts to advance race-conscious policy and practice geared toward serving Asian Americans and Pacific Islanders. In Chapter 5, Tracy Lachica Buenavista examines trends in policy related to undocumented students and calls for policy that educators and scholars use research to argue and advocate for social and economic sustainability for undocumented students and their communities. In Chapter 6, Natasha Saelua, Erin Kahunawaika'ala Wright, Keali'i Troy Kukahiko, Meg Malpaya

Thornton, and Iosefa Aina discuss the influence of institutionalized counter spaces, such as cultural centers transformed with art and images of Pacific Islander scholars, on student success. Chapter 7 discusses the ways in which Jeffrey Tangonan Acido, Jennifer Farrales Custodio, and Gordon Lee use social biography to transform higher education curricula. In Chapter 8, William Collins, Anna Chiang, Joshua Fisher, and Marie P. Ting discuss institutionalized efforts to provide programs that inform Hmong students of the college application process and financial aid options, and promote their self-efficacy, resilience, development of talents, and academic achievement. Chapter 9 revolves around Mary Ann Takemoto, Simon Kim, Karen Nakai, and Karen Quintilliani's experiences advancing a campus-wide initiative to increase access and success among Cambodian American college students. In Chapter 10, Niki Libarios discusses the underrepresentation of Filipinos at the state of Hawai'i's flagship four-year university and their overrepresentation in Hawai'i's community colleges. He recommends resources, support programs, and development of policy to enable Filipino American students to enroll directly from high school to four-year universities and increase the transfer of students from community colleges to four-year campuses.

The following three chapters focus on centering and highlighting the voices of marginalized populations within the Asian American and Pacific Islander community. In Chapter 10, Leilani Kupo discusses the complexities surrounding questions about the right to claim an identity, which are complicated by government, community, or societal influences. In Chapter 11, Phitsamay Sychitkokhong Uy shares her own narrative and the stories of Southeast Asian American students, and recommends policies to provide culturally relevant training for faculty and staff so that they are more equipped to meet their unique needs. And, in Chapter 12, Loan Dao and Linda Tran examine the voices of Vietnamese American women in college.

Finally, in the conclusion of this volume, Doris Ching and Amy Agbayani compare the challenges that Asian Americans and Pacific Islanders faced decades ago in higher education with those that they encounter today. They end this volume with a call to action and recommendations to advance higher education research, policy, and practice geared toward better serving Asian American and Pacific Islander communities.

NOTES

1. In the remaining sections of this introduction, I use "we" to refer collectively to scholars who have been advancing knowledge about Asian Americans and Pacific Islanders in higher education over the last two decades.

REFERENCES

Boehnlein, J. K., & Kinzie, J. D. (1997). Cultural perspectives on posttraumatic stress disorder. In T. W. Miller (Ed.), *Clinical disorders and stressful life events* (pp. 19–43). Madison, CT: International Universities Press.

Buenavista, T. L., & Chen, A. C. (2013). Intersections and crossroads: A counter-story of an undocumented Asian American college student. In S. D. Museus, D. C. Maramba, & R. T. Teranishi (Eds.), *The misrepresented minority: New insights on Asian Americans and Pacific Islanders, and the implications for higher education* (pp. 198–212). Sterling, VA: Stylus.

Chew, P. K. (1994). Asian Americans: The "reticent" minority and their paradoxes. *William and Mary Law Review, 36*(1), 1–94.

Chang, M. J., & Kiang, P. N. (Eds.). (2009). Higher education [Special issue]. *AAPI Nexus: Asian Americans & Pacific Islanders Policy, Practice, and Community, 7*(2).

Ching, D., & Agbayani, A. (2012). *Asian Americans and Pacific Islanders in higher education: Research and perspectives on identity, leadership, and success.* Washington, DC: National Association of Student Personnel Administrators.

Chhuon, V., & Hudley, C. (2008). Factors supporting Cambodian American students' successful adjustment into the university. *Journal of College Student Development, 49*(1), 15–30.

Cho, S. K. (2003). Converging stereotypes in racialized sexual harassment: Where the model minority meets Suzie Wong. In A. K. Wing (Ed.), *Critical race feminism: A reader* (2nd ed., pp. 349–366). New York, NY: New York University Press.

Chou, R., & Feagin, J. R. (2008). *The myth of the model minority: Asian Americans facing racism.* Boulder, CO: Paradigm.

Espiritu, Y. L. (2007). *Asian American women and men: Labor, laws, and love* (2nd Ed.). Lanham, MD: Rowman & Littlefield Publishers

Fullilove, R. E., & Treisman, E. M. (1992). Mathematics achievement among African American undergraduates at the University of California, Berkeley, CA: An evaluation of the mathematics workshop program. *Journal of Negro Education, 59*(3), 463–478.

Fultz, M., & Brown, A. (2008). Historical perspectives on African American males as subjects of educational policy. *American Behavioral Scientist, 51*(7), 854–871.

Halualani, R. T. (2002). *In the name of Hawaiians: Native identities and cultural politics.* Minneapolis, MN: University of Minnesota Press.

Hoffman, J., & Peña, E. V. (2013). Too Korean to be White and too White to be Korean: Ethnic identity development among transracial Korean American adoptees. *Journal of Student Affairs Research and Practice, 50*(2), 152–170.

Kanahele, P. (2005). I am this land, and this land is me. *Hūlili: Multidisciplinary Research on Hawaiian Well-being, 2*(1), 21–31.

Kiang, P. N. (2002). Stories and structures of persistence: Ethnographic learning through research and practice in Asian American Studies. In Y. Zou & E. T. Trueba (Eds.), *Ethnography and schools: Qualitative approaches to the study of education* (pp. 223–255). Lanham, MD: Rowman & Littlefield.

Kiang, P. N. (2009). A thematic analysis of persistence and long-term educational engagement with Southeast Asian American college students. In L. Zhan

(Ed.), *Asian American voices: Engaging, empowering, enabling* (pp. 21–58). New York, NY: NLN Press.

Kim, J. (1999). The racial triangulation of Asian Americans. *Politics and Society, 27*(1), 105–138.

Lee, S. J. (1994). *Unraveling the model minority stereotype: Listening to Asian American youth.* New York, NY: Teachers College Press.

Lee, S. J. (2006). Additional complexities: Social class, ethnicity, generation, and gender in Asian American student experiences. *Race, Ethnicity and Education, 9*(1), 17–28.

Lowe, L. (1996). *Immigrant acts: On Asian American cultural politics.* Durham, NC: Duke University Press.

Maramba, D. C. (2008). Immigrant families and the college experience: Perspectives of Filipina Americans. *Journal of College Student Development, 49*(4), 336–350.

Matsuda, M. J. (1996). *Where is your body?: And other essays on race, gender, and the law.* Boston, MA: Beacon Press.

McCoy, D. L., & Rodricks, D. J. (2015). Critical race theory in higher education: 20 years of theoretical and research innovations. *ASHE Higher Education Report, 41*(3). San Francisco, CA: Jossey-Bass.

McEwen, M. K., Kodama, C. M., Alvarez, A. N., Lee, S., & Liang, C. T. H. (2002). *Working with Asian American college students: New directions for student services.* San Francisco, CA: Jossey-Bass.

Mitchell, D., Jr. (Ed.). (2014). *Intersectionality and higher education: Theory, research, and practice.* New York, NY: Peter Lang.

Moynihan, D. P. (1965). *The Negro family: The case for national action.* Washington, DC: U.S. Department of Labor.

Museus, S. D. (2008a). The model minority and the inferior minority myths: Understanding stereotypes and their implications for student involvement. *About Campus, 13*(3), 2–8.

Museus, S. D. (2008b). The role of ethnic student organizations in fostering African American and Asian American students' cultural adjustment and membership at predominantly White institutions. *Journal of College Student Development 49*(6), 568–586.

Museus, S. D. (Ed.). (2009). Conducting research on Asian Americans in higher education [Special issue]. *New Directions for Institutional Research, 142.*

Museus, S. D. (2011). Generating Ethnic Minority Success (GEMS): A collective-cross case analysis of high-performing colleges. *Journal of Diversity in Higher Education, 4*(3), 147–162.

Museus, S. D. (2013a). Asian Americans and Pacific Islanders: A national portrait of growth, diversity, and inequality. In S. D. Museus, D. C. Maramba, & R. T. Teranishi (Eds.), *The misrepresented minority: New insights on Asian Americans and Pacific Islanders, and the implications for higher education.* Sterling, VA: Stylus.

Museus, S. D. (2013b). *Asian American students in higher education.* New York, NY: Routledge.

Museus, S. D. (2013c). Unpacking the complex and multifaceted nature of parental influences on Southeast Asian American college students' educational trajectories. *Journal of Higher Education, 84*(5), 708–738.

Museus, S. D. (2014). The culturally engaging campus environments (CECE) model: A new theory of college success among racially diverse student populations. In *Higher Education: Handbook of Theory and Research*. New York, NY: Springer.

Museus, S. D., & Chang, M. J. (2009). Rising to the challenge of conducting research on Asian Americans in higher education. *New Directions for Institutional Research, 142*, 95–105.

Museus, S. D., & Iftikar, J. (2014). Asian Critical Theory (AsianCrit). In M. Y. Danico and J. G. Golson (Eds.), *Asian American Society*. Thousand Oaks, CA: Sage Publications and Association for Asian American Studies.

Museus, S. D., & Jayakumar, U. M. (Eds.) (2012). *Creating campus cultures: Fostering success among racially diverse student populations*. New York, NY: Routledge.

Museus, S. D., & Kiang, P. N. (2009). Deconstructing the model minority myth and how it contributes to the invisible minority reality in higher education research. *New Directions for Institutional Research, 142*, 5–15.

Museus, S. D., Lam, S., Huang, C., Kem, P., & Tan, K. (2012). Cultural integration in campus subcultures: Where the cultural, academic, and social spheres of college life collide. In S. D. Museus & U. M. Jayakumar (Eds.), *Creating campus cultures: Fostering success among racially diverse student populations* (pp. 106–129). New York, NY: Routledge.

Museus, S. D., Ledesma, M. C., & Parker, T. L. (2015). *Racism and racial equity in higher education*. San Francisco, CA: Jossey-Bass.

Museus, S. D., & Maramba, D. C. (2011). The impact of culture on Filipino American students' sense of belonging. *The Review of Higher Education, 34*(2), 231–258.

Museus, S. D., Maramba, D. C., Palmer, R. T., Reyes, A., & Bresonis, K. (2013). An explanatory model of Southeast Asian American college student success: A grounded theory analysis. In R. Endo & X. L. Rong (Eds.), *Asian American educational achievement, schooling, and identities* (pp. 1–28). Charlotte, NC: Information Age.

Museus, S. D., Maramba, D. C., & Teranishi, R. T. (Eds.). (2013). *The misrepresented minority: New insights on Asian Americans and Pacific Islanders, and their implications for higher education*. Sterling, VA: Stylus.

Museus, S. D., & Park, J. J. (2015). The continuing significances of racism in the lives of Asian American college students. *Journal of College Student Development, 56*(6), 551–569.

Museus, S. D., & Saelua, N. (2014). The power of intersectionality in higher education research: The case of Asian Americans and Pacific Islanders in higher education. In D. Mitchell Jr. (Ed.), *Intersectionality and higher education: Theory, research, and practice*. New York, NY: Peter Lang.

Museus, S. D., Shiroma, K., & Dizon, J. P. (2016). A qualitative examination of the impact of community cultural connections on Southeast Asian American college student success. *Journal of College Student Development, 57*(5), 485–50.

Museus, S. D., & Truong, K. A. (2013). Racism and sexism in cyberspace: Engaging stereotypes of Asian American women and men to facilitate student learning and development. *About Campus, 18*(4), 14–21.

Museus, S. D., & Vue, R. (2013). A structural equation modeling analysis of the role of socioeconomic status in Asian American and Pacific Islander students' transition to college. *The Review of Higher Education, 37*(1), 45–67.

Nakanishi, D. T. (1995). A quota on excellence? The Asian American admissions debate. In D. T. Nakanishi and T. Y. Nishida (Eds.), *The Asian American educational experience: A source book for teachers and students* (273–284). New York, NY: Routledge.

Ngo, B. (2006). Learning from the margins: Southeast and South Asian education in context. *Race, Ethnicity, and Education, 9*(1), 51–65.

Ngo, B., & Lee, S. J. (2007). Complicating the image of model minority success: A review of Southeast Asian American education. *Review of Educational Research, 77*(4), 415–453.

Osajima, K. (1995). Racial politics and the invisibility of Asian Americans in higher education. *The Journal of Educational Foundations, 9*(1), 35.

Park, J. J. (2008). Race and the Greek system in the 21st Century: Centering the voices of Asian American women. *The NASPA Journal, 45*(1), 103–132.

Park, J. J. (2012). Asian American women's perspectives on historically White sorority life: A critical race theory and cultural capital analysis. *Oracle: The Research Journal of the Association of Fraternity/Sorority Advisors, 7*(2), 1–18.

Reyes, N. A. S. (2014). *A space for survivance: Locating Kānaka Maoli through the resonance and dissonance of critical race theory.* Paper presented at the 2014 annual meeting of the Association for the Study of Higher Education, Washington, DC.

Sasso, P. A., & DeVitis, J. L. (Eds.). (2015). *Today's college students.* New York, NY: Peter Lang.

Suzuki, B. H. (2002). Education and socialization of Asian Americans: A revisionist analysis of the "model minority" thesis. *Amerasia Journal, 4*(2), 23–51.

Takaki, R. (1998). *A history of Asian Americans: Strangers from a different shore.* New York: Little, Brown & Company.

Takeuchi, D., Hune, S., Andresen, T., Hong, S., Kang, J., Redmond, M. A., & Yeo, J. J. (2008). *Growing presence, emerging voices: Pacific Islanders and academic achievement in Washington.* University of Washington, Washington, DC.

Teranishi, R. (2010). *Asians in the ivory tower: Dilemmas of racial inequality in American higher education.* New York: Teachers College Press.

Teranishi, R. T., & Nguyen, T. K. (2012). Asian Americans and Pacific Islanders and the changing demography of the United States: Implications for education policy. *Harvard Journal of Asian American Policy Review, 22,* 17–27.

Tran, M., & Chang, M. J. (2013). To be mice of men: Gender identity and development of masculinity through participation in Asian American interest fraternities. In S. D. Museus, D. C. Maramba, & R. T. Teranishi (Eds.), *The misrepresented minority: New insights on Asian Americans and Pacific Islanders, and their implications for higher education* (pp. 68–92). Sterling, VA: Stylus.

Vue, R. (2013). Searching for self, discovering community: An examination of the experiences of Hmong American college students. In S. D. Museus, D. C. Maramba, & R. T. Teranishi (Eds.), *The misrepresented minority: New insights on Asian Americans and Pacific Islanders, and their implications for higher education* (pp. 214–234). Sterling, VA: Stylus.

Wright, E. K., & Balutski, B. J. N. (2013). The role of context, critical theory, and counter-narratives in understanding Pacific Islander indigeneity. In S. D. Museus, D. C. Maramba, & R. T. Teranishi (Eds.), *The misrepresented minority: New insights on Asian Americans and Pacific Islanders, and the implications for higher education* (pp. 140–158). Sterling, VA: Stylus.

Wu, F. H. (1995). Neither black nor white: Asian Americans and affirmative action. *BC Third World LJ, 15,* 225.

Yu, T. (2006). Challenging the politics of the "model minority" stereotype: A case for educational equity. *Equity & Excellence in Education, 39,* 325–333.

CHAPTER 1

THE STATE OF SCHOLARSHIP ON ASIAN AMERICANS AND PACIFIC ISLANDERS IN EDUCATION

Anti-Essentialism, Inequality, Context, and Relevance

Samuel D. Museus, anthony lising antonio, and Peter Nien-Chu Kiang (江念祖)

Hours after the murder of six Sikh community members—including one woman and two elders—at their Oak Creek, Wisconsin Gurdwara by a killer with White supremacist ties, Preeti Kaur posted her richly and righteously textured poem, "Letters Home," which included these lines:

Focusing on the Underserved, pages 1–51
Copyright © 2017 by Information Age Publishing

america:
enter
the gurdwara door is open
our bare feet like cracked glass
our covered heads bulletproof from ego
we turn our backs on Bellingham
build our gurdwaras from post traumatic cinder
of bombed birmingham Black church
nina simone sings tera bhaana meetha laage
to tune of mississippi goddamn[1]

Kaur provides a multi-lingual, multi-layered, cross-referencing of that murderous and tragic moment inside the sacred Sikh temple with the domestic terror that targeted African American children, families, communities, and culture during the Civil Rights era. Critical counterstories punctuate other stanzas of her remarkable poem as well—from Angel Island, smallpox blankets, and Hiroshima to napalm, Vincent Chin, post-9/11 murders, and decades of ignored, untaught Sikh American history.

Indeed, as both the local Oak Creek Sikh community and the global Sikh diaspora mobilized resiliently amidst shock and grief in early August 2012, politicians and journalists attempted, albeit briefly, to articulate ethnic-specific expertise regarding Sikh American demographic profiles, migration histories, spiritual practices, and community networks. Their breakthrough insight: Sikhs are not Muslims; Sikhs are not the enemy. Meanwhile, Asian American and Pacific Islander (AAPI) educators, researchers, and advocates collectively wept: "We have been here before … "

Just six weeks earlier, in July 2012, the Pew Research Center, an elite, mainstream public policy think tank, released its first-ever national report on Asian Americans based on census data and related datasets as well as their own nationally administered survey and telephone interviews. They asserted, "Asian Americans are the highest-income, best-educated and fastest-growing racial group in the United States" (Pew Research Center, 2012). National media coverage across print, broadcast, and social media platforms quickly repeated Pew's headline, "Asians Overtake Hispanics," while AAPI educators, researchers, and advocates collectively wailed, "We have been here before … "

These two relatively recent examples reveal deadly and deep gaps in knowledge about and lack of representation for Asian American populations in public and scholarly discourse in 2012 vis-à-vis national politics, research, and media across wide-ranging contexts and levels of analysis. These examples span the disturbing assumptions of an individual mass murderer to superficial portrayals that media professionals communicate to the public, to problematic interpretations by influential scholars that shape institutional priorities and public policies. At the same time, given their absence from these and countless other constructions by and about Asian Americans, Pacific Islander researchers and advocates continue to question the very premise of the AAPI category as a vehicle for indigenous and immigrant Pacific Islander visions (Diaz, 1995, 2004, 2011; Diaz & Kauanui, 2001; Panapasa, Crabbe, & Kaholokula, 2011; Taualii, Quenga, Samoa, Samanani, & Dover, 2011; Young, 2006): "Yes, we have been here before. And yes, we are here again now."

In other recent writings, some of us have optimistically highlighted a "changing landscape for AAPI educational research" (Museus & Kiang, 2009, p. 11), noting that "AAPIs have reached a critical moment in U.S. higher education—a moment described by sociologists as a 'tipping point'" (Chang & Kiang, 2009, p. ix). Chang and Kiang (2009, p. x) posit that "other signs of progress such as the growing AAPI interest group memberships of the American Educational Research Association and the Association for the Study of Higher Education signal a shift in the landscape of the field so that calling for disaggregated data and debunking the model minority myth may no longer need to be the primary points of our publications." This is not to say that disaggregated data and deconstructions of model minority stereotypes are not important. Indeed, they generate critical awareness of the need to pay attention to AAPI populations among those whose way of thinking is still dominated by the myth. Yet, AAPI education scholarship must transcend such analyses to develop diverse lines of inquiry and significant bodies of research that illuminate the realities of AAPI experiences.

By recognizing Kaur's ethnic-specific "post-traumatic cinder" and Pew's aggregate highest-best-fastest analysis as part of the current landscape, however, we are compelled to re-engage with previous generations of AAPI education researchers and practitioners who established and sustained critical national networks of advocacy, representation, and support based on visions of AAPI educational equity since the 1970s. These still-functioning groups include the following:

- National Association for Asian Pacific American Educators (NAAPAE), founded in 1977;
- National Association for the Educational Advancement of Cambodian, Laotian, and Vietnamese Americans (NAFEA), founded in 1979;
- Association for Asian American Studies (AAAS), founded in 1979;
- Association for Asian Pacific Americans in Higher Education (APAHE), in founded 1987;
- Southeast Asian Resource Action Center (SEARAC), founded in 1979;
- Leadership Education for Asian/Pacifics' Leadership Development Program for Higher Education (LDPHE), founded in 1997;
- National Pacific Islander Educator Network (NPIEN), founded in 2001;

- National Education Association's (NEA) Asian and Pacific Islander Caucus;
- National Asian Pacific Islander Scholarship Fund (APIASF), founded in 2003;
- National Commission on Asian American and Pacific Islander Research in Education (CARE), founded in 2008;
- Asian Pacific Islander American Association of Colleges and Universities (APIACU), founded in 2011; and
- Asian American Legal Defense and Education Fund (ALDEF), founded in 1974.

Pioneering associations such as NAAPAE, NAFEA, and AAAS have remained as vital professional resources for their members, despite fundamental shifts in both policy and demography across the areas of K–12 bilingual education, refugee resettlement, and ethnic studies since the 1980s. Nevertheless, questions of mission and capacity have challenged the leadership of every network, particularly as internal generational changes have also redefined their perspectives and priorities.

In addition, nationally convened, multi-year research, advocacy, and policy projects have also left footprints on the education field through their reports and findings, as well as through the networks of collaborative relationships across sectors and communities that they nurtured. These include the following:

- National Coalition of Advocates for Students (NCAS)'s National Asian Family/School Partnership Project, founded in 1997;
- Asian Americans and Pacific Islanders in Philanthropy (AAPIP)'s Project on the Educational Needs of Asian Pacific American Youth, founded in 1998; and
- Asia Society's National Commission on Asia in the Schools, founded in 2001.

"We have been here before . . . " But we choose to gather together again—freshly this time upon the volcanic landscape of a once-violently overthrown Kingdom. We are prepared to hear *tera bhaana meetha laage* with the tune of Nina Simon's *mississippi goddamn*, and more.

SETTING THE STAGE

In the following sections, we examine more than 250 pieces of existing literature on AAPIs in education and share insights that emerged from our analysis. In the next section, we discuss four perspectives from which AAPIs have been viewed as a subject in the literature, which offer an understanding of the ways in which this population is conceptualized and analyzed in educational research. Then, we delve into our review of literature and outline the four major themes that emerged from our analysis of existing scholarship. We conclude our discussion with critical considerations that emerged from this analysis and inform our collective journey to construct a unified voice that can catalyze a new area of research, policy, advocacy, and social justice among AAPIs in education.

Before presenting our analysis and synthesis, a few caveats are warranted. First, we find it appropriate to note that we approach this colossal task with a noticeable measure of humility. We take stock of a massive body of existing literature on an incredibly vast and diverse population and recognize that any effort of this magnitude has limitations. For example, in reviewing such a large body of research on this diverse community and providing a broad analysis and synthesis of that knowledgebase, we acknowledge that we will inevitably compromise some level of depth and complexity. However, the purpose of this endeavor is not to provide an in-depth and intricate understanding of any population or issue in the literature on AAPIs. Rather, we seek to offer one of the most comprehensive appraisals of this body of knowledge to date and identify areas of paucity and density within this research in order to construct a more coherent picture of the knowledgebase on AAPIs in education, provide a foundation for understanding critical directions for future scholarship on this population, and identify and synthesize the critical messages that this body of research has to offer educational policymakers who care about serving the needs of AAPI populations.

Second, we also approached this task with a high degree of determination and recognition that this analysis and synthesis of literature is one important step in a larger agenda to create a more collective and cohesive vision for the AAPI research community in education. Indeed, it is difficult to argue with the notion that we should understand the road that we have traveled and the path on which we find ourselves, in order to make informed decisions about the direction in which we should or must move forward. Thus, we execute this endeavor under the assumption that taking stock of the knowledge that has previously been generated and using that understanding to reflect upon the most pressing limitations of this existing knowledgebase and corresponding critical areas for future scholarly inquiry are essential steps in creating a collaborative and coherent agenda for the AAPI community in education.

Third, we are fully aware that some people—both within and outside of the AAPI community—might jump to conclusions that we are misguided or are being oppressive with the utilization of the AAPI racial categorization. However, we understand that there are histories of marginalization and exclusion of particular subgroups within the AAPI population (e.g., Southeast Asian Americans and Pacific Islanders). We have observed and studied the political tensions between and among various ethnic groups within the AAPI community and between AAPI interest groups with divergent political orientations. We discuss some of the historical, cultural, and structural differences across subgroups. Indeed, we acknowledge that these realities exist and must remain in our consciousness as we engage in any research and advocacy for and with AAPI populations. Yet, we refuse to let these tensions and the resulting dissonance lead us into a state of despair and we hold steadfast to our interest in advocating for and with *all* AAPI communities. Moreover, we intentionally engage these political conditions to inform this project by soliciting input from the AAPI Research Coalition—a group of AAPI scholars from a diverse array of ethnic backgrounds, communities, areas of scholarly expertise, and geographic regions—and asking the coalition to mind their communities' needs and ensure that analysis and synthesis coincide with interests of these AAPI subgroups as well as the common good.

Moreover, we approach this project with the belief that collective advocacy among AAPIs, combined with a continuous critical self-examination and consideration of the diversity and political tensions that exist within this population, can benefit all AAPI communities. We understand that such efforts to advocate for individual ethnic communities and the collective, while still valuing the many forms of diversity that exist throughout the population, is a difficult and continuous negotiation (Coloma, 2006). Nevertheless, historical narrative tells us that multiracial and multiethnic alliances are an important means to community building and advocacy to improve these communities (e.g., Bulosan, 1995; Chin, 1999; Kochiyama, 2004; Trask, 1999). And, we believe that such collective efforts, while challenging, are necessary to make progress in efforts to advocate for and improve the conditions of AAPI populations.

Finally, we review the literature on AAPIs in K–12 and higher education simultaneously, noting areas in which they diverge when appropriate. Our decision to avoid reviewing literature in these two sectors separately is due to our recognition that their two corresponding bodies of literature have more commonalities than differences; reviewing them simultaneously permits a more coherent discussion of the racial, historical, cultural, and structural realities that shape the experiences of AAPIs in navigating both K–12 and higher education systems. We do, however, acknowledge that the policy and organizational contexts that affect AAPIs vary between K–12 and postsecondary education, and we address these distinctions where relevant.

FOUR VIEWS OF THE ASIAN AMERICAN AND PACIFIC ISLANDER SUBJECT IN EDUCATIONAL RESEARCH

Although educational research on AAPI populations is a fairly recent movement, the work can be differentiated by the manner in which AAPIs are viewed as research subjects. We believe that it is important to delineate these views, as the implications of the different views for the continued progress of the research, and more importantly, the welfare and status of AAPI populations are quite important. In her short existence as a research subject in education, the AAPI has been seen as a monolith, subjected to fragmentation, imbued with emerging integrity, and recognized as a community engaged in self-determination. Some of these views have permeated the literature for decades; some have yet to establish visibility as a legitimate alternative subjectivity. All four can be found in current research, and each one contributes to a national conversation regarding the identities of AAPIs and the nature of their relationship to education. We present these four views herein to provide the reader with a thematic backdrop with which to consider past, present, and future educational research that informs policy directives and debates on AAPI individuals and communities.

The Monolith

According to this view, the Asian American, Asian Pacific American, Asian Pacific Islander American, or Asian American and Pacific Islander in educational research is more object than subject. Regardless of the pan-ethnic label used, this view aggregates and essentializes AAPIs into a single monolithic group. Although studies employing this perspective range from understanding positive outcomes (e.g., educational achievement) to negative ones (e.g., maladjustment and mental health issues), the AAPI subject is conceptually barren and culturally flat. These studies are generally comparative with another racial group—typically Whites—and, as such, provide valuable data (vis-à-vis Whites and others) to begin discussions about AAPIs, education, and educational policy. These monolithic portrayals, of course, have limited utility in such discussions as well.

A recent example of work utilizing this view is a comparative study of White-Asian American achievement gaps by Konstantopoulos (2009). Konstantopoulos examined mathematics and reading achievement score differences between the two groups with national survey data between the 1970s and 1990s. Asian Americans, according to the author's own terminology, are grouped together because of the unavailability of disaggregated group membership data, analysis limitations due to the reduction in sample size with disaggregation, and because research on group differences typically uses these broad designations.

Though valuable for providing a foothold on which to claim relevance in educational debates, this monolithic view potentially harms various ethnic and nationality-based AAPI populations in masking or muting positions of disadvantage. This critique has been discussed at length in the scholarly community with regard to the model minority myth, the stereotype portraying AAPIs as academically successful and financially prosperous (Chun, 1980; Suzuki 1977, 2002), which we discuss in greater detail below.

Clearly, much of the existence of this view of AAPIs is due to both the limited availability of educational data on specific AAPI ethnic groups, as well as a tacit acceptance of monolithic categories as legitimate and appropriate. Educational data at any systemic or organizational level—federal, state, local, or school—has rarely been available to researchers in disaggregated form or in large enough sample sizes, leaving the monolithic view as the only alternative to ignoring AAPI populations completely.

Fragmentation and Diversity

AAPI populations, when viewed as multifaceted and comprised of a number of distinctive groups, avoid some of the limitations of the monolithic view. Disaggregation and disambiguation by ethnicity, nationality, and socioeconomic status are the underlying charges of studies framed in this view, resulting in sharper distinctions among populations, visibility for underserved communities, and exposed problematics inherent in the monolithic view.

National census data has most often been used to present and compare various AAPI subgroups. Although the inclusion of and the specific names of groups have varied across administrations of the census, the large sample sizes have allowed researchers to conduct analyses of several AAPI communities, especially in a comparative manner. An early example of this research is Hirschman and Wong's (1984) study of education and socioeconomic inequality between Whites, Blacks, Hispanics, and Japanese, Chinese, and Filipino Americans. Using census data from the 1960s and 1970s, they compared educational effects on earnings across groups. For educational researchers, especially, census data has only limited use; to note, one drawback is that census data does not contain information on schooling characteristics and educational processes. We might think of AAPIs as fragmented in this view, since disaggregation separates, but does little to distinguish among, individual ethnic groups.

In forgoing a monolithic view, a number of researchers have collected their own data or drawn upon appropriate state and institutional education data to pursue an in-depth study of one or more AAPI populations. In addition, more recent Department of Education surveys contain large enough samples of some Asian American ethnic groups to enable disaggregated analyses. With richer databases, these studies bring a comparative picture of diversity in the AAPI educational experience. Examples include the early analysis of Chinese, Filipino, Japanese, Korean, Southeast Asian, and South Asian students with NELS data by Goyette and Xie (1999) and the more recent use of California state educational data by Pang, Han, and Pang (2011) in their study of seventh-grade achievement among 12 distinct AAPI subgroups.

Moving Towards Subjectivity—Integrity

As a more integrated subject, scholars have treated AAPIs as complex, contingent, and context-bound participants in society and education. Studies imagine AAPIs as fully subjective actors in organizations and a society complexly infused with racism, subcultures, and larger social structures. The depth, contours, differences, and similarities of numerous AAPI groups are both objectives and contingencies of scholarly inquiry.

Much of this work is necessarily ethnographic and localized, as scholars pursue non-stereotyped, taken-for-granted meanings and experiences that characterize the lives of specific communities inside and outside of educational contexts. Stacey Lee's (1996) work is characteristic of this integrated view, including her seminal book, *Unraveling the "Model Minority" Stereotype*. More recently, Nguyen and Brown (2010) explore language use and style behavior among adolescent Hmong to reveal heterogeneity within a group typically distinguished by little more than their status as refugee-immigrant AAPIs. Mixed method studies also demonstrate this view, such as Zhou and Kim's (2006) case studies of supplementary education in four Korean and Chinese American communities.

Moving Towards Self-Determination

This view envisions the potentials of power, position, and influence of AAPIs in education. Educational leadership, political involvement, and resistance over oppression are among the foci of scholarship that animate this view. Research that maintains this view of AAPIs is still relatively scarce. The most active line includes those studies that utilize perspectives drawn from critical race theory, which seeks to expose racism and racist structures that limit or constrain full AAPI engagement in educational processes and organizations (Buenavista, Jayakumar, & Misa-Escalante, 2009; Museus, Ravello,

& Vega, 2012; Teranishi, 2002). As we discuss below, empirical investigations of leadership are only beginning to emerge, such as Moua's and Riggs (2012) recent study of Hmong women leaders in education, politics, business, and health professions and Neilson and Suyemoto's (2009) study of Asian American executive administrators in higher education.

Grouped in this way, we can see how each view impacts how AAPIs are conceptualized, examined, and consequently, positioned in policy discourse. With these four views as a conceptual backdrop, we now turn to a discussion of the substantive research areas addressing AAPI education.

CORE AREAS OF SCHOLARSHIP ON ASIAN AMERICANS AND PACIFIC ISLANDERS IN EDUCATION

In the following sections, we provide our analysis and synthesis of the existing literature on AAPIs in education. First, we discuss four core areas of scholarship on AAPIs that are characterized by relatively high density, while also noting the limitations of research in these areas. Second, we provide an overview of areas of scholarly inquiry on AAPIs in which a paucity of literature exists. We structure this section on gaps in the knowledgebase around populations that are invisible in the literature (i.e., *who* we need to study as we move forward), critical issues that are understudied (i.e., *what* we need to examine to advance knowledge), and important considerations in methodology (i.e., *how* we should analyze these populations and issues). Finally, we conclude this chapter with a discussion about the implications of this analysis of existing scholarship for future research and policy in education.

Our analysis and synthesis of the literature on AAPIs reveals that education scholars have generated a significant amount of literature in four primary core areas. These four bodies of literature are not mutually exclusive, but rather overlap and are interconnected in many ways. The four areas in which scholars have created a knowledgebase with substantial density in AAPI education are *anti-essentialism, inequality, context,* and *relevance.*

Anti-Essentialism: Stereotype Deconstruction and Demystification

Arguably the most pervasive theme in the literature on AAPIs in education is the anti-essentialism that permeates this discourse. Essentialism refers to the notion of a uniform essence to a group's experience or, in the case of AAPIs, that there is a singular AAPI experience (Grillo, 1995; Harris, 2003). Put another way, essentialism is a process by which the dominant majority forces AAPIs and other racial groups "into an essentialized and totalized unit that is perceived to have little or no internal variation" (Ladson-Billings, 2000, p. 260). Thus, the dominant narrative categorizes, perceives, and treats the wide array of AAPI ethnic groups with diverse histories, cultures, communities, languages as one monolithic population (Kiang, 1996, 2006; Lee, 1994; 1996; Museus, 2009; Museus & Kiang, 2009; Suzuki, 1989, 2002), and assigns this group race-related attributes through the process of racialization (Omi & Winant, 2002).

Although the essentialization and racialization of AAPIs occur in many ways, and can depend on the actors involved (see, for example, Tavares, 2008), two stereotypes have been discussed more extensively than others in the literature on AAPIs in education (Ancheta, 2000): the aforementioned model minority myth and the perpetual foreigner stereotype. The most commonly discussed stereotype in this body of research is the model minority myth, which refers to the notion that AAPIs achieve uniform, universal, and unparalleled academic and occupational success (Lee, 1994; Museus, 2009; Museus & Kiang, 2009; Pendakur & Pendakur, 2012; Suzuki, 1989, 2002). In fact, a majority of researchers who study AAPIs in education are forced to demystify the model minority myth in order to justify the need to expend energy studying and learning about AAPIs (Museus & Chang, 2009; Museus & Kiang, 2009). Indeed, a substantial body of anti-essentialist literature demystifies this portrayal through a more complex picture of AAPIs. First, scholars have sought to better understand the nature of the model minority myth by deconstructing the stereotype and identifying the variety of assumptions that contribute to its perpetuation. Such assumptions include the misconceptions that AAPIs are not really racial minorities, do not face race-related challenges, do not require support, and are all socially awkward math nerds (e.g., Lee, 2011; Museus & Kiang, 2009; Museus & Park, 2012).

Second, researchers have invested a significant amount of energy in demystifying the myth and complicating existing understandings of the experiences of AAPIs in K–12 and higher education by disaggregating data and highlighting the ethnic, socioeconomic, and other heterogeneity that exists within this population (e.g., Baker, Keller-Wolff, & Wolf-Wendel, 2000; Buenavista et al., 2009; Chang, 2011; Chang, Park, Lin, Poon, & Nakanishi, 2007; Chou & Feagin, 2008; Government Accountability Office [GAO], 2007; Kiang, 1995, 1996, 2002, 2009; Lee, 1994, 1996, 2001, 2011; Lee & Kumashiro, 2005; Museus, 2009, 2011, 2013; Museus, Maramba, Palmer, Reyes, & Bresonis, 2013; Museus & Park, 2012; Museus & Truong, 2009; Ngo, 2006; Ngo & Lee, 2007; Suyemoto, Kim, Tanabe, Tawa, & Day, 2009; Teranishi, Ceja, Antonio, Allen, & McDonough, 2004). These scholars have engaged in anti-essentialism by disaggregating data to underscore important ethnic and socioeconomic disparities that exist within the AAPI category.

Researchers have also furthered anti-essentialist perspectives by examining how intersecting identities interact in complex ways to shape the experiences of AAPIs (Abbas, 2002; Awaya, 2000; Buenavista & Chen, 2013; Buenavista et al., 2009; Cho, 2003; James, 1994; Joshi, 2006; Kiang, 1991, 2002, 2009; Kumashiro, 1999, 2001; Lee, 2006, 2011; Lei, 2003; Maramba & Museus, 2011; Meyers, 2006; Museus, 2011; Museus & Griffin, 2011; Museus & Maramba, 2011; Museus & Vue, 2013; Nghe, Mahalik, & Lowe, 2003; Ngo, 2002, 2006; Ngo & Lee, 2007; Park, 2012; Pepin & Talbot, 2013; Tengan, 2002). This latter body of literature has begun to clarify how racial, ethnic, gender, sexual orientation, religion, socioeconomic, immigrant, and refugee identities interact to mutually shape individual experience. There is, however, much empirical research to be done in this area of intersectionality among AAPIs. For example, it is very difficult to find scholarship on how masculinities shape the experiences, academic choices, and educational outcomes of AAPIs. Similarly, there is a paucity of literature on experiences of South Asian Muslims in the education literature. And, to a large extent, the diverse ways in which lesbian, gay, bisexual, and transgender identities uniquely shape the experiences of AAPIs in education remains unexplored. These are just a few examples of areas that require further exploration and understanding; many more exist and are ripe for inquiry.

It is important to note that some groups occupy a unique space in the discourse on academic success (Chhuon & Hudley, 2011; Lee, 1994; Museus, 2013; Museus et al., 2013; Ngo & Lee, 2007). Specifically, Southeast Asian Americans and Pacific Islanders, while often being lumped into the AAPI category and racialized as model minorities in national contexts, are also essentialized as deviant minorities (e.g., school dropouts, welfare sponges, gang members) in other localized contexts. Consequently, education researchers studying Southeast Asian Americans have attempted to demystify both the model minority and deviant minority stereotypes in order to develop a more authentic understanding of this subpopulation (e.g., Lee, 2011; Ngo & Lee, 2007; Vue, 2013). Alternatively, how these contradictory stereotypes shape Pacific Islander experiences has not been systematically and thoroughly examined.

Third, researchers have begun to uncover some of the negative consequences of the model minority myth (Kiang, 2006; Kim & Yeh, 2002; Museus, 2008; Museus & Park, 2012; Suzuki, 1989, 2002). For example, scholars have discussed the reality that many K–12 and college educators hold stereotypical views of AAPIs that are characterized by the model minority myth, which ultimately and negligently results in an absence of programs, practices, and efforts to meet these students' needs (e.g., Kiang, 2006; Suzuki, 2002). In addition, researchers have asserted that AAPI students can face immense pressures to live up to the unrealistic expectations of perfection that are perpetuated by the myth (Chung, 1997; Fisher, Wallace,

& Fenton, 2000; Huang, 1997; Lee, 2011; Museus, 2008; Museus & Park, 2012; Siu, 1996). This pressure has also been associated with AAPI students choosing not to engage or seek help out of a fear of failing to conform to the model minority myth and revealing that they face challenges and need support (Lee, 2011; Museus, 2008; Museus & Park, 2012). Finally, there is some indication that the model minority stereotype can lead to "choking" in examinations under extreme pressures (Cheryan & Bodenhausen, 2000), but this relationship is not yet well understood.

In contrast to the model minority myth, the forever foreigner stereotype casts Asian Americans specifically as indefinite foreigners who can never be full citizens with equal status (Ng, Lee, & Pak, 2007; Tuan, 1998). While this stereotype emerged hundreds of years ago, relatively recent academic research suggests that this stereotype is alive and well (Jo, 2004; Lee, 2006; Lei, 2003; Museus & Park, 2012). However, while these studies show that the forever foreigner stereotype contributes to negative views of Asian Americans in general, the ways in which this stereotype shapes the experiences of Asian Americans in K–12 and higher education are not well understood (Ng et al., 2007). Also absent from the education literature is a thorough discussion of whether this perpetual foreigner stereotype affects the experiences of Pacific Islanders in education. Asian Americans are racialized as exotic Orientals and this is different than the way mainstream society racializes Pacific Islanders, but it can be argued that the dominant majority in the United States exoticizes and otherizes the latter group as well, albeit in different and unique ways. Yet, much remains to be learned about these stereotypes and their impact on Pacific Islanders' experiences in K–12 and higher education.

In sum, a large body of the existing literature focused on racial stereotypes of AAPIs has centered on deconstructing and demystifying the model minority myth. This scholarship has also examined ethnic and socioeconomic diversity within the population and begun to illuminate the complex ways that multiple identities shape the experiences of AAPIs. Yet, many gaps remain in this body of research on racial stereotypes in AAPI education. We believe that future research should shed further light on the myriad ways that intersecting identities shape the lives of AAPIs, as such scholarship both furthers anti-essentialist goals and illuminates a more realistic picture of the experiences of groups and individuals within this population. But, we also feel that researchers should develop a more thorough understanding of the ways that both the model minority and forever foreigner stereotypes might affect the experiences of AAPI administrators, faculty, and students in K–12 and higher education. Specifically, we believe that researchers should move beyond discussing the reality that the model minority myth leads to the dismissal of AAPIs' needs and explore the ways that both of these stereotypes systematically and directly influence AAPIs' interpersonal interactions, cognitive development, psychosocial well-being, identity formation, sense of belonging, and professional success in education.

Inequality: Excavating Disparities in the Education Pipeline

Interconnected with the first theme of anti-essentialism is the reality that scholars studying AAPIs in education have invested significant energy problematizing work on this population by illuminating inequality faced by AAPIs in various spheres of K–12 and higher education (Chang et al., 2007; Ching & Agbayani, 2012; GAO, 2007; Hune, 2002; Jayakumar & Museus, 2012; Kiang, 2002; Lee & Kumashiro, 2005; Museus, 2009, 2011, 2013; Museus & Chang, 2009; Museus & Kiang, 2009; Museus, Palmer, Davis, & Maramba, 2011; Ngo & Lee, 2007; Suzuki, 1989, 2002; Teranishi, Behringer, Grey, & Parker, 2009; Teranishi et al., 2004). These researchers have made efforts to construct convincing arguments regarding why education scholars should be concerned about and pay attention to AAPIs in education. As is often the case in educational research, these scholars have primarily made their case via the illumination of racial, ethnic, and socioeconomic disparities.

A substantial body of research underscores the ethnic and socioeconomic inequalities that exist within the AAPI population at the national level (e.g., Ching & Agbayani, 2012; Hune, 2002; Jayakumar & Museus, 2012; Kiang, 2002; Lee & Kumashiro, 2005; Museus, 2009, 2011, 2013a; Museus & Kiang, 2009; Museus et al., 2011; Teranishi et al., 2004). These analyses invariably show that Southeast Asian American and Pacific Islander students graduate from high school, transition into higher education, and graduate from college at lower rates than other AAPI groups and the overall national population. They also offer some indication that first-generation and low-income AAPIs, regardless of ethnicity, graduate high school, attend college, and attend selective colleges at lower rates than their continuing generation and more affluent counterparts. It is important to note, however, that analyses of ethnic and socioeconomic disparities in college degree attainment among those who matriculate into postsecondary education are virtually non-existent. Unfortunately, as we discuss below, data that permit such examinations are difficult to find.

Also noteworthy is the fact that the relationship between ethnicity and educational success within the nation is geographically context-specific (Museus, 2013). For example, researchers have noted that, while Filipino Americans have relatively high rates of success nationally, they earn high school diplomas, attend college, and graduate from higher education at lower rates than all AAPIs and the general population in the state of Hawai'i

(Museus, 2013; Okamura, 2008). Yet, empirical analyses that disaggregate by region and state are few and far between, and there is a need for a better understanding of disparities that exist within different geographic regions of the nation. Such analyses can generate a more complex picture of AAPIs in education, but also help state and local policymakers pinpoint and understand how to serve the AAPI communities most in need.

Existing evidence also indicates that AAPIs are underrepresented at post-college stages of the pipeline in education. In graduate education, for example, there is some existing evidence that AAPIs in doctoral education, as a whole, complete their degrees at lower rates than their majority peers (Council of Graduate Schools, 2009). Yet, with very few exceptions (Museus, Mueller, & Aquino, 2013), researchers have not yet thoroughly examined the experiences of AAPI students in graduate education. Such research is essential to understanding leaks in the pipeline to leadership in various professions, including the pipeline to leadership positions in both K–12 and postsecondary education.

Indeed, scholars have also shed light on the underrepresentation of AAPIs in educational leadership positions. In the K–12 sector, researchers have discussed the underrepresentation of AAPIs among school board members, principals, and K–12 teachers (e.g., Kiang, 2006). For example, in 2008, AAPIs constituted more than 4% of the national population (National Center for Education Statistics [NCES], 2011), but they made up less than 1% of the nation's elementary and secondary school principals. Moreover, Asian Americans comprised only 1.3% and Pacific Islanders comprised only 0.2% of the nation's high school teachers (NCES, 2011).

A cursory glance at aggregate statistics indicates that AAPIs are overrepresented in college faculty ranks. Whereas in 2010, AAPIs constituted approximately 6% of the national population, they made up 8.2% of faculty nationwide (NCES, 2011). However, these figures conflate international and domestic faculty, as well as faculty from many diverse ethnic groups, within the AAPI population. Unfortunately, sufficient data are not available that permits the disaggregation of this population to see whether particular subgroups are underrepresented in the faculty ranks or AAPIs are underrepresented in specific disciplines, and we discuss this in more detail below. AAPIs are also underrepresented in executive and managerial positions in higher education (NCES, 2011; Yamagata-Noji & Gee, 2012). In fact, they comprised only 3.4% of all full-time executive and managerial positions in colleges and universities, with slightly higher representation at four-year (3.5%) than at public two-year institutions (2.6%).

Unfortunately, in both K–12 and higher education, there is a paucity of research that sheds light on the factors that might contribute to this underrepresentation in educational leadership or the variables that positively and negatively influence AAPI administrators' career trajectories. At the K–12 level, one systematic analysis revealed that Asian Americans had low levels of interest in teaching because they felt obligated to enter fields that were more financially lucrative for their families, they perceived that perfection was required of educators, concerns about having to work with populations from different cultures, and a lack of understanding of the value of having Asian American teachers educating Asian American students (Gordon, 2000). One limitation of this inquiry was focused on first- and second-generation Asian Americans, whose ties to their ethnic heritages are still relatively strong (Ng et al., 2007). Another reason discussed for the lack of Asian Americans in K–12 leadership positions is the notion that they are likely to select ethnic enclave majors and professions, where they can find other Asian Americans and shield themselves from discrimination. Once again, inquiries into the barriers for Pacific Islanders' pursuit of educational leadership positions are virtually nonexistent.

At the higher education level, researchers have offered some hypotheses regarding the factors that might pose barriers to AAPIs progressing into executive leadership positions (Adrian, 2004; Committee of 100, 2005; Neilson & Suyemoto, 2009; Yamagata-Noji & Gee, 2012). These variables include institutional racism, negative perceptions of Asian cultural leadership styles, and the absence of a pool of qualified candidates to compete for executive level positions. However, these hypotheses are largely based on the viewpoints of a few senior administrators. Systemic empirical inquiries into the factors that hinder and catalyze AAPIs' decisions to pursue leadership positions in both K–12 and higher education are critical for expanding the knowledgebase on AAPIs in education. While there is some evidence that AAPI faculty are underrepresented in certain fields and they face a glass-ceiling within the faculty ranks, making them less likely to earn tenured positions or pay equal to their majority counterparts, this literature is sparse (Lee, 2002; Yan & Museus, 2013).

In conclusion, extant scholarship in K–12 and higher education underscores the reality that AAPIs are underrepresented in various spheres of education. However, in terms of empirical evidence that illuminates the causes of these disparities, we have much to research and learn. It is imperative that education scholars who study AAPI populations in education produce more research that examines the factors that influence Southeast Asian American and Pacific Islander students' educational trajectories, variables that hinder and promote AAPI graduate students' success, and the forces that positively and negatively influence AAPIs pathways to educational leadership positions in both K–12 and higher education.

Context: Analyzing Intersecting Historical, Cultural, and Structural Forces

The third theme that emerged from our review is the pervasive and critical role of context in shaping the experiences and outcomes of AAPIs in education. When we use the term context, we refer to the historical, racial, cultural, and structural factors that are external to educational institutions and create the conditions within which AAPI communities and individuals live. Existing literature underscores that these factors have a salient influence on the experiences and outcomes of AAPIs, particularly Asian Americans, in education.

Various AAPI ethnic communities have distinct historical contexts that include stories of immigrants, refugees, and indigenous peoples (Chan, 1991; Okihiro, 1994; Portes & Rumbaut, 1996; Takaki, 1989). These histories play a critical role in differentially shaping AAPI communities. For example, many East and South Asian communities migrated from societies in which educational attainment was a primary means to social mobility and immigrated to seek increased opportunity (Takaki, 1989; Zhou & Kim, 2006). In contrast, many Southeast Asian Americans entered the United States as war refugees after American military intervention in Southeast Asia. Thus, they migrated to the West to escape political persecution and most of them came to rebuild lives that had been disrupted by war and displacement. During migration, many Southeast Asian American refugees experienced or witnessed separation from family, disease, mass starvation, rape, murder, and mass execution (Abueg & Chun, 1996; Boehnlein & Kinzie, 1997; Kinzie, 1989). Southeast Asian American refugees and their children bring these experiences and, sometimes, resulting trauma into education classrooms (Han, 2008; Kiang, 2002). Alternatively, Native Hawaiʻian culture and identity has been, in part, shaped by a history of colonization by the West, American attempts to commit cultural genocide and force assimilation upon the Native Hawaiʻian community, and a movement to revitalize Hawaiʻian culture and community (Halualani, 2002; Kanahele, 2005; Labrador & Wright, 2011; Young, 2006). Finally, other Pacific Islander populations (e.g., Samoan, Chamorro, Guamanian, Micronesian, etc.) have a history that includes both U.S. colonization in their homeland and immigration to the United States (Heine, 2002). One of the most significant implications of these differences in histories is the fact that some communities have migrated to seek Western society, while Western society has been imposed upon others.

The aforementioned historical forces play an important role in shaping the conditions and experiences of AAPI students. First, these historical realities are intertwined with the cultures and structures that AAPI students' navigate throughout their educational careers, and we discuss these cultural and structural forces in more detail below. However, there is some evidence that these historical contexts also directly shape the experiences, perspectives, and strengths that AAPIs bring with them into the education system. For example, Southeast Asian American undergraduates' refugee stories can shape their views about survival, overcoming barriers, and persisting through college (Kiang, 2002, 2009). There is also a body of research indicating that second-generation Southeast Asian Americans' intergenerational knowledge of the struggles and sacrifices of their family can shape their views about succeeding in education (Museus, 2013; Ngo & Lee, 2007). Much remains to be learned about how historical contexts directly shape other AAPI groups' (e.g., Pacific Islanders) perspectives about academic success.

Many researchers have examined the influence of cultural contexts on AAPI students' experiences and outcomes (Caplan, Choy, & Whitmore, 1991; Freeman, 1995; Goto, 1997; Heine, 2002; Kiang, 2002, 2009; Kibria, 1993; Min, 2003; Museus, 2008, 2011, 2013; Museus, Lam, Huang, Kem, & Tan, 2012; Museus & Maramba, 2011; Museus & Quaye, 2009; Ngo, 2002, 2008; Penning, 1992; Qin, 2006; Robbins, 2004; Zhou & Bankston, 1998; Zhou & Kim, 2006). This body of research somewhat varies between K–12 and higher education. In the K–12 sector, a substantial body of existing literature has focused on how Asian American cultural values (i.e., community and family values) either facilitate or hinder their educational success (Ngo, 2002, 2006; Ngo & Lee, 2007). Specifically, scholars have discussed how cultural values that emphasize educational attainment and responsibility to family are responsible for the success of Asian American students (e.g., Min, 2003; Ogbu, 1987; Zhou & Bankston, 1998), while others have discussed how conflict between cultural values and the perspectives of mainstream society pose challenges for Southeast Asian Americans (Heine, 2002; Ngo, 2002). It has been noted that these cultural difference or cultural conflict perspectives must be used with caution because they can lead to oversimplified conceptualizations of complex family influences, contribute to the misconception that cultures are static, and foster a deficit way of thinking about students from particular undeserved AAPI ethnic groups and blame the cultures of Southeast Asians for their struggles (DePouw, 2006; Lee, 2006; Ngo, 2002, 2006; Ong, 1996; Zhou & Kim, 2006). While such blame-the-victim way of thinking has not been thoroughly analyzed in literature on Pacific Islanders in education, there is some indication that Samoan students in K–12 education have reported being stereotyped as uneducated troublemakers in Hawai'i (Mayeda, Pasko, & Chesney-Lind, 2006). Much more research is needed, however, to understand fully the ways that these stereotypes shape the experiences and outcomes of Samoan and other Pacific Islander students in varied geographical and social contexts.

In contrast, the literature on cultural influences on AAPI experiences and outcomes in postsecondary education is couched within a larger body of literature that focuses on the interactions between home and campus cultures (e.g., Chhuon & Hudley, 2008; Jayakumar & Museus, 2012; Kiang, 2002, 2009; Museus, 2008, 2011; Museus et al., 2012, Museus & Maramba, 2011; Museus, Maramba et al., 2013; Museus & Quaye, 2009). Whereas the aforementioned K–12 research focuses on cultural values, much of this higher education scholarship emphasizes how AAPI students who come from cultures that are more incongruent with those found on their respective college and university campuses than their peers are more likely to face increased challenges adjusting to, connecting to, and persisting through their respective institutions of higher education. Researchers producing knowledge in this area emphasize the importance of institutions adapting to bridge the distance between their campus cultures and the home cultures of their AAPI students. While this research is incredibly informative, almost all of it is qualitative in nature. We believe that this body of knowledge can be enhanced significantly by quantitative analyses of the effects of institutional adaptation to diverse AAPI ethnic groups' cultural backgrounds on AAPI experiences and outcomes.

Education scholars have underscored the fact that structural forces also play a role in shaping the experiences of AAPIs. For example, poverty has been identified as one barrier that negatively impacts Southeast Asian Americans (Conchas, 2006; Long, 1996; Root, Rudawski, Taylor, & Rochon, 2003; Smith-Hefner, 1999; Um, 1999, 2003; Xiong, 1996). In addition, unequal access to resources, limited access to high-quality teachers, fewer curricular options, and tracking practices have been discussed as salient influences on the experiences and opportunities of AAPI and other students (Darling-Hammond, 2003). In addition, some evidence suggests that social networks and the resources that are tied to these networks partly shape student success (Bourdieu, 1986; Lareau, 2011; Museus & Neville, 2012; Stanton-Salazar, 1997). Indeed, scholars have highlighted how social networks that are developed and exist within AAPI communities can provide critical support structures—namely supplementary education programs and youth advocacy organizations—for AAPI students as they navigate the education pipeline on the way to college (Kiang, 2006; Zhou & Kim, 2006).

Researchers have highlighted the fact that history, culture, and structure interact to shape the lives of AAPIs (McGinnis, 2007; Zhou & Kim, 2006). Drawing from a multiple case study, for example, Zhou and Kim (2006) illuminated how Chinese and Korean American communities' that originated in societies that valued education as means to social mobility were linked to cultural values that were brought with these communities and manifested in these groups investing existing resources to create community education structures. While Zhou and Kim's analysis made a major contribution to our understandings of the limitations of focusing on one contextual factor (e.g., culture or structure) and advanced our understandings of the ways that these larger social forces intersect, the scholarship in this area has only just begun to emerge.

A significant body of literature discusses the racial contexts that shape the experiences of Asian Americans and Pacific Islanders (Buenavista et al., 2009; Chang & Kiang, 2002; Chou & Feagin, 2008; Cress & Ikeda, 2003; Diver-Stamnes & Lomascolo, 2001; Hune & Yeo, 2010; Kiang, 1995, 1996, 2006; Lagdameo et al., 2002; Lew, Chang, & Wang, 2005; Lewis, Chesler, & Forman, 2000; Museus, 2008, 2011, 2013; Museus & Park, 2012; Museus & Truong, 2009; Smedley, Myers, & Harrell, 1993; Tang, 2006). As mentioned above, researchers have discussed how AAPIs face pressures to conform to the model minority stereotype. However, existing research also shows that AAPIs face linguistic discrimination via historical and contemporary assaults on bilingual education in K–12 education. AAPIs also face daily racial prejudice and discrimination in both K–12 and higher education. This racial prejudice and discrimination can vary in intensity and include racial isolation, racial exclusion from the curriculum, racial slurs and jokes, racial harassment and bullying, and racial hate crimes that even lead to murder (Cho, 2003; Davis & McDaid, 1992; Hune & Yeo, 2010; Kiang, 1996; Kiang & Kaplan, 1994; Kurashige, 2000; Museus & Park, 2012; Suyemoto, Kim et al., 2009). Despite the importance of racism in the lives of AAPI students, few systematic empirical inquiries focus specifically on developing holistic frameworks to understand the various ways that racism shapes the daily experiences of Asian Americans in educational institutions (Cress & Ikeda, 2003; Lewis et al., 2000; Museus & Park, 2012; Sue, Bucceri, Lin, Nadal, & Torino, 2007). With few exceptions (Hune & Yeo, 2010), empirical investigations into the ways that racism influences the everyday experiences of Pacific Islanders in education are difficult to find, suggesting that there is much work to be done in this area of inquiry.

It is important to note that there is evidence that ethnic prejudice and discrimination also exist *within* the AAPI population (Lee, 2001; Pyke & Dang, 2003). Although these dynamics are not thoroughly examined, the limited evidence that does exist suggests that divisions within the AAPI community can engender negative prejudicial attitudes toward Southeast Asian Americans who come from under-resourced communities (Lee, 2001). Scholars have also documented how Korean Americans and Vietnamese Americans label their co-ethnics—who are either seemingly assimilated or deemed too ethnic—as "Whitewashed" and "FOBs" (i.e., fresh-off-the-boat) (Pyke & Dang, 2003). They note that these dynamics result from larger societal racism that AAPIs internalize and enact to categorize their peers. Sometimes AAPIs' internalization of racism and racial categorization of members of their own ethnic groups are directly intertwined with education, as researchers have examined how working-class Korean Americans otherize their co-ethnics as "acting White" if they are too studious or academically oriented (Lew, 2006). Again, research on within-race prejudice and discrimination is sparse. And, while such scholarship might be difficult because it can uncover negative realities about AAPI communities, it is absolutely necessary to fully address the tensions that exist among AAPI populations.

The aforementioned racial contexts go beyond their effects on daily interactions among AAPIs and people in their environment, and they shape the actual identities of AAPIs themselves (Alvarez, 2002; Ibrahim, Ohnishi, & Sandhu, 1997; Kim, 1981; Museus, Vue, Nguyen, & Yeung, 2013; Nadal, 2004; Renn, 2000).

An emerging body of literature examines how racial contexts shape the individual identities of AAPIs. This literature has evolved from Kim's (1981) development of a progressive racial identity stage model, to state models that take both race and ethnicity into account (Ibrahim et al., 1997; Nadal, 2004), to models that paint a more complex picture of the ways that shifting racial contexts interact with individual identities in complex, non-static, non-linear, and continuously fluid ways (Accapadi, 2012; Kiang, 2002; Museus, Vue et al., 2013; Renn, 2000). This body of literature remains underdeveloped and more research needs to develop alternative ways of viewing various racial and ethnic identity development processes within the AAPI population in order to test whether these frameworks offer valid lenses for viewing AAPI identity development.

In sum, the literature on AAPIs in education underscores the ways that historical, cultural, structural, and racial contexts shape the lives of individuals within this population. Again, however, limitations in this body of knowledge exist. For example, research on how these larger societal forces shape the lives of Pacific Islanders is difficult to find. Moreover, the intersection of historical, cultural, structural, and racial forces are seldom the specific focus of empirical inquiry; much remains to be learned about the ways that these factors mutually shape the experiences of specific AAPI subpopulations.

Relevance: The Promise of Culture and Community in Transformative Education

The final theme that emerged from our analysis is the concept of relevance. Specifically, educational researchers have developed a small body of knowledge that focuses on the importance of educational systems and institutions constructing and delivering education that is relevant to the AAPI cultures and communities.

This body of research responds to the reality that AAPI populations are generally excluded from mainstream school, college, and university cultures (Jayakumar & Museus, 2012; Kiang, 2006; Museus, Lam et al., 2012) and it identifies culturally relevant spaces, curricula, and pedagogies as critical elements of transformative education—that is, education that stresses social justice by empowering people and communities from oppressed groups (Suyemoto et al., 2009).

At the K–12 level, scholars have discussed the positive impact of bilingualism and bilingual education on student development, cognitive development, cultural knowledge acquisition, English language learning, and community building (Crawford, 1986; Garcia, 1993; Hakuta, 1998; Hakuta & Diaz, 1985; Hakuta & Gould, 1987; Pang, Kiang, & Pak., 2003; Pease-Alvarez & Hakuta, 1992; Snow & Hakuta, 1992; Willig, 1985; Yamauchi, Lau-Smith, & Luning, 2008). Despite the range of potential positive outcomes of bilingual education programs, however, researchers have noted that federal education policies (including No Child Left Behind, among others), well-funded ballot initiatives, and relentless attacks on bilingual education by English-only movement advocates have successfully weakened bilingual education programs and hindered the nation's ability to fully realize the benefits of bilingual education (Kiang, 2006; Wright, 2007). In doing so, they have severely limited students' opportunities to learn multiple languages or learn and maintain their heritage language in particular (Beykont, 2000; Crawford, 1992).

It can be argued that all communities of color, and therefore all AAPIs, are forced to go through a process of language shifting or language loss as they become more integrated into Western society. However, it is important to note that scholars have distinguished between the language loss of immigrant and indigenous groups of color (Hinton, 2001). While immigrant groups' languages are maintained in their countries or regions of origin and immigrants of color often have the ability to learn their heritage language via courses or visits to their homeland, indigenous languages are at greater risk of becoming extinct. Arguably, this reality then makes language revitalization and maintenance higher stakes for indigenous populations such as Native Hawai'ians and corresponding research shows that the Native Hawai'ian community has developed promising bilingual education programming that are both generating positive results and can inform such efforts in other communities (Au, 1997; Au & Carroll, 1997; Warner, 2001; Yamauchi, 2003; Yamauchi et al., 2008). To clarify, however, we do not argue that language revitalization and maintenance is not important for immigrant groups of color as well. In fact, we believe that language revival and conservation of all AAPI groups has profound positive implications for individuals, as discussed above, as well as for enriching the diversity of the larger society.

Language is inextricably intertwined with culture. A small but growing body of research shows that institutional spaces, programs, practices, curricula, and pedagogies that incorporate elements of these students' cultural backgrounds and identities into programming and curriculum engage and validate the cultural backgrounds of AAPIs (Chan, 2000; Chang & Kiang, 2002; Kiang, 1997, 2002, 2009; Museus, 2008, 2011, 2013; Museus, Lam et al., 2012; Museus & Maramba, 2011; Museus & Quaye, 2009; Suyemoto, Tawa et al., 2009; Tang & Kiang, 2011; Vue, 2013; Yamauchi, 2003). By and large, this literature shows that such culturally engaging and validating education can promote a stronger sense of identity, foster a sense of belonging and cohesion, facilitate learning and success, and contribute to the creation of spaces in which students can develop a sense of civic responsibility. All too often, however, these culturally engaging and validating elements of education are isolated to ethnic enclaves that exist within broader school and college environments. Moving forward, we believe that this body of research has the potential to profoundly transform the way educators across society think about structuring education programs, practices, and curricula for AAPIs and other students of color. However, one limitation of this research is that it is almost all qualitative in nature; it lacks the development, testing, and validation of new theoretical frameworks that is necessary to generate a highly visible body of knowledge that can begin to tinker, let alone shift, mainstream discourse about the delivery of K–12 and higher education.

Education researchers have also discussed the potentially positive role of community and family engagement in the education of AAPIs in education (Chan, 2000; Kiang, 1997, 2002; Museus, Lam et al., 2012; Warren, Hong, Rubin, & Uy, 2009; Yamauchi et al., 2008). This body of literature underscores a possible bidirectional relationship whereby communities and families can make valuable contributions to AAPI students' educational experiences and outcomes, and schools and postsecondary institutions can create educational experiences that allow faculty, staff, and students to work together to positively impact communities. Regarding community impact on AAPIs' educational experiences and outcomes, Zhou and Kim's (2006) study shows that Chinese American and Korean American communities created vital supplementary education programs for their students, but the impact of community organizations on the education of AAPIs has not often been the focus of systematic empirical inquiry.

Regarding parental influences on education, research paints a complex and sometimes contradictory picture. Early research shows that Asian American parents were less involved and that their involvement negatively affected their students in K–12 education (Desforges, 2003), but more recent data and analyses suggest that Asian American parents are more involved than some other racial groups, and that this involvement is *positively* associated with expectations to achieve higher levels of education (Museus,

Harper, & Nichols, 2010; NCES, 2011). These contradictions could partially be a function of the socioeconomic status and level of acculturation of Asian American parents. Regarding the implications of socioeconomic status, there is some evidence that working-class Asian American parents work long hours and are unable to help their children navigate the education system (e.g., the college choice and application process), while middle- and upper-class Asian American parents have been found to gather information about various educational options from school administrators, teachers, and friends to inform their children's college-going decision-making processes (Lew, 2004; Louie, 2001). In addition, research indicates that newly immigrated Asian American parents who are less acculturated can experience intergenerational conflict with their children who adapt to Western society more quickly through their school and peer networks, resulting in these parents becoming detached from their children's lives (Louie, 2001; Qin, 2006).

The impact of culture differences on the involvement of Asian American parents in their children's lives, however, is further complicated by societal racism (Lee, 2001). Specifically, Lee found that 1.5-generation Asian American students maintain more traditional values about education in the eyes of their parents, remain isolated from mainstream peers at school, and downplayed the instances of racism because they were able to compare it with less desirable circumstances in their countries of origin. In contrast, she found that second-generation Asian Americans were viewed as having lost their traditional cultural heritage in the eyes of their parents and were skeptical that education was an effective means of social mobility that could overcome racial oppression in American society. Again, the cultural dynamics that exist within Pacific Islander families and how they shape the educational attitudes and experiences of Pacific Islander students are virtually nonexistent and require future exploration.

Finally, one of the many intersections between K–12 and higher education that has been discussed in the literature on AAPIs is the role of ethnic studies (e.g., Asian American studies, Hawai'ian studies, and Pacific Island studies) in teacher education programs (Furumoto, 2003; Kiang, 2004; Tintiangco-Cubales, Kiang, & Museus, 2010). It has been noted that most people who enter the K–12 teaching profession are White and have limited experience with Asian American students (Goodwin, 2002). Similarly, most of these individuals have limited experience and understanding of Pacific Islander populations. If left unaddressed, these individuals will likely view their students, at least partially, through the lens of racial and ethnic stereotypes. And, as discussed, above, this can be detrimental for AAPI students. Thus, scholars have underscored the potentially powerful positive impact that ethnic studies programs can have on a wide range of outcomes, including teacher professional development, positive AAPI student outcomes, and engagement of AAPI communities and parents in education (Kiang, 2006).

While the role of ethnic studies programs in the development of faculty and staff in higher education has not been discussed in-depth in the literature, this area also holds potential for conducting informative and transformative future scholarly inquiry and improving the experiences of AAPI college students. Indeed, many institutions of higher education have centers for teaching and learning, as well as professional development courses and workshops for college faculty and staff. Moreover, at some institutions, such as UMass Boston, ethnic studies programs have been intentionally engaged in the delivery of these programs. Nevertheless, this remains an understudied area in the literature on AAPIs in education.

In summation, the literature on AAPIs emphasizes the importance of education that is relevant to the cultures and communities of AAPI students. However, there is much more room for high-impact work in this area, including the role of relevance in the experiences of Pacific Islanders, the development and (in)validation of theories testing the impact of cultural relevance on AAPI outcomes, and the role of AAPI ethnic studies programs in the professional development of teachers in both K–12 and higher education.

In the previous section, we reviewed extant literature to identify areas of relative density in the knowledgebase on AAPIs and the limitations of research in each of these areas. This review allows us to also identify areas in which little empirical knowledge exists. In the following "Critical Populations" section, we briefly summarize the AAPI groups that are the most invisible in the education knowledgebase and that we believe are essential target populations for future inquiry. Then, in the "Critical Foci" section, we discuss areas for future scholarly inquiry that are most pressing and deserve immediate attention. Finally, in the "Critical Issues" in educational research section, we present vital considerations in constructing a scholarly agenda that is aimed at effecting change through educational policy.

CRITICAL POPULATIONS FOR FUTURE RESEARCH ON ASIAN AMERICANS AND PACIFIC ISLANDERS IN EDUCATION: TOWARD GREATER INCLUSION AND UNDERSTANDING

One of the most troubling conclusions from our comprehensive review of literature on AAPIs is the fact that various subgroups within this population have been marginalized or excluded from educational research. We find several groups that lack voice in the AAPI education knowledgebase. Although many of these groups are highlighted in some articles and book chapters, the research lacks any holistic picture of their experiences and lives.

Three groups of AAPI ethnic populations remain understudied and are not well understood. In addition to AAPI ethnic populations, several other groups can be distinguished by various social identities and are marginalized or excluded from existing educational research:

- *Pacific Islanders* exhibit some of the lowest rates of educational attainment of all racial and ethnic groups in the nation (Museus, 2011, 2013; Wright & Balutski, 2013). Yet, while these groups are often invoked when discussing inequalities in K–12 and higher education, disheartening is the reality that they are virtually invisible in the literature that is aimed at generating an authentic picture of the conditions, realities, and lives of AAPIs in both sectors of education. Perhaps it should be said here that we find important studies on Native Hawaiʻian education often outside of the mainstream educational literature (e.g., Goodyear-Kaopua, 2009; hoʼomanawanui, 2008; Kaomea, 2009, 2011). We recognize that this reflects back to and implicates larger structural factors. We strive to make this literature visible to the educational community as we see such work having the potential to frame the ways in which we can approach and critique teaching and learning in Native Hawaiʻian communities and perhaps extend these approaches to other PI communities.

- *Southeast Asian Americans* also face drastic disparities in educational attainment. And, like their Pacific Islander counterparts, they are often invoked in discussions about disparities within the AAPI category in higher education research, but rarely the focus of empirical analysis, particularly in higher education. While this reality is beginning to shift and there is an increasing body of knowledge on Southeast Asian American students in postsecondary education (e.g., Chhuon & Hudley, 2008; Kiang, 2002, 2009; Museus, 2013; Museus, Maramba et al., 2013; Vue, 2013), much work needs to be done to excavate the challenges and success of these populations.

- *South Asian Americans* are virtually invisible in the literature on AAPIs. South Asian Americans' high rates of educational attainment might lead to difficulty problematizing scholarly inquiry on this group and their automatic dismissal as a viable focus of empirical research. Indeed, with few exceptions (e.g., Abbas, 2002; Cole & Ahmadi, 2010), they have not achieved a noticeable level of voice and visibility in research on AAPIs in education and, given the post-9/11 rise in xenophobia targeted toward this population, the black box in knowledge that obscures their experiences, challenges, and needs is highly problematic.

- *Multiracial AAPIs* are almost invisible in the education literature. While a handful of studies explore mixed-race identity in college and experiences with prejudice and discrimination in higher education (Museus, Lambe Sariñana, & Kawamata-Ryan, 2015; Museus, Lambe Sariñana, Yee, & Robinson, in press; Renn, 2000), these inquiries are few and far between. Given that multiracial individuals comprise a significant and growing proportion of the population, particularly among AAPIs, this is a critical area for future inquiry.

- *Transracial AAPI Adoptees* are yet another population that is virtually invisible in the education knowledgebase. Although these individuals comprise a significant population in the United States and have been examined in fields outside of education (e.g., Hoffman & Vallejo Peña, 2013; Johnston, Swim, Saltsman, Deater-Deckard, & Petrill, 2007), there is little existing knowledge regarding the unique challenges and experiences encountered by them as they navigate the education system.

- *Low-Socioeconomic AAPIs* (e.g., low-income, first-generation in college, urban) are another critical population for future examination. The little evidence that does exist on this group suggests that they face distinct inequalities and unique challenges that are not well understood but must be comprehended if policymakers and educators hope to provide these students with optimal educational opportunity (e.g., Museus, 2013; Teranishi et al., 2004).

- *Lesbian, Gay, Bisexual, Transgender, Queer, and Ally (LGBTQA) AAPIs* have been labeled a double-minority because they can become marginalized within both their racial and sexual orientation identity groups. Indeed, LGBTQA AAPIs' racial, sexual orientation, and other identities mutually shape their experiences in complex and unique ways (Chan, 1989). Given the continued systemic and individual prejudice and discrimination that exists toward sexual orientation minorities in society, it can be argued that education scholars have a moral obligation to understand the experiences of these individuals within the AAPI community in ways that can effectively inform policy and practice toward this segment of the population.

- *Undocumented AAPIs* are another AAPI subpopulation that has rarely been the focus of scholarly debate or systematic empirical inquiry. With few exceptions (Buenavista & Chen, 2010; Buenavista & Chen, 2013), scholars have not made efforts to understand the unique experiences of this population. Given the malicious attacks that have continuously been launched against this population over the past decade and the negative implications of these assaults for undocumented AAPIs, we believe it is essential that AAPI scholars develop a foundation of knowledge that can both expand our understanding of the diverse and unique experiences that exist within the AAPI category, but also inform larger debates about immigration and immigrant education.

- *AAPI Military Recruits and Veterans* who navigate a life to and through the U.S. military also have distinct experiences that can help us better understand the AAPI population and inform larger social discourse around the intersection of education and militarization. On one hand, both literature and common sense tell us that some AAPIs, like other students of color, choose to enlist in the military as a means to access higher education. However, only a few studies exist on this population in education (Kiang, 1991), and the implications of these choices on the lives of AAPIs who seek a higher education and eventually enter college campuses constitute another black box.

- *AAPIs in Community Colleges* comprise 40% of the AAPI college student population and 15% of all two-year college students (Kiang, 1992; Lew et al., 2005). Yet, only a few studies examine these students' experiences and outcomes (Makuakane-Drechsel & Hagedorn, 2000; Yang, Rendón, & Shearon, 1994). Therefore, this is a critical area for future scholarship. Such scholarship can not only demystify assumptions about model minority AAPIs all attending prestigious colleges and universities, but can also help generate a more authentic understanding of AAPI experiences in education.

- *The "Other"* is also a critical population of future inquiry on AAPIs. When we say the "other," we refer to non-AAPIs' perceptions, attitudes, and perspectives about AAPI populations. A few studies have begun to shed light in this area (Delucchi & Do, 1996; Liang & Sedlacek, 2003), and these inquiries shed useful light on the negative racialzed views that college educators hold toward Asian American students and how it negatively affects the experiences of the latter, as well as provide insight on how to identify problematic misperceptions and target resources to address them to improve the educational experience for these students. These studies, however, are sparse.

CRITICAL FOCI FOR FUTURE RESEARCH ON ASIAN AMERICANS AND PACIFIC ISLANDERS IN EDUCATION: TOWARD A MORE HOLISTIC PICTURE OF OUR LIVES IN CONTEXT

Our second area for future inquiry centers on critical foci. To frame this section, we adapt an existing theoretical model that highlights the varied layers of an individual's environment (Bronfenbrenner, 1979). In doing so, we identify four levels of environment that shape the experiences of AAPIs in education, for better or worse, and can and should be better understood through scholarly inquiry on this population. We do not claim to cover every critical area of inquiry in each of these environmental levels, but we offer some examples that emerged from our literature analysis and synthesis:

- *Global and Geopolitical Environments* are the most macro-level environmental layer that shapes the lives of AAPIs in education. As such, these environments are not typically the focus of empirical inquiry in education. However, they do play a profound role in the experiences and outcomes of AAPI students. For example, higher education scholars have written about the trend toward the internationalization of higher education and popular press has underscored the influx of international Asian students entering American college and university campuses (e.g., McMurtrie, 2001). Not only does this influx signal another growing population of Asian descent that college educators know little about and are ill-equipped to serve, but it also has implications for how domestic Asian Americans are viewed and beg questions regarding the extent to which colleges and universities are able to meet the needs of this population once they matriculate.

  At the same time, post-9/11 discourse around terrorism and war undoubtedly have negative effects on the experiences of South Asian Americans and as education scholars, researchers, and activists from AAPI communities, we have a moral responsibility to understand and address these realities. Moreover, as the years pass and an increasing number of AAPI and other veterans return home and enter postsecondary education with post-traumatic stress disorder and other war-induced challenges, college educators must be equipped with knowledge of how to effectively serve and educate this population.

  Beyond individual AAPIs' entrance into and return from the military, scholars have noted that militarization intersects with education to shape the experiences of AAPIs. Moreover, these intersecting factors impact the lives of indigenous Native Hawai'ian and Other Pacific Islander populations in unique ways (Wright & Balutski, 2013). However, the small body of literature addressing these realities in education focuses on describing the historical context and the importance of understanding it. This makes sense, given that, clearly a majority of K–12 and postsecondary educators across the nation probably do not understand the historical context of militarization in the Pacific and its damaging effects on Pacific Islander populations. However, moving forward, we believe that we should begin to ask more questions about how this militarization affects the choices, identities, and educational pathways of Pacific Islander populations.

And, because of their intimate knowledge of these realities and connections to these communities, more Pacific Islander researchers must be developed and authentically engaged in this work.

- *Political and Policy Environments* at the national level are another source of environmental influences on AAPI students' educational trajectories. Although not often discussed in the literature on AAPIs, some scholars have discussed the complex intersections between federal education policies on AAPIs in K–12 education (e.g., Kiang, 2006). This discourse suggests that, as federal policymakers make decisions about accountability systems, standardized testing, reward structures, and funding allocations, many of the real social problems faced by AAPI populations, such as the intentional efforts to eradicate bilingual education and blatant exclusion of AAPI voices from school curricula, go unaddressed and continue to fester.

We also see critical national political and policy issues that span both K–12 and higher education affecting AAPI populations, while simultaneously failing to include and reflect voices from these communities. Over the last decade, immigration policies, policing and deportation of immigrants, and immigrant access to higher education have emerged as some of the most controversial topics in political and policy areas. Yet, while these issues affect both Asian Americans and Pacific Islanders who are undocumented, these populations have been silenced and their voices excluded in this discourse.

As political tensions around undocumented immigrant populations has emerged, 35 year-old national debates about the need, morality, and future of affirmative action have re-emerged, as the Supreme Court gears up to hear the third case challenging the use of race-conscious admissions policies in the last decade. As Chang (forthcoming) notes, while AAPIs have been relegated to the role of serving as a tool to support both pro- versus anti-Affirmative Action debates in the past, the current case has excavated AAPI voices, signaling a possible movement toward self-determination in policy arenas. Future scholarship, however, must shed light on the ways that AAPIs are affected by affirmative action, and the elimination of race-conscious admissions policies to inform the debates that exist within the AAPI community and between AAPI and other racial and ethnic groups.

In the area of federal financial aid policies, research on financial aid in higher education clarifies a trend toward increasing tuition costs coupled with increasing sizes of financial aid awards and an increased reliance on loans in the construction of financial aid packages (Museus, 2010). Given that AAPI students and other students of color are less likely than their peers to view it as appropriate to go deeply into debt to pay for their education, this trend could prove detrimental for many AAPIs. This is a particularly important area of inquiry with regard to Southeast Asian Americans and Pacific Islanders, who already face racial and ethnic disparities that could be exacerbated by these trends.

- *Community and Family Environments* have been underscored in the scholarly discourse on AAPIs and, as discussed above, play a critical role in the lives of AAPI students (Kiang, 1996; Museus, 2013; Museus et al., 2016; Warren et al., 2009; Zhou & Kim, 2006). However, while the influences of community and family on Asian American students' outcomes have been the focus of extensive scholarly inquiry in K–12 education (Ng et al., 2007; Ngo & Lee, 2007), literature systematic empirical research has been conducted on the influence of Asian American communities and families on their students' outcomes in college or the impact of Pacific Islander communities and families on their students' outcomes in both K–12 and higher education.

As we mentioned in the preceding sections of this discussion, the exclusion of AAPI cultures and communities from school, college, and university curricula is problematic. The message sent by this omission is that AAPIs have not contributed to the development of America, do not have valuable knowledge and voices to be heard, and should detach from their cultural heritage and communities to be a full member of American society. Such exclusion may not only hinder the engagement and success of AAPI students, but the absence of AAPI voices from the knowledge that is shared in educational institutions can also be devastating to the identity development and psychological well being of AAPIs and other students of color. While scholars have noted this exclusion (Kiang, 2006; Lewis et al., 2000; Museus, 2013), we must begin utilizing empirical research to unpack the ways that the systemic exclusion negatively affects the academic, psychological, and social outcomes on AAPI students and the ways that this reality can be addressed. As we discuss above, ethnic studies programs provide salient models regarding how to address this exclusion. Moreover, research that examines the impact of these programs on student outcomes can strengthen the case for their institutionalization (e.g., Kiang, 2009; Museus et al., 2016). However, given that a larger number of students never have the opportunity to connect with ethnic studies programs, we must not be content with the creation and maintenance of these programs, but instead link them to a broader agenda of institutional transformation in schools, colleges, and universities through diversification of faculty bodies and the professional development of faculty and staff in educational institutions. And, these efforts at institutional transformation must also be evaluated.

In the preceding sections, we mention that the relationship between educational institutions and communities is bidirectional, with each having the potential to positively transform the other. Again, however, a comprehensive knowledgebase that details the ways in which ethnic studies programs and classes, co-curricular community engagement activities, and service-learning initiatives specifically impact AAPI communities is missing. Such information can contribute to greater understandings regarding the possibilities of fostering flourishing university-community partnerships that positively transform both entities in profound ways.

- *Institutional Environments* comprise the most fourth and final environmental influences that we discuss herein. While there are many areas that can be further explored to benefit current levels of understanding about AAPIs, we focus on three of them. First, a fairly large body of literature has now revealed how racialized institutional (and societal) environments affect the experiences of AAPI faculty and students in both K–12 and higher education (e.g., Buenavista & Chen, 2013; Buenavista et al., 2009; Cress & Ikeda, 2003; Kiang, 1992, 1996; Lewis et al., 2000; Museus, 2008; Museus & Park, 2012; Museus & Truong, 2009; Tavares, 2008). However, some gaps remain and, as we discuss above, we need a fuller understanding of how environmental stereotypes negatively affect the experiences, choices, and outcomes of AAPIs. We need a more established knowledgebase of the ways that racism manifests in the experiences of Pacific Islanders in education.

  Ethnic enclaves provide safe havens for AAPIs and other people of color in relatively unwelcoming larger institutional environments in education (Museus, 2008; Museus & Quaye, 2009), and ethnic studies programs offer one type of critical enclave for AAPI students across the nation. Yet, on some campuses, AAPI students continue to struggle to establish ethnic studies courses and programs (Museus & Park, 2012). And, we suspect that research plays a role in clarifying the potential benefits of such programs to better inform institutional decision-makers and communities about whether they should be advocating for the development of such structures. Indeed, we believe a clearer picture about the potential challenges and benefits of the development of ethnic studies programs is critical to informing such decisions.

  A fairly recent development in the policy arena is the federal designation of Asian American Native American and Pacific Islander

Serving Institutions (AANAPISIs). Several institutions serving large numbers of AAPI and low-income students have applied to and been approved for the federal designation, as well as federal funds that have been developed to support AAPIs at the AANAPISI campuses. The federal funds that have been allocated are being utilized for a variety of different purposes depending on the institutions' student bodies, their existing structures, and their missions. A critical area of inquiry at these sites is whether or not the programs and activities that are being implemented significantly affect student experiences and outcomes. Thus, examinations of the AANAPISI campuses must go beyond descriptive comparisons and encompass the utilization of qualitative, longitudinal survey, and experimental studies so that we can develop a better understanding of what does and does not work, in order to inform future programmatic efforts geared toward AAPIs at AANAPISI and other institutions.

CRITICAL ISSUES IN FUTURE EDUCATIONAL RESEARCH ON AAPIS: TOWARD A PRESENCE IN THE SCHOLARSHIP–POLICY–PRACTICE NEXUS

As a research community, there are a number of issues to consider with regard to the process of producing future scholarship on AAPI education. Our concern here is to identify those with particular importance to the scholarship–policy–practice nexus, a space where research not only has policy implications and not only where policy and practice reference a particularly supportive study, but rather, a space where research and policy agendas or programs are jointly developed, discussed, prepared, and pursued. We identify three essential elements to fostering a scholarship–policy–practice nexus that can thrive: the availability of rich disaggregated data, communication, and crucial collaboration.

Availability of Rich Disaggregated Data

As is clear from the preceding discussion, data on AAPIs—its availability and form—is central to the specific formation of the AAPI subject and consequently, the nature of the scholarship–policy–practice nexus. Monolithic views invite solidarity and coalition building to the scholarship–policy–practice nexus, but they can also render smaller communities and their policy and programmatic concerns invisible. Diverse, integrated AAPI subjects may be more visible but contribute to a fragmented view of AAPIs as a whole. Aggregation and disaggregation of AAPI data, therefore, is not an either/or proposition for educational researchers. Approaches to the aggregation issue must be strategic.

The analysis of aggregated data is often the only option for researchers. Large federal databases like the National Education Longitudinal Survey of 1988 (NELS), the Education Longitudinal Study of 2002 (ELS), and the High School Longitudinal Study of 2009 (HSLS) oversample AAPI students to produce sample sizes large enough for cross-racial analyses. As racial issues in education are often publicly imagined and politically engaged in as comparative—the Black–White achievement gap, affirmative action as helping Blacks, Latino/as, and Native Americans and hurting Whites and Asian Americans, ethnic studies as anti-White—aggregated data provides researchers with samples that allow for AAPI representation in the analysis of such issues. Disaggregated samples in these databases are only borderline adequate for some AAPI subgroup analyses and wholly inadequate for smaller communities (e.g., Hmong, Vietnamese, Samoan, Thai) and analyses that require further sample identification (e.g., Filipina women, Japanese American immigrants). When national data is preferred, particularly for reasons of representativeness and generalizability, they should be used with full understanding—and disclosure—of the implications of aggregated data for providing actionable data for all AAPI communities. Further, analytical steps should be taken where possible to counter tendencies to overlook critical differences between AAPI subgroups, such as the use of interaction terms with subgroup identifiers and control variables that help identify important sources of intra-AAPI variation such as gender, student/parent/grandparent immigrant status, native language, parents' educational attainment, and family income/wealth.

Two of the major themes in AAPI educational research that we have identified in this paper are best supported by analyses of rich, disaggregated data of individual AAPI populations. Disaggregated data is required both to produce anti-essentialist scholarship and to expose educational disparities suffered by AAPIs in both the K–12 and higher education sectors. The stumbling block, of course, is the availability of data rich enough and expansive enough to pursue such research agendas. Researchers have taken advantage of public datasets that allow disaggregation, and significantly, have undertaken their own data collection efforts when national or state programs have been insufficient. While we graciously recognize these efforts, we also highlight the poor availability of public data programs that are designed to fully disaggregate AAPI populations and collect data that is necessary to inform the critical policy and programmatic issues that emanate from the themes we have labeled anti-essentialism and inequality. Efforts to simply oversample a monolithic AAPI population do not produce the necessary data. The collection of student data at any level—federal, state, district—needs to maintain the objective of producing data capable of characterizing both the larger communities (i.e., Chinese, Japanese, Korean,

Filipino, and Indian Americans) and the smaller but critical ones for educational policy and programming (i.e., Hmong, Vietnamese, Lao, Pakistani, Hawai'ian, Samoan, Guamanian). In other words, data programs should be designed to generate samples that achieve statistical representation *and* be appropriately augmented to facilitate detailed subgroup analyses.

Communication

A crucial element of a productive scholarship–policy–practice nexus is the ability of researchers to make policy- and program-relevant research accessible and on the attention screen of policymakers and practitioners. Here we consider "policymakers" broadly and include formal lawmakers as well as government staffers, school district leadership and analysts, judges and lawyers, and governing boards at all levels of education. Policymaking, in this view, includes processes of agenda-setting, development, and implementation, and a large number of different actors come into play. We also consider "practitioners" to broadly include college educators and community members engaging in efforts to address AAPI issues that are relevant to educational contexts. Communication with the actors at each stage of the policymaking or program development process is vital for the research community to be positioned as central to policy and programs that impact AAPI populations, not simply interested observers.

Communication framed in this way goes beyond "getting the word out" about research findings and recommendations for policy and practice. That is, it is more than the necessary but insufficient tasks of distributing press releases, issuing policy reports, and publishing opinion pieces in major news outlets. It is certainly far beyond the minimal effort of publishing books and articles in scholarly journals. Communication serves two purposes here—establishing voice and begetting collaboration.

As a community of scholars intent on addressing and improving the lives of AAPI populations across the country within the sphere of education, we need to establish a prominent, authoritative voice on policy and programmatic matters that can be informed by scholarly knowledge. Establishing voice involves expanding our circle of scholars and developing networks that link that circle to the policymaking and program development actors listed above. Expanding our circle of scholars refers to discovering and forging linkages to researchers across disciplinary and institutional bounds. Our potential colleagues reside not only in colleges of education and ethnic studies programs, but also in departments of economics, public policy, sociology, psychology, and political science, and schools of engineering, law, business, and medicine. Expanding our circle, then, also infers an expansion of publishing venues to mainline disciplinary journals and professional practice publications.

Developing networks to policymaking actors is probably the most difficult task for educational researchers, as generating such relationships typically is not what we were trained for and most likely, is not a goal or outcome in which we are encouraged, incentivized, or evaluated upon by our institutions. Nevertheless, developing these relationships and establishing communication with these actors is a vital pre-condition for collaboration.

Crucial Collaboration

Our call for communication should not be read as to presuppose collaboration. Collaboration in our scheme closely follows communication. The essential premise here is that effective social activism via scholarship must occur in collaboration. By collaboration, we do not refer to the typical image of two or more scholars working together on a research project or publication. Collaboration for social change through the scholarship–policy–practice nexus requires collaboration between scholars, policymakers (as defined above), and activists. Currently, scholars are rarely engaged in or invited into the processes of agenda-setting, policy and program development, and policy and program implementation. While the professional expectations for such collaboration are weak, there are notable examples of scholars' critical involvement in education policymaking and program development. Scholarly knowledge has played roles in consequential legal cases (e.g., *Brown v. Board of Education, Lau v. Nichols, Gratz and Grutter v. University of Michigan*) and individual scholars have been involved in fashioning or furthering education policy agendas via their appointments to public office. Perhaps the most notable example is that of sociologist, James Coleman, whose 1966 report to Congress formed the basis of national school desegregation policy. These are exceptional examples, however, and they are generally not illustrative of how scholar *communities* can utilize their expertise and be more centrally involved in education policymaking and program development.

Crucial collaboration, as we envision it, is a dialogical process of policymaking and program development undertaken by researchers, policymakers, educators, and activists working together. Agenda-setting, for example, is simultaneously the purview of researchers who can help identify and/or validate acute areas of need, of government policymakers who understand the political realities and roadblocks of implementing successful policies, of educators who bring practical and contextual knowledge to policy design, and of activists who represent community will, desire, and sense of priority in discussions that ultimately affect students and their communities. Researcher involvement in crucial collaboration will bring our work to the "ground floor" of policymaking, promising both greater participation in the process and a tighter tailoring of research agendas to contemporary policy debates and programmatic needs.

CONCLUSION

Yes. We have been here before, and we choose to gather again for the 2012 ARC Summit to forge new alliances, to construct a fresh vision, and establish a national research agenda for the future. We gather as a socially and critically conscious group of Asian Americans and Pacific Islanders that, like the AAPI community, reflect a vast array of ethnic backgrounds, cultures, and communities. We gather as researchers and activists that possess a wide range of rich scholarly and community perspectives and methodological strengths. But most importantly, we gather to fuse our energies and minds so that we can unite to move forward—*pupukahi i holomua*.

NOTE

1. For the entire poem, see http://phulkari.blogspot.com/2012/08/letters-home.html

REFERENCES

Abbas, T. (2002). The home and the school in the educational achievements of South Asians. *Race, Ethnicity and Education, 5*(3), 291–316.

Abueg, F. R., & Chun, K. M. (1996). Traumatization stress among Asian and Asian Americans. In A. J. Marsella, M. J. Friedman, E. T. Gerrity, & R. M. Scurfield (Eds.), *Ethnocultural aspects of posttraumatic stress disorder: Issues, research, and clinical applications* (pp. 285–299). Washington, DC: American Psychological Association.

Accapadi, M. M. (2012). Asian American identity consciousness: A polycultural model. In D. M. Ching & A. Agbayani (Eds.), *Asian Americans and Pacific Islanders in higher education: Research and perspectives on identity, leadership, and success* (pp. 57–94). Washington, DC: National Association of Student Personnel Administrators.

Adrian, L. (2004). *Asian American leaders in higher education: An exploration of a dynamic constructivist approach to leadership* (Unpublished doctoral dissertation). The Claremont Graduate University, Claremont, CA, and San Diego State University, San Diego, CA.

Alvarez, A. N. (2002). Racial identity and Asian Americans: Supports and challenges. *New Directions for Student Services, 97*, 33–44.

Ancheta, A. (2000). *Race, rights and the Asian American experience.* New Brunswick, NJ: Rutgers University Press.

Au, K. H. (1997). Schooling, literacy, and cultural diversity in research and personal experience. In A. Neumann & P. L. Peterson (Eds.), *Learning from our lives: Women, research, and autobiography in education* (pp. 71–90). New York, NY: Teachers College Press.

Au, K. H., & Carroll, J. H. (1997). Improving literacy achievement through a constructivist approach: The KEEP demonstration classroom project. *The Elementary School Journal, 97*(3), 203–221.

Awaya, A. (2000). *Fa'afafine (Third Gender) teachers of American Samoa* (Unpublished master's thesis). University of Hawaii, Manoa.

Baker, B. D., Keller-Wolff, C., & Wolf-Wendel, L. (2000). Two steps forward, one step back: Race/ethnicity and student achievement in education policy research. *Education Policy, 14*(4), 511–529.

Beykont, Z. F. (2000). *Lifting every voice: Pedagogy and politics of bilingualism.* Cambridge, MA: Harvard Educational Review.

Boehnlein, J. K., & Kinzie, J. D. (1997). Cultural perspectives on posttraumatic stress disorder. In T. W. Miller (Ed.), *Clinical disorders and stressful life events* (pp. 19–43). Madison, CT: International Universities Press.

Bourdieu, P. (1986). The forms of capital. In J. G. Richardson (Ed.), *Handbook of theory and research for the sociology of education* (pp. 241–258). New York, NY: Greenwood.

Bronfenbrenner, U. (1979). *The ecology of human development: Experiments by nature and design.* Cambridge, MA: Harvard University Press.

Buenavista, T. L., & Chen, A. C. (2013). Intersections and crossroads: A counter-story of an undocumented Asian American college student. In S. D. Museus, D. C. Maramba, & R. T. Teranishi (Eds.), *The misrepresented minority: New insights on Asian Americans and Pacific Islanders, and the implications for higher education* (pp. 198–212). Sterling, VA: Stylus.

Buenavista, T. L., Jayakumar, U. M., & Misa-Escalante, K. (2009). Contextualizing Asian American education through Critical Race Theory: An example of U.S. Pilipino college student experiences. *New Directions for Institutional Research, 142,* 69–81.

Bulosan, C. (1995). *On becoming Filipino: Selected writings of Carlos Bulosan.* Philadelphia, PA: Temple University Press.

Caplan, N., Choy, M. H., & Whitmore, J. K. (1991). *Children of the boat people: A study of educational success.* Ann Arbor, MI: University of Michigan Press.

Chan, C. S. (1989). Issues of identity development among Asian-American lesbians and gay men. *Journal of Counseling & Development, 68*(1), 16–20.

Chan, S. (1991). *Asian Americans: An interpretive history.* Boston, MA: Twayne.

Chan, K. S. (2000). Rethinking the Asian America Studies project: Bridging the divide between "campus" and "community." *Journal of Asian American Studies, 3*(1), 17–36.

Chang, M. J. (2011). Battle hymn of the model minority myth. *Amerasia Journal, 37*(2), 137–143.

Chang, M. J. (forthcoming). *Multiple representations but shared aspirations: Asian American organizations weigh in on affirmative action.* Paper presented at the Asian American and Pacific Islander Coalition Summit, Honolulu, HI.

Chang, M. J., & Kiang, P. N. (2002). New challenges of representing Asian American students in U.S. higher education. In W. A. Smith, P. G. Altbach, & K. Lomotey (Eds.), *The racial crisis in American higher education: Continuing challenges for the twenty-first century* (pp. 137–158). Albany, NY: State University of New York Press.

Chang, M. J., & Kiang, P. N. (Eds.). (2009). Higher education [Special issue]. *AAPI Nexus: Asian Americans & Pacific Islanders Policy, Practice, and Community, 7*(2).

Chang, M. J., Park, J., Lin, M. H., Poon, O. A., & Nakanishi, D. T. (2007). *Beyond myths: The growth and diversity of Asian American college freshmen, 1971–2005.* Los Angeles, CA: Higher Education Research Institute, University of California, Los Angeles.

Cheryan, S., & Bodenhausen, G. V. (2000, September). When positive stereotypes threaten intellectual performance: The psychological hazards of "model minority" status. *Psychological Science, 11*(5), 399–402.

Chhuon, V., & Hudley, C. (2008). Factors supporting Cambodian American students' successful adjustment into the university. *Journal of College Student Development, 49*(1), 15–30.

Chhuon, V., & Hudley, C. (2011). Ethnic and panethnic Asian American identities: Contradictory perceptions of Cambodian students in urban schools. *Urban Review, 43*(5), 681–701.

Chin, S.-Y. (1999). *Doing what had to be done: The life narrative of Dora Yum Kim.* Philadelphia, PA: Temple University Press.

Ching, D., & Agbayani, A. (2012). *Asian Americans and Pacific Islanders in higher education: Research and perspectives on identity, leadership, and success.* Washington, DC: National Association of Student Personnel Administrators.

Cho, S. K. (2003). Converging stereotypes in racialized sexual harassment: Where the model minority meets Suzie Wong. In A. K. Wing (Ed.), *Critical race feminism: A reader* (2nd ed., pp. 349–366). New York, NY: New York University Press.

Chou, R., & Feagin, J. R. (2008). *The myth of the model minority: Asian Americans facing racism.* Boulder, CO: Paradigm.

Chun, K.-T. (1980). The myth of Asian American success and its educational ramifications. *IRCD Bulletin, 15*(1/2), 1–12.

Chung, W. (1997). Asian American children. In E. Lee (Ed.), *Working with Asian Americans: A guide for clinicians* (pp. 165–174). New York, NY: Guilford.

Cole, D., & Ahmadi, S. (2010). Reconsidering campus diversity: An examination of Muslim students' experiences. *The Journal of Higher Education, 81*(2), 121–139.

Coloma, R. S. (2006). Disorienting race and education: Changing paradigms on the schooling of Asian Americans and Pacific Islanders. *Race, Ethnicity and Education, 9*(1), 1–15.

Committee of 100. (2005). *Asian Pacific Americans (APAs) in higher education report card.* New York, NY: Committee of 100. Retrieved from http://www.committee100.org/initiatives/initiative-herc.htm

Conchas, G. Q. (2006). *The color of success: Race and high-achieving youth.* New York, NY: Teachers College Press.

Council of Graduate Schools. (2009). *PhD completion and attrition: Findings from exit surveys of Ph.D. completers.* Washington, DC: Council of Graduate Schools Ph.D. Completion Project.

Crawford, J. (1986, April 23). Immersion method is fairing poorly in bilingual study. *Education Week, 5*(1), 1.

Crawford, J. (Ed.). (1992). *Language loyalties: A source book on the official English controversy.* Chicago, IL: University of Chicago Press.

Cress, C. M., & Ikeda, E. K. (2003). Distress under duress: The relationship between campus climate and depression in Asian American college students. *NASPA Journal, 40*(2), 74–97.

Darling-Hammond, L. (2003). What happens to a dream deferred? The continuing quest for equal educational opportunity. In J. A. Banks (Ed.), *Handbook of research on multicultural education* (pp. 607–630). New York, NY: Macmillan.

Davis, D. G., & McDaid, J. L. (1992). Identifying second-language students' needs: A survey of Vietnamese high school students. *Urban Education, 27*(1), 32–40.

Delucchi, M., & Do, H. D. (1996). The model minority myth and perceptions of Asian Americans as victims of racial harassment. *College Student Journal, 30*(3), 411–414.

DePouw, C. (2006). *Negotiating race, navigating school: Situating Hmong American university student experiences* (Unpublished doctoral dissertation). University of Illinois, Urbana-Champaign.

Desforges, C. (2003). *The impact of parental involvement, parental support and family education on pupil achievements and adjustment: A literature review* (Report No. 433). Washington, DC: Department of Education.

Diaz, V. M. (1995). Bye bye Miss American pie: Chamorros and Filipinos and the American dream. *Isla: Journal of Micronesian Studies, 3*(1), 147–160.

Diaz, V. M. (2004). "To "P" or not to "P"?": Marking the territory between Pacific Islander and Asian American studies. *Journal of Asian American Studies, 7*(3), 183–208.

Diaz, V. M. (2011). Tackling Pacific hegemonic formations on the American gridiron. *Amerasia Journal, 37*(3), 90–113.

Diaz, V. M., & Kauanui, J. K. (2001). Native Pacific Cultural Studies on the edge. *The Contemporary Pacific, 13*(2), 315–342.

Diver-Stamnes, A. C., & Lomascolo, A. F. (2001). The marginalization of ethnic minority students: A case study of a rural university. *Equity & Excellence in Education, 34*(1), 50–57.

Fisher, C. B., Wallace, S. A., & Fenton, R. E. (2000). Discrimination distress during adolescence. *Journal of Youth and Adolescence, 29*(6), 679–695.

Freeman, J. M. (1995). *Changing identities: Vietnamese Americans 1975–1995.* Boston, MA: Allyn & Bacon.

Furumoto, W. (2003). Reconnecting education to social justice. *Amerasia Journal, 29*(2), 1–7.

Garcia, E. E. (1993). Language, culture, and education. *Review of Research in Education, 19,* 51–98.

Goodyear-Ka'ōpua, J. N. (2009). Rebuilding the "Auwai": Connecting ecology, economy and education in Hawaiian schools. *AlterNative: An International Journal of Indigenous Peoples, 5*(2), 47–77.

Government Accountability Office [GAO]. (2007). *Information sharing could help institutions identify and address challenges some Asian American and Pacific*

Islander Students face. Washington, DC: United States Government Accountability Office.

Goodwin, A. L. (2002). Teacher preparation and the education of immigrant children. *Education and Urban Society, 34*(2), 156–172.

Gordon, J. (2000). Asian American resistance to selecting teaching as a career: The power of community and tradition. *Teachers College Record, 102*(1), 173–196.

Goto, S. T. (1997). Nerds, normal people, and homeboys: Accommodation and resistance among Chinese American students. *Anthropology & Education Quarterly, 28*(1), 70–84.

Goyette, K., & Xie, Y. (1999). Educational expectations of Asian American youths: Determinants and ethnic differences. *Sociology of Education, 72*(1), 22–36.

Grillo, T. (1995). Anti-essentialism and intersectionality: Tools to dismantle the master's house. *Berkeley Journal of Gender, Law & Justice, 10*, 16–30.

Hakuta, K. (1998, February 13–16). *Improving education for all children: Meeting the needs of language minority children.* Paper presented for the Aspen Institute Congressional Program meeting, "Education and the development of American youth," Charleston, SC.

Hakuta, K., & Diaz, R. M. (1985). The relationship between degree of bilingualism and cognitive ability: A critical discussion and some new longitudinal data. In K. E. Nelson (Ed.), *Children's language* (Vol. 5, pp. 319–344). Hillsdale, NJ: L. Erlbaum.

Hakuta, K., & Gould, L. J. (1987, March). Synthesis of research on bilingual education. *Educational Leadership, 44*(6), 38–45.

Halualani, R. T. (2002). *In the name of Hawaiians: Native identities and cultural politics.* Minneapolis, MN: University of Minnesota Press.

Han, M. (2008). Relationship among perceived parental trauma, parental attachment, and sense of coherence in Southeast Asian American college students. *Journal of Family Social Work, 9*(2), 25–45.

Harris, A. P. (2003). Race and essentialism in feminist legal theory. In A. K. Wing (Ed.), *Critical race feminism: A reader* (2nd ed., pp. 34–41). New York, NY: New York University Press.

Heine, H. C. (2002). *Culturally responsive schools for Micronesian immigrant students.* Honolulu, HI: Pacific Resources for Education and Learning.

Hinton, L. (2001). Language revitalization: An overview. In L. Hinton & K. Hale (Eds.), *The green book of language revitalization in practice* (pp. 3–18). San Diego, CA: Academic Press.

Hirschman, C., & Wong, M. G. (1984). Socioeconomic gains of Asian Americans, Blacks, and Hispanics: 1960–1976. *American Journal of Sociology, 90*(3), 584–607.

ho'omanawanui, k. (2008). 'Ike 'Āina: Native Hawaiian culturally based Indigenous literacy. *Hūlili: Multidisciplinary Research on Hawaiian Well-Being, 5*, 203–244.

Hoffman, J., & Vallejo Peña, E. (2013). Too Korean to be White and too White to be Korean: Ethnic identity development among transracial Korean American adoptees. *Journal of Student Affairs Research and Practice, 50*(2), 152–170

Huang, L. N. (1997). Asian American adolescents. In E. Lee (Ed.), *Working with Asian Americans: A guide for clinicians* (pp. 175–195). New York, NY: Guilford.

Hune, S. (2002). Demographics and diversity of Asian American college students. *New Directions for Student Services, 97*, 11–20.

Hune, S., & Yeo, J. (2010). How do Pacific Islanders fare in U.S. education? A look inside Washington state public schools with a focus on Samoans. *AAPI Nexus: Asian Americans & Pacific Islanders Policy, Practice, and Community, 8*(1), 1–16.

Ibrahim, F., Ohnishi, H., & Sandhu, D. S. (1997). Asian American identity development: A culture specific model for South Asian Americans. *Journal of Multicultural Counseling & Development, 25*(1), 34–50.

James, K. E. (1994). Effeminate males and changes in the construction of gender in Tonga. *Pacific Studies, 17*(2), 39–69.

Jayakumar, U. M., & Museus, S. D. (2012). Mapping the intersection of campus cultures and equitable outcomes among racially diverse student populations. In S. D. Museus & U. M. Jayakumar (Eds.), *Creating campus cultures: Fostering success among racially diverse student populations* (pp. 1–27). New York, NY: Routledge.

Jo, J.-Y. (2004). Neglected voices in the multicultural America: Asian American racial politics and its implication for multicultural education. *Multicultural Perspectives, 6*(1), 19–25.

Johnston, K. E., Swim, J. K., Saltsman, B. M., Deater-Deckard, K., & Petrill, S. A. (2007). Mothers' racial, ethnic, and cultural socialization of transracially adopted Asian children. *Family Relations, 56*(4), 390–402.

Joshi, K. Y. (2006). The racialization of Hinduism, Islam, and Sikhism in the United States. *Equity & Excellence in Education, 39*(3), 211–226.

Kanahele, P. (2005). I am this land, and this land is me. *Hūlili: Multidisciplinary Research on Hawaiian Well-Being, 2*(1), 21–31.

Kaomea, J. (2009). Contemplating Kuleana: Reflections on the rights and responsibilities of non-indigenous participants in programmes for indigenous education. *AlterNative: An International Journal of Indigenous Peoples, 5*(2), 78–99.

Kaomea, J. (2011). Hawaiian math for a sustainable future: Envisioning a conceptual framework for rigorous and culturally relevant 21st-century elementary mathematics education. *Hūlili: Multidisciplinary Research on Hawaiian Well-Being, 7*, 290–306.

Kaur, P. *Letters home.* Retrieved from http://phulkari.blogspot.com/2012/08/letters-home.html

Kiang, P. N. (1991). About face: Recognizing Asian & Pacific American Vietnam veterans in Asian American Studies. *Amerasia, 17*(3), 22–40.

Kiang, P. N. (1992). Issues of curriculum and community for first-generation Asian Americans in college. *New Directions for Community Colleges, 80*, 97–112.

Kiang, P. N. (1995). Bicultural strengths and struggles of Southeast Asian Americans in school. In A. Darder (Ed.), *Culture and difference: Critical perspectives on the bicultural experience in the United States* (pp. 201–225). New York, NY: Bergin & Garvey.

Kiang, P. N. (1996). Persistence stories and survival strategies of Cambodian Americans in college. *Journal of Narrative and Life History, 6*(1), 39–64.

Kiang, P. N. (1997). Pedagogies of life and death: Transforming immigrant/refugee students and Asian American Studies. *Positions, 5*(2), 551–577.

Kiang, P. N. (2002). Stories and structures of persistence: Ethnographic learning through research and practice in Asian American Studies. In Y. Zou & E. T. Trueba (Eds.), *Ethnography and schools: Qualitative approaches to the study of education* (pp. 223–255). Lanham, MD: Rowman & Littlefield.

Kiang, P. N. (2004). Linking strategies and interventions in Asian American Studies to K–12 classrooms and teacher preparation. *International Journal of Qualitative Studies in Education, 17*(2), 199–225.

Kiang, P. N. (2006). Policy challenges for Asian Americans and Pacific Islanders in education. *Race, Ethnicity, and Education, 9*(1), 103–115.

Kiang, P. N. (2009). A thematic analysis of persistence and long-term educational engagement with Southeast Asian American college students. In L. Zhan (Ed.), *Asian American voices: Engaging, empowering, enabling* (pp. 21–58). New York, NY: NLN Press.

Kiang, P. N., & Kaplan, J. (1994). Where do we stand?: Views of racial conflict by Vietnamese American high-school students in a Black-and-White context. *The Urban Review, 26*(2), 95–119.

Kibria, N. (1993). *Family tightrope: The changing lives of Vietnamese Americans.* Princeton, NJ: Princeton University Press.

Kim, J. (1981). *The process of Asian-American identity development: A study of Japanese American women's perceptions of their struggle to achieve positive identities* (Unpublished doctoral dissertation), University of Massachusetts, Amherst.

Kim, A., & Yeh, C. J. (2002). *Stereotypes of Asian American students.* ERIC Digests, ED462510.

Kinzie, J. D. (1989). Therapeutic approaches to traumatized Cambodian refugees. *Journal of Traumatic Stress, 2*(1), 75–91.

Kochiyama, Y. (2004). *Passing it on.* Los Angeles, CA: UCLA Asian American Studies Center Press.

Konstantopoulos, S. (2009). The mean is not enough: Using quantile regression to examine trends in Asian-White differences across the entire achievement distribution. *Teachers College Record, 111*(5), 1274–1295.

Kumashiro, K. K. (1999). Supplementing normalcy and otherness: Queer Asian American men reflect on stereotypes, identity, and oppression. *Qualitative Studies in Education, 12*(5), 491–508.

Kumashiro, K. K. (2001). *Troubling intersections of race and sexuality: Queer students of color and anti-oppressive education.* Lanham, MD: Rowman & Littlefied Publishers.

Kurashige, S. (2000). Pan-ethnicity and community organizing: Asian Americans United's campaign against anti-Asian violence. *Journal of Asian American Studies, 3*(2), 163–190.

Labrador, R. N., & Wright, E. K. (2011). Engaging Indigeneity in Pacific Islander and Asian American Studies. *Amerasia Journal, 37*(3), 135–147.

Ladson-Billings, G. (2000). Racialized discourses and ethnic epistemologies. In N. Denzin & Y. Lincoln (Eds). *Handbook of Qualitative Research* (2nd Ed., pp. 257–277). Thousand Oaks, CA: Sage.

Lagdameo, A., Lee, S., Nguyen, B., Liang, C. T. H., Lee, S., Kodama, C. M., & M. K. McEwen. (2002). Voices of Asian American students. *New Directions for Student Services, 97,* 5–10.

Lareau, A. (2011). *Unequal childhoods: Class, race, and family life.* Berkeley, CA: University of California Press.

Lee, S. J. (1994). Behind the model-minority stereotype: Voices of high- and low-achieving Asian American students. *Anthropology & Education Quarterly, 25*(4), 413–429.

Lee, S. J. (1996). *Unraveling the model minority stereotype: Listening to Asian American youth.* New York: Teachers College Press.

Lee, S. J. (2001). More than "model minorities" or "delinquents": A look at Hmong American high school students. *Harvard Educational Review, 71*(3), 505–528.

Lee, S. J. (2006). Additional complexities: Social class, ethnicity, generation, and gender in Asian American student experiences. *Race, Ethnicity, and Education, 9*(1), 17–28.

Lee, S. J. (2011). *Unraveling the "model minority" stereotype: Listening to Asian American youth* (2nd Ed.). New York, NY: Teachers College Press.

Lee, S. J., & Kumashiro, K. K. (2005). *A report on the status of Asian Americans and Pacific Islanders in education: Beyond the "model minority" stereotype.* Washington, DC: National Education Association.

Lee, S. M. (2002). Do Asian American faculty face a glass ceiling in higher education? *American Educational Research Journal, 39*(3), 695–724.

Lei, J. L. (2003). (Un)necessary toughness?: Those "loud Black girls" and those "quiet Asian boys." *Anthropology & Education Quarterly, 34*(2), 158–181.

Lew, J. (2004). The "other" story of model minorities: Korean American high school dropouts in an urban context. *Anthropology & Education Quarterly, 35*(3), 303–323.

Lew, J. (2006). Burden of acting neither White nor Black: Asian American identities and achievement in urban schools. *The Urban Review, 38*(5), 335–352.

Lew, J., Chang, J. C., & Wang, W. W. (2005). The overlooked minority: Asian Pacific American students at community colleges. *Community College Review, 33*(2), 64–84.

Lewis, A. E., Chesler, M., & Forman, T. A. (2000). The impact of "colorblind" ideologies on students of color: Intergroup relations at a predominantly White university. *The Journal of Negro Education, 69*(1/2), 74–91.

Liang, C. T. H., & Sedlacek, W. (2003). Attitudes of White student services practitioners toward Asian Americans. *NASPA Journal, 40*(3), 30–42.

Long, P. D. P. (1996). *The dream shattered: Vietnamese gangs in America.* Boston, MA: Northeastern University Press.

Louie, V. (2001). Parents' aspirations and investment: The role of social class in the educational experiences of 1.5- and second-generation Chinese Americans. *Harvard Educational Review, 71*(3), 438–474.

Makuakane-Drechsel, T., & Hagedorn, L. S. (2000). Correlates of retention among Asian Pacific Americans in community colleges: The case for Hawaiian students. *Community College Journal of Research and Practice, 24*(8), 639–655.

Maramba, D. C., & Museus, S. D. (2011). The utility of using mixed-methods and intersectionality approaches in conducting research on Filipino American students' experiences with the campus climate and on sense of belonging. *New Directions for Institutional Research, 151*, 93–101.

Mayeda, D. T., Pasko, L., & Chesney-Lind, M. (2006). "You got to do so much to actually make it": Gender, ethnicity, and Samoan youth in Hawaii. *AAPI Nexus: Asian Americans & Pacific Islanders Policy, Practice, and Community, 4*(2), 69–94.

McGinnis, T. (2007). "Khmer pride": Being and becoming Khmer American in an urban migrant education program. *Journal of Southeast Asian American Education & Advancement, 2,* 1–19.

McMurtrie, B. (2001, November 26). Foreign enrollments grow in the U.S., but so does competition from other nations. *The Chronicle of Higher Education,* pp. A45–A47.

Meyers, J. (2006). Pho and apple pie: Eden Center as a representation of Vietnamese American ethnic identity in the Washington, D.C. metropolitan area, 1975–2005. *Journal of Asian American Studies, 9*(1), 55–85.

Min, P. G. (2003). Social science research on Asian Americans. In J. A. Banks & C. M. Banks (Eds.), *Handbook of research on multicultural education* (pp. 332–348). San Francisco, CA: Jossey-Bass.

Moua, L., & Riggs, J. (2012). Navigating multiple worlds: A qualitative study of the lived experiences of Hmong women leaders. *Journal of Southeast Asian American Education and Advancement, 7,* 1–24.

Museus, S. D. (2008). The role of ethnic student organizations in fostering African American and Asian American students' cultural adjustment and membership at predominantly White institutions. *Journal of College Student Development, 49*(6), 568–586.

Museus, S. D. (Ed.). (2009). Conducting research on Asian Americans in higher education [Special issue]. *New Directions for Institutional Research, 142.*

Museus, S. D. (2010). Understanding racial/ethnic differences in the direct and indirect effects of loans on degree completion. *Journal of College Student Retention: Theory, Research, and Practice, 11*(4), 499–527.

Museus, S. D. (2011). Generating Ethnic Minority Success (GEMS): A collective-cross case analysis of high-performing colleges. *Journal of Diversity in Higher Education, 4*(3), 147–162.

Museus, S. D. (2013). Unpacking the complex and multifaceted nature of parental influences on Southeast Asian American college students' educational trajectories. *Journal of Higher Education, 84*(5), 708–738.

Museus, S. D. (2013a). Asian Americans and Pacific Islanders: A national portrait of growth, diversity, and inequality. In S. D. Museus, D. C. Maramba, & R. T. Teranishi (Eds.), *The misrepresented minority: New insights on Asian Americans and Pacific Islanders, and the implications for higher education.* Sterling, VA: Stylus.

Museus, S. D., & Chang, M. J. (2009). Rising to the challenge of conducting research on Asian Americans in higher education. *New Directions for Institutional Research, 142,* 95–105.

Museus, S. D., & Griffin, K. A. (2011). Mapping the margins in higher education: On the promise of intersectionality frameworks in research and discourse. *New Directions for Institutional Research, 151,* 5–13.

Museus, S. D., Harper, S. R., & Nichols, A. H. (2010). Racial differences in the formation of postsecondary educational expectations: A structural model. *Teachers College Record, 112*(3), 811–842.

Museus, S. D., & Kiang, P. N. (2009). Deconstructing the model minority myth and how it contributes to the invisible minority reality in higher education research. *New Directions for Institutional Research, 142,* 5–15.

Museus, S. D., Lam, S., Huang, C., Kem, P., & Tan, K. (2012). Cultural integration in campus subcultures: Where the cultural, academic, and social spheres of college life collide. In S. D. Museus & U. M. Jayakumar (Eds.), *Creating campus cultures: Fostering success among racially diverse student populations* (pp. 106–129). New York, NY: Routledge.

Museus, S. D., Lambe Sariñana, S. A., & Kawamata-Ryan, T. (2015). Qualitative examination of multiracial students' coping responses to experiences with prejudice and discrimination in college. *Journal of College Student Development, 56*(4), 331–348.

Museus, S. D., Lambe Sariñana, S. A. L., Yee, A. L., & Robinson, T. E. (in press). Multiracial prejudice and discrimination in college. *Journal of College Student Development.*

Museus, S. D., & Maramba, D. C. (2011). The impact of culture on Filipino American students' sense of belonging. *The Review of Higher Education, 34*(2), 231–258.

Museus, S. D., Maramba, D. C., Palmer, R. T., Reyes, A., & Bresonis, K. (2013). An explanatory model of Southeast Asian American college student success: A grounded theory analysis. In R. Endo & X. L. Rong (Eds.), *Asian American educational achievement, schooling, and identities* (pp. 1–28). Charlotte, NC: Information Age.

Museus, S. D., Mueller, M. K., & Aquino, K. (2013). Engaging Asian American and Pacific Islander culture and identity in graduate education. In S. D. Museus, D. C. Maramba, & R. T. Teranishi (Eds.), *The misrepresented minority: New insights on Asian Americans and Pacific Islanders, and the implications for higher education* (pp. 106–123). Sterling, VA: Stylus.

Museus, S. D., & Neville, K. M. (2012). Delineating the ways that key institutional agents provide racial minority students with access to social capital in college. *Journal of College Student Development, 53*(3), 436–452.

Museus, S. D., Vue, R., Nguyen, T. K., & Yeung, F. (2013). A Southeast Asian American identity model: Merging theoretical perspectives and considering intersecting identities. In S. D. Museus, D. C. Maramba, & R. T. Teranishi (Eds.), *The misrepresented minority: New insights on Asian Americans and Pacific Islanders, and the implications for higher education* (pp. 47–66). Sterling, VA: Stylus.

Museus, S. D., Palmer, R., Davis, R. J., & Maramba, D. C. (2011). *Racial and ethnic minority students' success in STEM education: ASHE higher education report* (Vol. 36, Issue 6). San Francisco, CA: Jossey-Bass

Museus, S. D., & Park, J. J. (2012). *The significance of race and racism in the lives of Asian American college students.* Paper presented at the Annual Meeting of the Association for the Study of Higher Education, Las Vegas, NV.

Museus, S. D., Ravello, J. N., & Vega, B. E. (2012). The campus racial culture: A critical race counterstory. In S. D. Museus & U. M. Jayakumar (Eds.), *Creating campus cultures: Fostering success among racially diverse student populations* (pp. 28–45). New York, NY: Routledge.

Museus, S. D., & Quaye, S. J. (2009). Toward an intercultural perspective of racial and ethnic minority college student persistence. *The Review of Higher Education, 33*(1), 67–94.

Museus, S. D., & Truong, K. A. (2009). Disaggregating qualitative data on Asian Americans in campus climate research and assessment. *New Directions for Institutional Research, 142,* 17–26.

Museus, S. D., & Vue, R. (2013). A structural equation modeling analysis of the role of socioeconomic status in Asian American and Pacific Islander students' transition to college. *The Review of Higher Education, 37*(1), 45–67.

Nadal, K. L. (2004). Pilipino American identity model. *Journal of Multicultural Counseling and Development, 32*(1), 45–62.

National Center for Education Statistics [NCES]. (2011). *Digest of Education Statistics.* Retrieved from http://nces.ed.gov/programs/digest/2008menu_tables.asp

Neilson, P. A., & Suyemoto, K. L. (2009). Using culturally sensitive frameworks to study Asian American leaders in higher education. *New Directions for Institutional Research, 142,* 83–93.

Ng, J. C., Lee, S. S., & Pak, Y. K. (2007). Contesting the model minority and perpetual foreigner stereotypes: A critical review of literature on Asian Americans in education. *Review of Research in Education, 31,* 95–130.

Nghe, L. T., Mahalik, J. R., & Lowe, S. M. (2003). Influences on Vietnamese men: Examining traditional gender roles, the refugee experience, acculturation, and racism in the United States. *Journal of Multicultural Counseling and Development, 31*(4), 245–261.

Ngo, B. (2002). Contesting "culture": The perspectives of Hmong American female students on early marriage. *Anthropology & Education Quarterly, 33*(2), 163–188.

Ngo, B. (2006). Learning from the margins: Southeast and South Asian education in context. *Race, Ethnicity and Education, 9*(1), 51–65.

Ngo, B. (2008). The affective consequences of cultural capital: Feelings of powerlessness, gratitude and faith among Hmong refugee parents. *Journal of Southeast Asian American Education & Advancement, 3,* 1–14.

Ngo, B., & Lee, S. J. (2007). Complicating the image of model minority success: A review of Southeast Asian American education. *Review of Educational Research, 77*(4), 415–453.

Nguyen, J., & Brown, B. B. (2010). Making meanings, meaning identity: Hmong adolescent perceptions and use of language and style as identity symbols. *Journal of Research on Adolescence, 20*(4), 849–868.

Ogbu, J. (1987). Variability in minority school performance: A problem in search of an explanation. *Anthropology & Education Quarterly, 18*(4), 312–334.

Okamura, J. Y. (2008). *Ethnicity and inequality in Hawaii.* Philadelphia, PA: Temple University Press.

Okihiro, G. Y. (1994). *Margins and mainstreams: Asian in American history and culture.* Seattle, WA: University of Washington Press.

Omi, M., & Winant, H. (2002). Racial formations. In T. E. Ore (Ed.), *Social construction of difference and inequality: Race, class, gender, and sexuality* (2nd ed., pp. 13–22). Columbus, OH: McGraw-Hill.

Ong, A. (1996). Cultural citizenship as subject-making: Immigrants negotiate racial and cultural boundaries in the United States. *Current Anthropology, 37*(5), 737–762.

Panapasa, S. V., Crabbe, M. K., & Kaholokula, J. K. (Fall 2011). Efficacy of federal data: Revised Office of Management and Budget Standard for Native Hawaiian and other Pacific Islanders examined. *AAPI Nexus: Asian Americans & Pacific Islanders Policy, Practice, and Community, 9*(1/2), 212–220.

Pang, V. O., Han, P., & Pang, J. (2011). Asian American and Pacific Islander students: Equity and the achievement gap. *Educational Researcher, 40*(8), 378–389.

Pang, V. O., Kiang, P. N., & Pak, Y. K. (2003). Asian Pacific American students: Challenging a biased educational system. In J. A. Banks & C. A. MgGee Banks (Eds.), *Handbook of research on multicultural education* (pp. 542–563). New York, NY: Macmillan.

Park, J. J. (2012). Asian American women's perspectives on historically White sorority life: A critical race theory and cultural capital analysis. *Oracle: The Research Journal of the Association of Fraternity/Sorority Advisors, 7*(2), 1–18.

Pease-Alvarez, L., & Hakuta, K. (1992). Enriching our views of bilingualism and bilingual education. *Educational Researcher, 21*(2), 4–6, 19.

Pendakur, S., & Pendakur, V. (2012). Let's get radical: The theory and praxis of being a practitioner-ally for Asian Pacific Islander American college students. In D. M. Ching & A. Agbayani (Eds.), *Asian Americans and Pacific Islanders in higher education: Research and perspectives on identity, leadership, and success* (pp. 31–50). Washington, DC: National Association of Student Personnel Administrators.

Penning, K. (1992). Tradition and pragmatism: An exploration into the career aspirations of Vietnamese refugee college students. In P. A. DeVoe (Ed.), *Selected papers on refugee issues* (pp. 89–99). Arlington, VA: American Anthropological Association.

Pepin, S., & Talbot, D. (2013). Negotiating the complexities of being self-identified as both Asian American and lesbian, gay, or bisexual. In S. D. Museus, D. C. Maramba, & R. T. Teranishi (Eds.), *The misrepresented minority: New insights on Asian Americans and Pacific Islanders, and the implications for higher education* (pp. 227–244). Sterling, VA: Stylus.

Pew Research Center. (2012, July 12). *The rise of Asian Americans* (pp. 1–36). Retrieved from http://www.pewsocialtrends.org/files/2012/06/SDT-The-Rise-of-Asian-Americans-Full-Report.pdf

Portes, A., & Rumbaut, R. G. (1996). *Immigrant America: A portrait* (2nd ed.). Berkeley, CA: University of California Press.

Pyke, K., & Dang, T. (2003). "FOB" and "Whitewashed": Identity and internalized racism among second generation Asian Americans. *Qualitative Sociology, 26*(2), 147–172.

Qin, D. B. (2006). "Our child doesn't talk to us anymore": Alienation in immigrant Chinese families. *Anthropology & Education Quarterly, 37*(2), 162–179.

Renn, K. A. (2000). Patterns of situational identity among biracial and multiracial college students. *Review of Higher Education, 23*(4), 399–420.

Robbins, K. (2004). Struggling for equality/ struggling for hierarchy: Gender dynamics in an English as an additional language classroom for adolescent Vietnamese refugees. *Feminist Teacher, 15*(1), 66–79.

Root, S., Rudawski, A., Taylor, M., & Rochon, R. (2003). Attrition of Hmong students in teacher education programs. *Bilingual Research Journal, 27*(1), 137–148.

Siu, S.-F. (1996, December). *Asian American students at risk: A literature review* (Report No. 8). Baltimore, MD: Johns Hopkins University, Center for Research on the Education of Students Placed At Risk.

Smedley, B. D., Myers, H. F., & Harrell, S. P. (1993). Minority-status stresses and the college adjustment of ethnic minority freshmen. *Journal of Higher Education, 64*(4), 434–52.

Smith-Hefner, N. J. (1999). *Khmer American: Identity and moral education in a diasporic community.* Berkeley, CA: University of California Press.

Snow, C. E., & Hakuta, K. (1992). The costs of multilingualism. In J. Crawford (Ed.), *Language loyalties* (pp. 384–394). Chicago, IL: The University of Chicago Press.

Stanton-Salazar, R. D. (1997). A social capital framework for understanding the socialization of racial minority children and youths. *Harvard Educational Review, 67*(1), 1–40.

Sue, D. W., Bucceri, J. M, Lin, A. I., Nadal, K. L., & Torino, G. C. (2007). Racial microaggressions and the Asian American experience. *Cultural Diversity and Ethnic Minority Psychology, 13*(1), 72–81.

Suyemoto, K. L., Kim, G. S., Tanabe, M., Tawa, J., & Day, S. C. (2009). Challenging the model minority myth: Engaging Asian American students in research on Asian American college student experiences. *New Directions for Institutional Research, 142*, 41–55.

Suyemoto, K. L., Tawa, J., Kim, G. S., Day, S. C., Lambe, S. A., Nguyen, P. T., & Ahn-Allen, J. M. (2009). Integrating disciplines for transformative education in health services: Strategies and effects. In L. Zhan (Ed.), *Asian American voices: Engaging, empowering, enabling* (pp. 41–55). New York, NY: National League for Nursing.

Suzuki, B. H. (1977). Education and socialization of Asian Americans: A revisionist analysis of the "model minority" thesis. *Amerasia Journal, 4*(2), 23–51.

Suzuki, B. H. (1989, November/December). Asian Americans as the "model minority": Outdoing Whites? Or media hype? *Change: The Magazine of Higher Learning, 21*(6), 13–19.

Suzuki, B. H. (2002). Revisiting the model minority stereotype: Implications for student affairs practice and higher education. *New Directions for Student Services, 97*, 21–32.

Takaki, R. (1989). *Strangers from a different shore: A history of Asian Americans.* Boston, MA: Little, Brown.

Tang, S. S. (2006). Community-centered research as knowledge/capacity building in immigrant and refugee communities. In C. R. Hale (Ed.), *Engaging contradictions: Theory, politics, and methods of activist scholarship* (pp. 237–264). Los Angeles, CA: University of California Press.

Tang, S. S., & Kiang, P. N. (2011). Refugees, veterans, and continuing pedagogies of PTSD in Asian Amrican Studies. *New Directions for Teaching and Learning, 125*, 77–87.

Taualii, M., Quenga, J., Samoa, R., Samanani, S. & Dover, D. (Fall 2011). Liberating data: Accessing Native Hawaiian and Other Pacific Islander data from national data sets. *AAPI Nexus Asian Americans & Pacific Islanders Policy, Practice, and Community, 9*(1/2), 249–255.

Tavares, H. M. (2008). When the familiar is strange: Encountering the cultural politics of Hawaii in the college classroom. *Discourse: Studies in the Cultural Politics of Education, 29*(3), 377–385.

Tengan, T. K. (2002). (En)gendering colonialism: Masculinities in Hawaii and Aotearoa, *Cultural Values, 6*(3), 239–256.

Teranishi, R. T. (2002). Asian Pacific Americans and critical race theory: An examination of school racial climate. *Equity and Excellence in Education, 35*(2), 144–154.

Teranishi, R. T., Behringer, L. B., Grey, E. A., & Parker, T. L. (2009). Critical race theory and research on Asian Americans and Pacific Islanders in higher education. *New Directions for Institutional Research, 142,* 57–68.

Teranishi, R. T., Ceja, M., Antonio, A. L., Allen, W. R., & McDonough, P. M. (2004). The college-choice process for Asian Pacific Americans: Ethnicity and socioeconomic class in context. *The Review of Higher Education, 27*(4), 527–551.

Tintiangco-Cubales, A., Kiang, P. K., & Museus, S. D. (Eds.). (2010). Intersections between secondary and postsecondary education [Special Issue]. *AAPI Nexus: Asian Americans & Pacific Islanders Policy, Practice, and Community, 8*(1).

Trask, H. K. (1999). *From a native daughter: Colonialism and sovereignty in Hawaii.* Honolulu, HI: University of Hawaii Press.

Tuan, M. (1998). *Forever foreigners or honorary Whites? The Asian ethnic experience today.* New Brunswick, NJ: Rutgers University Press.

Um, K. (1999). Scars of war: Educational issues and challenges for Cambodian-American students. In C. C. Park & M. M.-Y. Chi (Eds.), *Asian-American education: Prospects and challenges* (pp. 263–284). Westport, CT: Bergin & Garvey.

Um, K. (2003). *A dream denied: Educational experiences of Southeast Asian American youth.* Washington, DC: Southeast Asia Resource Action Center and Berkeley Southeast Asian Student Coalition.

Vue, R. (2013). Campus contexts and Hmong students' experiences negotiating identity and higher education. In S. D. Museus, D. C. Maramba, & R. T. Teranishi (Eds.), *The misrepresented minority: New insights on Asian Americans and Pacific Islanders, and the implications for higher education* (pp. 182–197). Sterling, VA: Stylus.

Warner, S. L. N. (2001). The movement to revitalize Hawaiian language and culture. In L. Hinton & K. Hale (Eds), *The green book of language revitalization in practice* (pp. 133–146). New York, NY: Academic Press.

Warren, M. R., Hong, S., Rubin, C. H., & Uy, P. S. (2009). Beyond the bake sale: A community-based relational approach to parent engagement in schools. *Teachers College Record, 111*(9), 2209–2254.

Willig, A. C. (1985). A meta-analysis of selected studies on the effectiveness of bilingual education. *Review of Educational Research, 55*(3), 269–317.

Wright, E. K., & Balutski, B. J. N. (2013). The role of context, critical theory, and counter-narratives in understanding Pacific Islander indigeneity. In S. D. Museus, D. C. Maramba, & R. T. Teranishi (Eds.), *The misrepresented minority: New insights on Asian Americans and Pacific Islanders, and the implications for higher education* (pp. 140–158). Sterling, VA: Stylus.

Wright, W. E. (2007). Heritage language programs in the era of English-only and No Child Left Behind. *Heritage Language Journal, 5*(1), 1–26.

Xiong, M. (1996). *Hmong college student attitudes towards counseling services* (Unpublished master's thesis). California State University, Northridge.

Yamagata-Noji, A., & Gee, H. (2012). Asian American and Pacific Islander leadership: Pipeline or pipedream? In D. M. Ching & A. Agbayani (Eds.), *Asian Americans and Pacific Islanders in higher education: Research and perspectives on identity, leadership, and success* (pp. 173–192). Washington, DC: National Association of Student Personnel Administrators.

Yamauchi, L. A. (2003). Making school relevant for at–risk students: The Wai'anae High School Hawaiian Studies program. *Journal of Education for Students Placed At Risk, 8*(4), 379–390.

Yamauchi, L. A., Lau-Smith, J.-A., & Luning, R. J. I. (2008). Family Involvement in a Hawaiian language immersion program. *The School Community Journal, 18*(1), 39–60.

Yan, W., & Museus, S. D. (2013). Asian American and Pacific Islander faculty and the glass ceiling in higher education: Findings from the national study of postsecondary faculty. In S. D. Museus, D. C. Maramba, & R. T. Teranishi (Eds.), *The misrepresented minority: New insights on Asian Americans and Pacific Islanders, and the implications for higher education* (pp. 249–265). Sterling, VA: Stylus.

Yang, X., Rendón, L. I., & Shearon, R. W. (1994). A profile of Asian students in North Carolina community colleges. *Community College Review, 22*(1), 19–32.

Young, K. (2006). Kuleana: Historiography of Hawaiian national consciousness 1780–2001. *Hawaiian Journal of Law and Politics, 2,* 1–33.

Zhou, M., & Bankston, C. L. (1998). *Growing up American: How Vietnamese children adapt to life in the United States.* New York, NY: Russell Sage.

Zhou, M., & Kim, S. (2006). Community forces, social capital, and educational achievement: The case of supplementary education in the Chinese and Korean immigrant communities. *Harvard Educational Review, 76*(1), 1–29.

PART I

RACISM, RACIAL POLITICS,
AND RACE CONSCIOUSNESS

CHAPTER 2

BEYOND BOBA TEA AND SAMOSAS

A Call for Asian American Race Consciousness

Sumun L. Pendakur and Vijay Pendakur

So, like, where are you from? Like, really from?

This question haunts the Asian American[1] experience. In particular, at a time in their lives when young people are trying to define themselves in relation to the world around them, Asian American college students continue to be otherized in subtle, yet pervasive, ways. When viewed in isolation of history, power, and oppression, this simple question might be understood as individual curiosity, laced with a hint of ignorance. Alternately, when examined through a lens of critical race theory (CRT) along with an intimate knowledge of the Asian American sociohistorical experience, this question is a manifestation of racism in the form of a powerful microaggression, tied to a much larger framework of racialization, xenophobia, and exclusion.

Asian Americans experience racism. Sadly, in our current political climate, this fact has to be stated overtly, as well as proven empirically (Alvarez,

Focusing on the Underserved, pages 55–71
Copyright © 2017 by Information Age Publishing
All rights of reproduction in any form reserved.

Juang, & Liang, 2006; Ching & Agbayani, 2012; Chou & Feagin, 2008; Museus, 2013). We borrow from Harper's (2012) synthesized definition of racism: " . . . individual actions (both intentional and unconscious) that engender marginalization and inflict varying degrees of harm . . . ; structures that determine and cyclically remanufacture racial inequity; and institutional norms that sustain White privilege and permit the ongoing subordination of minoritized persons" (p. 10). This chapter is not about whether or not Asian Americans experience racism in its many forms. We are taking this as a given. This chapter is about what happens—developmentally and ideologically—for Asian American college students in a lived context where they will undoubtedly be racialized and experience racism as part of existing in a system of hegemonic Whiteness.

As student affairs educators, we have been working with Asian American college students for more than a decade. Geographically, at the time of writing this chapter, we lived and worked in very different regions of the country, the Midwest and Southern California. And yet, we have observed disturbingly similar patterns of identification, behavior, and ideology among the Asian American students we have met. In our experience, Asian Americans tend to enter collegiate life identifying with their specific ethnic group or groups, rather than as Asian Americans. This personal observation is also supported by a growing body of scholarship on Asian American college students (Alvarez et al., 2006; Junn & Masuoka, 2006, 2008). When asked, "How do you identify, racially?" students tend to answer ethno-culturally, such as "Vietnamese and Chinese" or "Pakistani." Rarely do we hear college freshmen readily identify as Asian American, even when specifically asked about their *racial identity*. While there is enormous value to ethnic identification and cultural enrichment (as well as critical importance in disaggregating our communities' experiences), we contend that this ethnicity-over-race paradigm represents a form of *racial alienation* that places Asian American college students at risk. In the groundbreaking *Asian American Psychology: Current Perspectives,* Alvarez (2009) notably documents the numerous adverse physical and psychological consequences of racism on Asian Americans (pp. 409–410). Interestingly, however, the majority of higher education researchers themselves have overwhelmingly focused on "variables related to ethnicity and culture and given relatively minimal attention to understanding how Asian Americans internalize and cope with race and racism" (Alvarez, 2002, p. 32, citing Helms, 1995). Students are left in a research and programming limbo that renders their racialized experiences as invisible, to themselves and others.

However, Junn and Masuoka (2006) posit, " . . . a shared racial identity can act as an ascriptive tie binding together members of a racial group as well as a mobilizing tool to activate political action" (p. 3). They draw from a rich body of political science research to make a case for the importance of racial identity, racial group consciousness, and resulting political behavior. Taken in the context of this chapter, Junn and Masuoka's work challenges us to think about the barriers to, and the value of, racial identity and racial group consciousness for Asian American college students. They explain:

> As an individual adopts a sense of group consciousness, that individual begins to realize that her individual life chances are interrelated with those of her group. This consciousness becomes politicized when a racial minority begins to attach the social and political problems of the group to systemic causes that require political action in order to be resolved. (2006, p. 8)

Research and programming needs to be dedicated to the specific issues of individual Asian American ethnic groups. Our chapter, however, argues that Asian American college students, *as a racial group*, are underserved and depoliticized due to the unique contours of their racial formation. We seek to serve Asian American college students by giving higher education faculty and staff the critical framework—along with the relevant programming model and curricula—to make a much-needed intervention in this issue. We are particularly interested in this linkage between racial identity and political group consciousness; we see Asian Americans as marginalized within the dominant racial order and feel the imminent need for an Asian American movement for racial justice.

This chapter emerges from our concern regarding the schism between Asian American college students' identification as ethnic subjects and their *racialized* experience of the world as Asian Americans. Within a White hegemonic frame, Asian people are otherized according to tropes that obscure ethnic identities in favor of an essentialized Asianness that is unassimalable, inscrutable, and expendable (Alvarez et al., 2006; Buenavista, Jayakumar, & Misa-Escalante, 2009; Chen, LePhuoc, Guzman, Rude, & Dodd, 2006; Junn, 2007; Kawai, 2005; Ng, Lee, & Pak, 2007). Whether it is the repeated deployment of the forever foreigner trope through questions such as "Where are you really from?" or the killing of Sikhs by Islamophobic fundamentalists, race and racism shape the experiences of Asian Americans. The mismatch between the extant politics of race and the individual adherence to an ontology of ethnicity leaves Asian American college students particularly vulnerable to the harmful effects of racism. Simultaneously, this mismatch offers little stable ground for movements of resistance, as it is extremely difficult to organize around ethnic identities. In the next section of this chapter, we explain this phenomenon of Asian American racial alienation by locating it in the broader literature on color-blind racism and Asian American CRT. Then, we conclude by reviewing existing best practices in the field of higher education student affairs that work to develop Asian American race consciousness.

COLOR-BLIND RACISM, MODEL MINORITY TYPOLOGY, AND RACIAL ALIENATION: ASIAN AMERICAN COLLEGE STUDENTS AT THE CROSSROADS OF RISK

Scholars attempting to map the contours of modern racism have generated a multitude of explanations for the shift from the overt, juridical racism of the Jim Crow era to the covert, *de facto* racism that remained after the 1964 Civil Rights Act. For the majority of White Americans, however, the legal protections for race and ethnicity that civil rights activists won in the late 1950s and 1960s marked the end of racism as a salient issue in American society (Bonilla-Silva, 2006). Popularly, this shift gave rise to the notion that the public sphere was now truly egalitarian and meritocratic, and that people of color no longer had any excuses for not succeeding. In this new era, race no longer had the meaning once conferred by overt, legalized racism. Hence, a corollary rhetoric of color-blindness emerged in the 1970s, supported by the logic that simply *not seeing race* will guarantee that *race does not matter* (Williams & Land, 2006; Wise, 2010). Ideologies that normalize this logic are often labeled as color-blind attitudes, color-blind discourse, or color-blind politics. Crucial to the overall argument of this chapter is an understanding that these ideologies buttress the current form of racial hegemony[2] in that they support the extant, racist, White power structure (Aleinikoff, 1991; Bonilla-Silva, 2006; Crenshaw, 1988; Forman, 2004; Gotanda, 1991; Smith, 2008). Hence, we use the language of color-blind *racism* throughout this chapter to indicate the hegemonic system of racial domination that is bolstered by color-blind ideologies.

Color-blind attitudes and color-blind racism have been studied and defined differently by scholars across multiple disciplines. In our reading of these works, several definitions arose as notable representations of the general concept. In his seminal work, *Racism Without Racists: Color-Blind Racism and the Persistence of Racial Inequality in the United States,* Bonilla-Silva (2006) deepens the scholarship on color-blind racism by breaking the central concept into four dominant frames. Bonilla-Silva agrees that color-blind racism is the racial discourse that supports the nuanced, covert, institutional racism of the post-Civil Rights Era. The author, however, explains that racial ideology always has dominant frames through which information is disseminated, ingested, filtered, and perpetuated. Bonilla-Silva constructs his four frames using wide-scale interviews conducted with college students from several different types of institutions and non-college students from the Detroit-area:

1. *Abstract liberalism* combines key concepts from political liberalism, like "meritocracy" and "equal opportunity," with the tenets of economic liberalism—namely, individual choice—to explain racial realities.

2. *Naturalization* suggests that racial realities result from some sort of natural order, such as explaining urban racial segregation through the logic of "people like to live near others like themselves" (p. 28).

3. *Cultural racism* asserts that the inequity found in communities of color is the result of cultural tendencies that negatively impact those communities. For example, the *cultural racism* frame is present when individuals conclude that Black people are often poor because they are—or Black *culture* is—prone to apathy and/or victimhood.

4. *Minimization of racism* is a frame that asserts that racism is no longer an issue after the legal reforms of the Civil Rights Movement and no longer a key factor affecting minorities' lives.

As these four frames add structure to the pathways through which a racist ideology exerts its influence in pervasive and continuing ways in our society, they are an important contribution to the definition of color-blind racism.

Departing from sociological analysis, Guinier and Torres (2003) historicize the color-blind racist framework and unpack its workings through Critical Legal Studies (CLS) and CRT lenses. They explain that the color-blind racist framework that emerged after the passing of the Civil Rights Acts in 1964 and 1968, which banned overt discrimination based on race, religion, and national origin, generates the narrative that "after formal, state-sanctioned barriers to individual mobility are removed, any continuing inequality must result from the personal failure of individuals . . . " (p. 35). Through their use of CLS and CRT lenses, Guinier and Torres are able to clearly explain how color-blind racism also works to problematize individuals of color while freeing the state from owning the burden of historical, as well as current, systemic racism.

Much like Bonilla-Silva (2006), Guinier and Torres (2003) attempt to distill the complexities of color-blind racism down to its essential components. They argue that color-blind racism endorses three axioms: (a) race is simply skin color, (b) the recognition of race is the invocation of fixed biological notions of race, and (c) racism is now a personal problem. These three rules work in concert to strip race of its historical and material context by reducing it to skin color while simultaneously silencing any meaningful engagement with race by problematizing racial talk as contributing to racism. The third rule of color-blind racism in this framework de-systematizes common constructions of race and racism and frames them as irrational, personal issues. Guinier and Torres' scholarship on color-blind racism, as well as the other scholarship reviewed in this section, provides us with both a multifaceted definition for this construct and a basic schema for how this form of racism works.

While color-blind racism poses challenges to all racialized communities and movements for racial justice, we hold that this modern form of racial hegemony poses a unique risk for Asian Americans, due to how Asian American racial identity is framed in the present. Junn (2007) writes that the model minority stereotype is a sharp departure from the nineteenth century racialization of Asian American laborers as coolies. Junn traces the movement of the dominant Asian American stereotype—from coolie to model minority—in the U.S. policy shift during the 1960s Cold War space race. In an attempt to compete with the Soviet Union in the science theater of the Cold War, the United States revised its long-standing ban on Asian immigration through the 1965 Immigration Act, allowing for Asians to once again enter America in large numbers.

The model minority typology, however, is created by selective immigration criteria tied to the Immigration Act (1965) that prioritized legal entry for Asians with science, math, and medical degrees that could help the United States advance research and development and compete with the Soviet Union. This selection criteria resulted in an artificially constructed community of post-1965 Asian Americans that, due to the broader sociopolitical circumstance, happened to be academically gifted, extremely hard working, focused on upward mobility, and ready to play "within the lines" of White-dominated society. Drawing on racial formation theory (Omi & Winant, 1994), Junn's (2007) analysis casts the model minority stereotype as a racial project that the nation-state built to address specific domestic labor needs, as well as foreign policy interests.

This historical background is imperative, as the model minority stereotype is the dominant narrative that shapes Asian American college student experience (Ng et al., 2007). Critical scholarship on this trope uncovers the various ways that it supports White hegemony while concurrently socializing and oppressing Asian American students. An embedded narrative within the model minority framework is the idea that Asian Americans have "succeeded" and that they have "done it on their own." This assertion supports post-Civil Rights claims that America represents a racial meritocracy, which is a key master narrative of White hegemony and color-blind racism (Buenavista et al., 2009; Kawai, 2005). Beyond supporting meritocratic mythologies, the model minority trope works as a wedge tool, positioning Asian Americans against other "unsuccessful" people of color groups who have supposedly "failed to do it on their own" in the post-Civil Rights era. Ng et al. (2007) argue that this valorization of Asian Americans by the White state contributes to the marginalization and isolation of Asian Americans from other communities of color. This "wedge-tool" argument is important for understanding the way that Asian Americans have been discursively invoked to oppress other people of color, strengthen the neoliberal state, and extend White hegemony.

This politics of racial triangulation also has serious consequences for the way Asian Americans conceptualize their own racial identity. Junn (2007) notes that Asian Americans are, within the context of the White-Black binary, offered an "honorary Whiteness" that has resulted in higher levels of racial alienation for Asian Americans. Being positioned as *discursive Whites* is an integral component of the background context for understanding the racial experience of Asian American college students. In higher education, this honorary Whiteness moves from the background to the foreground as Asian Americans are often lumped with Whites in the discourse surrounding affirmative action and student success (Buenavista et al., 2009).

After several decades of enduring under the auspices of honorary whiteness, Asian Americans also face many barriers to developing strong racial group consciousness (Junn & Masuoka, 2008). By examining survey results on racial consciousness affinity and racial political identity, Junn and Masuoka (2008) offer the following list of factors that may lead Asian American group members to possess lower racial consciousness:

- The salience of ethnic group identity over racial identity;
- Having more economic and social mobility in U.S. society than Blacks or Latina/os (tied to model minority selection criteria);
- The connection between increased social mobility and the dissolution of ethnic enclave communities that can preserve racial consciousness;
- Due to the relatively nascent nature of the Asian American community—most arrived after 1965 (again, precipitated by U.S. immigration policy and the Asian Exclusion Acts [1875, 1882, 1917, 1924])—this recent immigration cuts most of the Asian American community off from the legacy of overt racial oppression in the nineteenth and early twentieth century;
- The model minority stereotype offers a more "positive" and individualistic framework of thinking of one's self that may lessen tendencies towards racial group consciousness.

CRITICAL INTERVENTIONS
AND PROGRAMMING DIRECTIONS

As discussed in previous sections, the construction of a racialized Asian American identity is mitigated by a variety of hegemonic forces that are currently nested in the politics and actions of color-blind racism. Asian American college students, ostensibly in a period of dynamic growth during their college years, are often confined by the processes of racialization that have impacted their development of a critically raced consciousness. In fact, students we dialogue with often enter college accepting the model minority stereotype: "Well, at least it's a positive stereotype!" is a claim we have heard many times. As Junn and Masuoka (2006) describe,

> So while Asian Americans might connect their racial identity with a particular set of stereotypical characteristics, the positive and more individualistic frame of their identity as a model minority provides fewer motives to form group racial identity. Similarly, if Asian Americans believe they have greater opportunities and hold higher status than others in society, there may be less reason to engage in group solidarity to achieve political ends. (pp. 12–13)

Junn and Masuoka (2006) offer two key factors that can lead to collective race consciousness: knowledge of historical racist oppression and knowledge of present-day racial marginalization. It is our argument that Asian American college students tend to enter college thinking of their identity individualistically and they are often missing the transformative learning experiences that could engender collective race consciousness. Therefore, as Alvarez (2002) writes: "For Asian American students, the goal of developing one's racial identity can be an ambiguous and emotionally evocative process" (p. 41).

In the context of color-blind racism, substantive works that challenge the dominant narrative of integration and meritocracy, like *The Myth of the Model Minority: Asian Americans Facing Racism* (Chou & Feagin, 2008), may not enter the popular discourse on race and racialization. Overlooking this research means that stories of direct racism and discrimination, the impact of the forever foreigner trope, hate crimes against Asian Americans (Chou & Feagin, 2008; Tuan, 1998), and knowledge of Asian American political movements and group mobilization may be rendered invisible. In addition, there is simply less research available on Asian American experiences in general and Asian Americans in higher education in particular (Alvarez, 2002; Junn & Masuoka, 2006, 2008; Museus & Kiang, 2009). Moreover, racism often tends to be viewed as "extreme acts committed by an ignorant or ill-intentioned few" (Harper, 2012, p. 10), a rigid definition that does not allow for nuanced understandings of the multiple directions of racism and subordination in U.S. society or in higher education. These manifold elisions contribute to a series of missed opportunities in our field to directly engage Asian American college students in a process of conscientization, or consciousness-raising, that could provide them with a strong collective race consciousness.

In an era of color-blind racism, the need for race consciousness has never been greater. For Asian American college students in particular, the pathways to racial salience hold unique challenges due to the historic and present contours of White hegemony. College educators aim to develop a strong, holistic sense of self in college students, and racial identity is a critical component of students' identities. It is our contention that Asian American students often require intentional, developmental experiences to build a critical race consciousness. The final section of this chapter will highlight several recommendations that can assist college educators as they seek to develop consciousness-raising programs.

First, while much of this chapter laid out the sociological, political, and historical barriers to Asian American race consciousness, we strongly believe that Asian American racial consciousness programs can operate as critical interventions in two key arenas: (a) providing Asian American students a language, voice, and tools to understand their raced experiences and resist the harmful effects of subordination and hegemony, as well as (b) a necessary space for Asian American youth to learn organizing, coalition-building, and allyship with other marginalized communities. The personal and the political are directly linked in this racial project.

Nearly fifteen years ago, Alvarez (2002) posed a challenge for student affairs professionals in terms of developing an Asian American racial identity, "What facilitates this process of racial consciousness?" (p. 33). We take this opportunity to respond to Alvarez by offering ideas for an Asian American empowerment and conscientizing/critical consciousness program. Empowerment here is defined as both an active and participatory process for the marginalized to gain access to resources and the ability to make decisions that impact their lives and their communities (Maton & Salem, 1995). Critical consciousness (or "conscientização") is derived from Freire's (1970, 1974) body of work. Critical consciousness represents a two-fold process of first understanding the oppressive and contradictory world around us, and then taking action against the hegemonic elements that are illuminated by that understanding. It is a praxis-oriented philosophy of education, as opposed to theory without practice or vice versa.

A number of colleges and universities across the country offer Asian American leadership development and mentoring programs that directly take into account race and racism, as well as sexism, heteronormativity, classism, etc. But many campuses are still "stuck" in a mindset of traditional programming—boba tea and samosas served at culture shows, film screenings, heritage festivals, and events that are largely centered on one-time exposure—without deeper educational content or space for analysis. Quaye and Baxter Magolda (2007) note that students have seldom developed a clear understanding of their own racial identities. Therefore, programming opportunities and interventions must take into account differences in developmental readiness to grapple with the realities of race and racism. So, what would an Asian American conscientizing/racial consciousness program look like? We posit that any long-term (semester-length or longer) program would optimally focus on two key areas: knowledge and organizing.

Knowledge

It is essential to situate the programming in CRT to cover counter-narrative history, the formation of the model minority stereotype, U.S. labor and foreign policy strategy, and the interrelationship of racial identity formation with class, gender, sexuality, ability, ethnicity, and more (Pendakur & Pendakur, 2012, p. 48). Given that Asian American students will enter any program at different developmental stages, it is important not to rely on positivistic stage models or a narrow progression of developmental goals. Accapadi (2012) proposes a highly valuable point of entry model for Asian American identity consciousness. She elaborates, "This model allows for the possibility of multiple points of entry...on one's racial identity journey, which is fluid, continuous, and dynamic..." (p. 72). Racial identity consciousness informs the student's relationship with their other identities, and vice versa. Accapadi's (2012) point of entry model takes into account ethnic attachment, self as other (treatment based on phenotype), familial influence, immigration history, external influences and perceptions (from experiences of discrimination to political climate), and other social identities.

Accapadi (2012) notes that we must not force students to choose among, or place in a hierarchy, their identities. We extend that argument by stating that a concrete exploration of intersectionality of identities—essentially situating the multiplicity of identities in the context of a hegemonic society—can lead to much more complex and nuanced understanding of power, oppression, domination, and forms of resistance. An intersectional approach can also help students relate to concepts of structural oppression by employing multiple facets of identity, in addition to race (Almandrez & Lee, 2011).

Not every campus has the ability to offer Asian American studies courses and not every student may want to "use" their course credits to take such courses. However, if campuses have Asian American resource centers or cultural centers, those are optimal places out of which to offer leadership, mentoring, and social justice programs in the co-curriculum.

Organizing

In addition to knowledge building, it is incredibly important to work with students to help them learn to effectively see and counter bias and subtle manifestations of racism. This is where we move from the intellectual to the actualized—How do we transform knowledge into action? Can students name racism when they see it, feel it, or experience it? When it is experienced (often codified by class, gender, and sexuality), can students speak up? Are students empowered with the know-how to advocate for themselves and others in their community, whether challenging racism or demanding resources and services? Do they know campus resources (where to go, with whom to speak) to deal with bias and discrimination? A racial consciousness program would work with students to help them articulate a clear understanding of power, resources, access, and tools at their disposal to make change. Beyond individual agency, an ideal program would resource students with language and provide opportunities for students to practice their organizing skills, whether on campus or in the community. Embedding the works of Chicana scholar activists, queer theorists, feminist writers, and more can help students locate their own experiences to those of others in a web of relationships. This is an important building block to true allyship—standing up and speaking out, even in discomfort, because a complex understanding of the interrelationships of systemic oppression has been developed.

Finding Pathways and Inspiration

Nationally, programs and best practices exist from which to derive inspiration and ideas. One of the authors directed the Asian Pacific American Student Services (APASS) department at the University of Southern California for a number of years. A flagship programmatic offering of APASS is Critical Issues in Race, Class, and Leadership Education (CIRCLE). Explicitly naming racial consciousness as a key facet of successful, progressive, and social change-oriented leadership, the program offers approximately 60 Asian American students an immersive, seven-week consciousness-raising and activism-training curriculum. Connecting Asian American history and stereotypes, racial formation, class, gender and gender identity, sexual orientation, community organizing, power analysis, and ally-building, the program culminates in an intensive two-day retreat that focuses on dismantling privilege and learning organizing skills. The program actively challenges normative definitions of leadership and overtly positions leadership as embedded in community and social change. In 2011, an evaluation of the program's impact and effectiveness revealed that 72% of the participants strongly agreed and 28% agreed that CIRCLE helped them to critically analyze the issue of race. As Alvarez et al. (2006) empirically demonstrate, "Explicit discussions about race and racism may be instrumental in normalizing the issue as a topic of concern as well as preparing Asian Americans to encounter such incidents" (p. 489). A 2011 CIRCLE participant shared the following reflection on their growth:

> I think I learned to think about race in a critical way. I never examined race, specifically Asian American issues, in this much depth before. It really made me analyze and think about stereotypes, sensitivity, and where racism comes from (why it forms). There are so many ways to look at racism, and at school we never really focus on Asian struggles and hardships. I liked how we talked about how prevalent racism is today, since it is something we like to pretend is mostly in the past. I think my participation in CIRCLE will help me be more sensitive, aware, and active in fighting racism in my everyday life.

Providing the safe, yet challenging, space in order to grapple with complex issues as related to Asian American identity affords students the opportunity to acknowledge the fact that the master narrative denies so much of our history and reality to us. Another 2011 participant went on to share how their commitment to being a change agent had evolved:

> I am now more focused and committed to making an impact both on and off campus, because I have explored on a deeper level the various issues that affect the Asian American community today, and have really questioned what it means to be a leader, and what it means to be an agent of social change. Overall, the program made me feel more empowered as an individual knowing I have a support group where my peers and I have a mutual understanding of the struggles each of us has faced and can relate with one another.

A number of participants similarly explained how their consciousness about race, class, gender, sexuality, and the disparities within our communities had shifted, empowering them with a desire to actively participate in making positive societal change.

Another APASS program, the PEER (Positive Experiences, Enriching Relationships) first-year success mentoring program extensively trains the 25–30 mentors in immigration history, Asian American identity and racial development, and first-year experiences, in addition to communication and counseling skills, training on the coming-out process, myth-busting around alcohol and sexual activity, body image, and handling crises. Many departments and centers offer mentoring programs that involve upperclassmen and first-year students. Although those programs do not always embed teaching about race and other constructs at their core, they are prime examples of ways to integrate racial consciousness and training that increases identity knowledge and complexity. Through all of APASS' programmatic offerings, the top 5 social issues about which participants increased their awareness were: (a) racism and stereotypes/race relations;

(b) gender and sexuality; (c) class inequities/SES disparities; (d) impact of colonialism, capitalism, and militarism; and (e) access to education. Many other institutions, including the University of Pennsylvania and Pomona College, offer other excellent models of peer mentoring and leadership development programs that are rooted in empowerment and race consciousness.

Existing and emerging literature substantiates our ideas around knowledge and organizing by offering a variety of best practices that can be implemented through Asian American resource/cultural centers, or through campus-based leadership centers or multicultural centers. Patton's (2010) *Culture Centers in Higher Education: Perspectives on Identity, Theory, and Practice* and Stewart's (2011) *Multicultural Student Services on Campus: Building Bridges, Re-visioning Community* are two excellent anthologies that offer historical and theoretical approaches to our work in student affairs, but also provide the reader practical guidance on embedding race consciousness and a conscientizing, or consciousness-raising, approach into programming. For example, Liu, Cuyjet, and Lee's (2010) chapter thoroughly explains the advantage of "safe space" training atmospheres and includes examples for mentorship and leadership development programs, as well as intergroup and intragroup relationship programs. Similarly, Quaye and Baxter Magolda (2007) pull from literature on intercultural maturity to make programming suggestions around learning partnerships, a multicultural education framework, and intergroup dialogue for practitioners. Liang, Lee, and Ting (2002) offer specific model programs at universities across the country that explicitly embed racial identity development in their curriculum and equip students with both knowledge and skills to engage in socially conscious leadership.

Directly confronting the on-going project of color-blind racism and the deracination and loss of identity salience experienced by Asian American students is a complex task. Harper (2012) argues that "ongoing attempts to study race without racism are unlikely to lead to racial equity." We would echo Harper's argument for our field of student affairs and assert that working with Asian American students without actively engaging race and racism in intersectional and transdisciplinary ways will not lead to justice for our communities. Rather, head-on confrontation of neoliberal forms of individual achievement is necessary if we are to enact broader change in students' lives and beyond. Returning to our opening critique of an ethnicity-over-race paradigm, adhering to an ethnicity-only model may provide students a foundation for a subsequent investment in color-blind racism by offering them a rich sense of personal identity, which, although valuable, can come at the expense of an understanding of group relationships within the context of state power, history, and hegemony.

Conclusion: Where We Are, Like, Really From...

We began revising this chapter in August of 2014, haunted by the backdrop of racial violence and police brutality in Ferguson, Missouri. Now, in the early months of 2016, we look back on the last year of campus upheaval and activism, the likes of which had not been seen for decades. By our accounts, it has been a time to call attention to the politics of race and racism, yet they are both discursively and substantively marginalized in the priorities and investments of our nation. Similarly, in the ever-evolving literature on higher education, race occupies spaces at both the center and the margins of the scholarship. Centrally, we are inundated with data points and press releases on the changing racial demographics of higher education while our own masters and doctoral programs teach about the importance of race and racism in understanding American society. Marginally, however, Harper (2012) notes that explicit scholarship on race and racism is still scarce in top-tier, peer-reviewed higher education journals. Within this glaring lacuna, work on race and racism in the Asian American context is even more rare.

We identify as radical Asian Americans and this chapter is our attempt to answer the "Where are you from?" question. As student affairs scholar-practitioners, we often find ourselves in dialogue about our own processes of conscientization, reflecting on powerful experiences of race and racism from our early childhood, high school, and college years. These formative experiences, in essence, represent where we are from. Over the years, we have worked with many Asian-identifying college students who share similar experiences of race and racism, but have not made meaning of these phenomena to form a critical Asian American race consciousness. Luckily, we do not have to leave this identity development opportunity up to chance. Well-researched and assessed programs that exist to support Asian American college students on their developmental journey and critical race praxis can interrupt processes of deracination and color-blind racism in powerful ways. A key factor for both scholars and practitioners to take into account is the crucial role of context in the formation of Asian American race consciousness. In the current milieu of race and politics in American society, Asian American college students are often denied their race and class reality by the context of model minoritization and their positioning within affirmative action discourses. This triangulization between race consciousness, model minority typology (which positions them as honorary Whites), and political discourses places Asian American students at risk. In addition, student affairs practitioners must be alerted to this phenomenon if they want to effectively engage Asian American students in co-curricular programs focused on politics and race. For Asian American students, staff, and faculty that stand on the periphery of higher education, we hope that this chapter can inspire spirited dialogue, action, and transformation.

NOTES

1. The term Asian American is a political, coalitional term used to group a wide variety of ethnic groups that can trace their roots back to the Asian continent. Within the literature on Asian Americans, intense debates address whether this *umbrella* term does justice to the deep heterogeneity of the community. Alternative terms such as Asian Pacific Islander American or Asian Pacific Islander Desi American are attempts to be more inclusive of often overlooked, and uniquely situated, groups within the Asian American pan-ethnic community. For the purpose of this chapter on race and racism, we will use the term Asian American because of the socio-historical and political legacy of this language in the American struggle for racial justice. We acknowledge that this choice comes with attendant problems and limitations, as do all choices in the parlance of race and ethnicity.

2. Omi and Winant (1994) draw from Gramsci to define hegemony as a system of control based on both coercion and consent. In a hegemonic system, the ruling elite incorporate key interests of subordinated groups to pacify resistance while also perpetuating a *common sense* ideology that leads subordinated group members to act in ways that enforce the rule of the elites. This complex interplay between incorporation, ideology, and resistance offers us a way to understand American racial rule, particularly in its shift from overt dominance to covert coercion and consent in the post-Civil Rights era.

REFERENCES

Accapadi, M. M. (2012). Asian American identity consciousness: A polycultural model. In D. Ching & A. Agbayani (Eds.), *Asian Americans and Pacific Islanders in higher education: Research and perspectives on identity, leadership, and success* (pp. 57–94). Washington, DC: National Association of Student Personnel Administrators.

Aleinikoff, T. A. (1991). A case for race consciousness. *Columbia Law Review, 91*(5), 1060–1125.

Almandrez, M. G., & Lee, F. J. (2011). Bridging integrated identities to integrated services. In D. L. Stewart (Ed.), *Multicultural student services on campus: Building bridges, re-visioning community* (pp. 107–121). Sterling, VA: Stylus.

Alvarez, A. N. (2002). Racial identity and Asian Americans: Supports and challenges. *New Directions for Student Services, 97*, 33–44.

Alvarez, A. N. (2009). Racism: "It isn't fair." In N. Tewari & A. N. Alvarez (Eds.), *Asian American psychology: Current perspectives* (pp. 399–419). New York, NY: Taylor & Francis Group.

Alvarez, A. N., Juang, L., & Liang, C. T. (2006). Asian Americans and racism: When bad things happen to "model minorities." *Cultural Diversity and Ethnic Minority Psychology, 12*(3), 477–492.

Asian Exclusion Acts, (1875, 1882, 1917, 1924).

Bonilla-Silva, E. (2006). *Racism without racists: Color-blind racism and the persistence of racial inequality in the United States* (2nd ed.). Lanham, MD: Rowman & Littlefield.

Buenavista, T. L., Jayakumar, U. M., & Misa-Escalante, K. (2009). Contextualizing Asian American education through Critical Race Theory: An example of U.S. Pilipino college student experiences. *New Directions for Institutional Research, 142,* 69–81.

Chen, G. A., LePhuoc, P., Guzman, M. R., Rude, S. S., & Dodd, B. G. (2006). Exploring Asian American racial identity. *Cultural Diversity and Ethnic Minority Psychology, 12*(3), 461–476.

Ching, D., & Agbayani, A. (Eds.). (2012). *Asian Americans and Pacific Islanders in higher education: Research and perspectives on identity, leadership, and success.* Washington, DC: NASPA Foundation.

Chou, R., & Feagin, J. R. (2008). *The myth of the model minority: Asian Americans facing racism.* Boulder, CO: Paradigm.

Civil Rights Act, Pub. L. 88–352, 78 Stat. 241 (1964).

Crenshaw, K. W. (1988). Race, reform, and retrenchment: Transformation and legitimation in antidiscrimination law. *Harvard Law Review, 101*(7), 1331–1387.

Forman, T. A. (2004). Color-blind racism and racial indifference: The role of racial apathy in facilitating enduring inequalities. In M. Krysan & A. E. Lewis (Eds.), *The changing terrain of race & ethnicity* (pp. 43–66). New York, NY: The Russell Sage Foundation.

Freire, P. (1970). *Pedagogy of the oppressed.* (M. B. Ramos, Trans.). New York, NY: Herder and Herder.

Freire, P. (1974). *Education for critical consciousness.* New York, NY: Continuum International Group.

Gotanda, N. (1991). A critique of "Our Constitution is color-blind." *Stanford Law Review, 44*(1), 1–68.

Guinier, L., & Torres, G. (2003). *The miner's canary: Enlisting race, resisting power, transforming democracy.* Cambridge, MA: Harvard University Press.

Harper, S. R. (2012). Race without racism: How higher education researchers minimize racist institutional norms. *The Review of Higher Education, 36*(1), 9–29.

Helms, J. E. (1995). An update of Helms's White and people of color racial identity models. In J. G. Ponterotto, J. M. Casas, L. A. Suzuki, & C. M. Alexander (Eds.), *Handbook of multicultural counseling* (pp. 181–198). Thousand Oaks, CA: Sage.

Immigration Act, H.R. 2580; Pub.L. 89–236, 79 Stat. 911 (1965).

Junn, J. (2007). From coolie to model minority: U.S. immigration policy and the construction of racial identity. *Du Bois Review, 4*(2), 355–373.

Junn, J., & Masuoka, N. (2006, March). *Asian pride or ambiguous identities? The influence of Asian American racial group consciousness on participation.* Paper presented at the Western Political Science Association Annual Meeting, Albuquerque, NM.

Junn, J., & Masuoka, N. (2008). Asian American identity: Shared racial status and political context. *Perspectives on Politics, 6*(4), 729–740.

Kawai, Y. (2005). Stereotyping Asian Americans: The dialectic of the model minority and the yellow peril. *The Howard Journal of Communications, 16*(2), 109–130.

Liang, C. T. H., Lee, S., & Ting, M. P. (2002). Developing Asian American leaders. *New Directions for Student Services, 97,* 81–90.

Liu, W. M., Cuyjet, M. J., & Lee, S. (2010). Asian American student involvement in Asian American culture centers. In L. Patton (Ed.), *Culture centers in higher education: Perspectives on identity, theory, and practice* (pp. 26–45). Sterling, VA: Stylus.

Maton, K. I., & Salem, D. (1995). Organizational characteristics of empowering community settings: A multiple case study approach. *American Journal of Community Psychology, 23*(5), 631–656.

Museus, S. D. (2013). *Asian American students in higher education.* New York, NY: Routledge.

Museus, S. D., & Kiang, P. N. (2009). Deconstructing the model minority myth and how it contributes to the invisible minority reality in higher education research. *New Directions for Institutional Research, 142,* 5–15.

Ng, J. C., Lee, S. S., & Pak, Y. K. (2007). Contesting the model minority and perpetual foreigner stereotypes: A critical review of literature on Asian Americans in education. *Review of research in education, 31,* 95–130.

Omi, M., & Winant, H. (1994). *Racial formation in the United States: From the 1960s to the 1990s* (2nd ed.). New York, NY: Routledge.

Patton, L. D. (Ed.). (2010). *Culture centers in higher education: Perspectives on identity, theory, and practice.* Sterling, VA: Stylus.

Pendakur, S., & Pendakur, V. (2012). Let's get radical: The theory and praxis of being a practitioner-ally for Asian Pacific Islander American college students. In D. M. Ching & A. Agbayani (Eds.), *Asian Americans and Pacific Islanders in higher education: Research and perspectives on identity, leadership, and success* (pp. 31–50). Washington, DC: National Association of Student Personnel Administrators.

Quaye, S. J., & Baxter Magolda, M. B. (2007). Enhancing racial self-understanding through structured learning and reflective experiences. *New Directions for Student Services, 120,* 55–66.

Smith, B. (2008). Far enough or back where we started: Race perception from Brown to Meredith. *Journal of Law & Education, 37*(2), 297–305.

Stewart, D. L. (Ed.). (2011). *Multicultural student services on campus: Building bridges, re-visioning community.* Sterling, VA: Stylus.

Tuan, M. (1998). *Forever foreigners or honorary Whites? The Asian ethnic experience today.* New Brunswick, NJ: Rutgers University Press.

Williams, D. G., & Land, R. R. (2006). The legitimation of black subordination: The impact of color-blind ideology on African American education. *Journal of Negro Education, 75*(4), 579–588.

Wise, T. J. (2010). *Colorblind: The rise of post-racial politics and the retreat from racial equity.* San Francisco, CA: City Lights Books.

CHAPTER 3

CRITICAL RACE CONSCIOUSNESS OR THE INTEREST CONVERGENCE OF "DIVERSITY"

Examining the Initiative for Hmong Studies

Christin DePouw

Although institutional racism is not often named as an important character-istic of the higher education experiences of Asian American students, rac-ism exhibits a significant influence on the experiences of Asian Americans on campus (DePouw, 2012; Museus & Park, 2015; Teranishi, 2010). Indeed, racially hostile campus environments for students of color have increasingly become topics of discussion in academic and mainstream media. Recently, various groups of students of color on campuses throughout the United States have waged protests and social media campaigns to draw attention to the problematic racial climates at their respective universities and to name institutional racism as the cause of racially hostile educational environments

Focusing on the Underserved, pages 73–87
Copyright © 2017 by Information Age Publishing
73

(Beck, 2014; Flaherty, 2013; Hing, 2014). Many of these students report being devalued intellectually and stereotyped culturally and racially, as well as receiving ongoing messages that they are not full members of their campus communities. In the current study, Hmong American interview participants reported similar environments on their campus and named institutional racism as a significant factor in their higher educational experiences.

Hmong American undergraduate students in Midwestern states like Minnesota and Wisconsin often comprise a significant portion of students of color on campus, particularly for the non-flagship, comprehensive campuses (University of Wisconsin [UW] System Office of Policy Analysis and Research, 2013). Despite their numerical presence, however, Hmong Americans are often rendered invisible in university curricula, programming, institutional decision-making processes, and power distributions (DePouw, 2012). For example, while several Midwestern campuses provide Hmong language classes, few actually offer courses beyond language that substantively engage in studies of Hmong and Hmong American communities. Many of these campuses have staff members who are Hmong American, though very few have Hmong American faculty and administrators (University of Wisconsin System, 2014).

This chapter uses critical race theory (CRT) to illustrate the centrality of race and racism in Hmong American students' experiences in higher education within campus climate, academic experiences, and interpersonal relationships (Taylor, Gillborn, & Ladson-Billings, 2009). It also uses CRT as an analytical framework to explore the value of critical race consciousness as key to empowering Hmong American students to resist and transform institutional racism (Lee, 2009; Ngo & Lee, 2007; Xiong, 2010). CRT concepts that are particularly relevant to this analysis include Whiteness as Property, racial microaggressions, and critical race consciousness (Harris, 1993; Stovall, 2006; Yosso, Smith, Ceja, & Solórzano, 2009). These concepts reveal the institutional nature of race and racism and expose the inequitable power arrangements within systems of education (Taylor et al., 2009). Interviews with Hmong American undergraduate participants in the Initiative for Hmong Studies[1] (IHS) at a four-year Midwestern university reveal the deeply embedded nature of race and racism in their higher education experiences, and highlight the importance of healthy cultural identities, the development of critical race consciousness, and social justice activism.

CRITICAL RACE THEORY

As an outgrowth of Critical Legal Studies (CLS), CRT examines the relationships between race and the law (Crenshaw, Gotanda, Peller, & Thomas, 1995). Within education, CRT can expose the ways in which race impacts various aspects of education, including material inequities, policy, and the lived experiences of students and teachers (Ladson-Billings, 1998). While there is much theoretical diversity within CRT, Dixson and Rousseau (2006) identified six major unifying themes within CRT: (a) recognition that race is endemic to American life; (b) skepticism toward dominant legal claims of neutrality, objectivity, colorblindness, and meritocracy, which is often articulated as a critique of liberalism; (c) challenges to ahistoricism and an insistence on contextual and historical analyses of the law; (d) recognition of the experiential knowledge of people of color and communities of origin in analyzing law and society; (e) a need for interdisciplinary scholarship; and (f) support for activist work to eliminate racial oppression as part of the broader goal of ending all forms of oppression. Together, these unifying themes provide tools to examine and reveal institutional racism in a colorblind era (Bonilla-Silva, 2006) and validate the experiential knowledge of communities of color (Solórzano & Yosso, 2002).

Whiteness as Property

The notion of Whiteness as property fits within the critique of dominant discourses mentioned above because the property rights of Whiteness are largely protected through seemingly neutral legal discourses that privilege individual rights and claim colorblindness. Property rights of Whites are also protected through assumptions of "universal" definitions of humanity whose seemingly neutral sameness, in practice, constructs ideal citizens within a norm of Whiteness and maleness (Nelson, 1998; Sanchez-Eppler, 1993). The normative construction of humanity as White and male is also linked to colorblindness and to race neutrality in the sense that universal humanity is positioned in opposition to specificity—that is to say, in opposition to the possession of a distinctive and racialized culture (Rosaldo, 1993).

CRT in education is largely built around the intersection of race and property rights (Dixson & Rousseau, 2006; Ladson-Billings & Tate, 1995). Naming Whiteness as a form of property is "rooted in the notion that race and property rights have been inextricably intertwined since the creation of the United States" (DeCuir-Gunby, 2006, p. 101). Harris (1993) was among the first to theorize the relationship between Whiteness and property, arguing that Whiteness historically had been afforded legal protection in ways that were similar to property, and that this protection of Whiteness made it a powerful resource and form of protection under the law.

Racial Microaggressions

One of the most common ways in which institutional behaviors become individualized experiences of racism and White supremacy is through racial microaggressions (Kwan, 2015; Solórzano, Ceja, & Yosso, 2000; Yosso et al., 2009). Racial microaggressions are defined as the following:

> Subtle, innocuous, preconscious, or unconscious degradations, and put-downs, often kinetic but capable of being verbal and/or kinetic. In and of itself a microaggression may seem harmless, but the cumulative burden of a lifetime of microaggressions can theoretically contribute to diminished mortality, augmented morbidity, and flattened confidence. (Pierce, 1995, p. 281 as cited in Yosso et al., 2009, pp. 660–661)

These subtle racial putdowns actually cause "mundane but extreme stress" (Yosso et al., 2009, p. 661), in part because they are pervasive and difficult to address.

Although racial microaggressions in postsecondary education are often experienced interpersonally, it is important to recognize that they are indicative of a deeper institutional issue—the ways in which relationships, resource distribution, opportunities, and ways of knowing are racialized and inequitable in higher education settings (Solórzano et al., 2000; Yosso et al., 2009). This context of institutionally sanctioned racial inequity, coupled with Whiteness as property in most areas of institutional life (Gillborn, 2005; Leonardo, 2003), makes racially hostile college and university environments characterized by pervasive racial microaggressions much more likely to persist.

Critical Race Consciousness

Resisting institutional racism and White supremacy requires a critical race consciousness of the ways in which racism and other systems of oppression function, as well as the empowerment to dismantle all forms of oppression (Romero, Arce, & Cammarota, 2009; Stovall, 2006). Critical race consciousness can involve the use of CRT to develop consciousness of racial oppression and appreciation for communities of color toward the goal of critical transformation (Bernal, 2002; Yosso, 2005, 2006).

As the work of Romero et al. (2009) reveals, students of color are often inundated with negative messages about race and culture that encourage the internalization of these deficit discourses. Through a pedagogy that centers race and critical consciousness within rigorous academic experiences, educators can foster a deeper awareness of and value for culture, language, and community that prior educational and social experiences had undermined.

METHODS

Through critical race methodology, this project is based on the relationships between me, a White faculty member at Riverview University at the time of the study, and many Hmong American students. The research project was initiated to create an academic source relevant to their experiences and validate their experiential knowledge. The research participants are a selected group of 10 Hmong American undergraduates who were identified by their peers as student leaders. I conducted one individual hour-long interview with each participant. Interviews were held in locations chosen by students—sometimes a reserved room on their university campus, a restaurant, or a familiar coffee shop.

In Fall 2012, in addition to the individual interviews with Hmong American student leaders, three Hmong American undergraduates and I conducted focus group interviews with larger groups of Hmong American undergraduates at Riverview University. Together, we also collected survey data in order to get a sense of the racial campus climate and broader Hmong American student attitudes about Hmong studies and their university experiences. This project is ongoing and we will continue to utilize the data as a means of support for broader academic, social, and political initiatives around race and Hmong American communities.

The project is a purposeful effort to utilize research as a way to expose and take action against institutional racism in the specific context of the research participants' educational lives (Hylton, 2012; Parker & Castro, 2013). As our relationships gained more trust and confidence, we began to have more in-depth conversations about race, culture, and racial microaggressions in campus life. Although students often struggled to find the vocabulary to name their experiences or describe the feelings that accompanied racial microaggressions, they recognized that the ability to verbalize and validate their experiences was necessary for them individually as well as a means toward substantive institutional remedies.

THE CONTEXT: THE INITIATIVE FOR HMONG

The IHS was created primarily by Hmong American students and later joined by a multiracial group of faculty. The initiative's goal is to develop and implement a Hmong studies program at Riverview University. The initiative has its roots in both the academic and personal experiences of Hmong American students, particularly their ongoing experiences with racial microaggressions on campus and in the surrounding community, and their ongoing invisibility in the vast majority of university courses.

The IHS began as a much smaller self-education project called the Hmong Education Circle (HEC), which attempted to use student-led discussions about race to make up for the absence of Hmong-related curricula at Riverview. We invited presenters to speak about race, culture, and related issues relevant to Hmong American students. Initially, these talks were organized by a group of Hmong American students and me. However, Hmong American students soon took ownership of this project and I stepped back as more of an ad-hoc advisor.

My removal from the project leadership was particularly appropriate in the current context because, as a White female professor, there were limits to the extent to which I could be expected to effectively lead conversations in areas of Hmong studies. Beyond these limits, it was important to de-center my involvement because we did not want to reproduce the broader institutional power dynamics inherent in a top-down decision-making process in which White faculty had authority over and often spoke for Hmong American students.

As HEC students developed deeper consciousness about race and racism, they also expanded their social justice activism focus, which led to the more formal IHS. While Hmong American students have been working hard to realize this goal, the IHS continues to struggle for greater inclusion at all levels of university life. In this sense, it has only been partially successful and is evidence of the ways in which maintenance of Whiteness as property often signals the divergence of interest between Hmong American students and the university with regard to issues of race. While the university publicly voices support for the IHS, dedicated resources such as faculty lines, staffing resources, and other material forms of support remain inadequate. In this way, the university resists challenges to Whiteness as property by offering the complexities of institutional policy and bureaucracy as seemingly neutral roadblocks for the substantive university-led implementation of an institutionalized Hmong studies program.

This development of critical race consciousness fostered by IHS has allowed Hmong American students to understand the racial power inequities present in how the larger university has responded to advocates of Hmong studies curricula. Through an analysis of our individual interview data, the following sections illuminate these dynamics.

RECOGNIZING RACISM IN COLLEGE

Participants described a wide range of experiences with racial microaggressions. For example, one student reported a similar experience as many research participants in terms of how her earlier reluctance to speak Hmong connected to her experiences in school:

> I was always complimented while I was growing up on being able to speak English. I don't know…that just helped reinforce the idea that English is more valuable than Hmong because no one ever valued my ability to speak Hmong.

In this context, English became a proxy for Whiteness, reinforcing other messages that devalued Hmong characteristics. This resulted in shame of or desire to hide being Hmong, and was often reinforced through racial microaggressions that the Hmong American students experienced. Another Hmong American student explained that the exclusion of Hmong voices from the curricula led her to believe that it was not possible to study Hmong-related things in formal education settings:

> And, I don't think it was so much that I didn't want to, but that I never thought that I could. Because it always seemed like, "I need to do this for school, this for school" but I never thought that I *could* do [Hmong-related stuff] for school.

The Hmong curricular invisibility identified by students sent powerful messages of devaluation and marginalization to them and their non-Hmong peers.

Several participants recognized the absence or distorted nature of Hmong-related information available to White peers in particular, and stated that racial power inequities converged with ignorance to create racially charged and sometimes hostile educational settings. One Hmong American female undergraduate remembered a gender studies course she took that included an article, *Hmong Speak*, by a Hmong American feminist author:

> [A]fter people got done reading *Hmong Speak,* people were like "Oh, I'm so proud of her. She found her voice. Before she was using Hmong speak but now she has a voice because she has American speech." And for me it was like, "Well, it's not that she had no voice. It was like she didn't know how to use her voice in a way that fits in with the context." Because I felt like there's always a dominant communication norm that you have to fit into . . . I got really upset because I didn't realize until then when they were making these remarks that they think these things . . . my teachers didn't really . . . they really wanted to teach Hmong material, but they didn't have anything to say about it. They just wanted . . . to see how the other students react.

As this student indicated, lack of instructor preparation to engage Hmong knowledge systems sometimes led to an unintended message of Hmong culture as deficient or backwards, which marginalized Hmong American students. The participant later explained that in her opinion, these messages of deficiency reinforced other stereotypes held by White peers, such as generalizations that Hmong people are profoundly different, Hmong culture is oppressive to women, and Hmong people ultimately need White Western values to improve.

Another incident that took place in a living learning community at Riverview further illustrates the connection between the lack of accurate information about Hmong Americans and racially hostile educational environments at the postsecondary level. During their time at Riverview, several Hmong American students participated in a living learning community in one of the residence halls. The focus of the living learning community was Hmong American studies, and the majority of students who elected to participate were Hmong American. This meant that there was a racially identifiable Hmong American space within the residence hall. White student residents, who were not prepared to be the numerical minority within that resident hall context, responded with ongoing racial harassment of Hmong American students. For example, two Hmong American female undergraduates recounted their experience with manifestations of racism in the residence hall showers:

> Me and [another Hmong American female student] were having a conversation while taking a shower and we were speaking in Hmong...These White girls walked in and they just kind of (clears throat) with loud voices like "I'm here," you know, so we could hear them and everything, and then [we] just stopped talking...I felt like the girls were right outside of my shower curtain...And we could hear them...I don't know, it sounded like they were making fun of us because of our language. What I heard was, "We're gonna open their shower curtains." With that, just knowing that they were that close to me, I really felt like they were gonna open it. So I just turned off my shower, wrapped myself with my towel and I just got out. I didn't even look at them because I just felt so embarrassed already because we were talking in our own language and when the moment when they came in, we totally hushed. We did not have any more conversations after that. I just got out.

As these remarks illustrate, these students felt threatened when speaking Hmong language in public areas of the residence halls. The behavior of their White peers indicated that Hmong language was not respected and, in fact, was a racializing marker upon which racially hostile White students focused (Bonilla-Silva, 2006). Such incidents of cultural racism were accompanied by other racist acts, such as targeting Hmong American students in the residence hall for cooking and eating "smelly food," mocking Asian accents, and the posting of a racist sign in the women's bathroom.

Some Hmong American participants also reported that White students made negative remarks about them not being "American," which demonstrated how White people often equated American with being White as they made these remarks. Many Hmong American students reported White professors who spotlighted them in class and asked them to explain aspects of traditional Hmong spiritual practice or culture without knowing whether the student actually knew this information. Other Hmong Americans were consistently tokenized by having photos taken of them on campus for use on the university website—photos intended to emphasize the institution's "diversity"—even as the overall campus population was close to 95% White.

Hmong American participants in the study felt subjected to the "use and enjoyment" of Whites on campus and sensed that a refusal to participate would result in exclusion (Harris, 1993). The day-to-day experiences of Hmong American students who participated in the study indicated that "racial spotlighting"—unwanted hypervisibility—was coupled with "racial ignoring" or racial invisibility when students wanted to be visible (Carter Andrews, 2012). One student illuminated these realities in her interview:

> Definitely, in my science classes, I have the spotlighting thing happen. You know, when I first got onto campus, I was expecting to have White friends because, in high school, I had White friends . . . I thought I would be able to connect to other White students the way I had in the past and then I realized that, no matter how . . . I didn't really understand why, but no matter how hard I tried, it didn't work. And, I was like, why is it that I can't connect with White students the way I did in high school? So, there was that sense of alienation.

For the Hmong American research participant, being able to name her experiences as racial spotlighting, which is a form of racial microaggression, was important. Through her engagement with IHS and peer study of CRT and ethnic studies, she gained the academic knowledge to analyze and the language to name her experiences through a CRT lens. This allowed her to reflect on her experiences of alienation within an institutional context instead of internalizing negative racial messages about who she is and what she deserves.

RISING RACIAL CONSCIOUSNESS

Prior to developing a critical race consciousness within the IHS, many Hmong American students reported awareness of overt racism and subtle feelings of marginalization and invisibility. However, because they were never taught about institutional racism, they lacked the knowledge and vocabulary necessary to name their experiences as manifestations of systemic racism. Instead, students often adopted a colorblind lens that individualized or minimized racism. One Hmong American male participant describes this in his own history: "I was basically . . . a White kid in an Asian kid's body. Well, I became that over time because that's what, that's kind of what my school and my town and I guess society made me into." Having grown up in an overwhelmingly White rural environment, this student had been taught a colorblind approach to race and racism, which meant being a "White kid in an Asian kid's body."

Similarly, prior to development of a critical race consciousness, other Hmong American students reported that they participated in institutional "diversity" initiatives in sincere but uncritical ways, thereby often solidifying

Whiteness as property embedded within the institution even as they believed they were dismantling it. One student, for example, sent IHS updates to a broad list of faculty even though other Hmong American students had asked her not to be concerned that the process would be coopted. The emails did result in faculty attempts at cooptation, which led to this realization on the part of the student:

> The thing I didn't realize was going to happen was the part where people would actually speak for you without asking what you want. That was very strange for me...I remember one of the members, one of the faculty who I've been speaking to for a long time, who was really supportive and I really appreciated that, but her good intent didn't mean that she had a good approach. And she came to a meeting one day and she announced that she was doing something for us and it was the exact opposite of what we had been trying to do, of what we wanted.

This experience politicized the student and taught her that institutional racism was the reason why the struggle for Hmong studies was so difficult. According to her, her initial desire for universal participation was not surprising since her prior educational experiences emphasized colorblindness and a more simplistic "diversity" focus. This led her to an uncritical engagement with representatives of the university, which then allowed the university to coopt Hmong American students' social justice activism while marginalizing their voices.

Accordingly, Hmong American college students at Riverview University engaged in an ongoing process of collective and individual reflection on race, culture, language, identity, and institutional inequities. Through this process of critical race education, the students developed stronger and more nuanced understandings of institutional racism and other systems of oppression. Through CRT and critical race consciousness, students understood the relationship between a depoliticized "diversity" focus and Hmong American students' concomitant inability to name institutional racism. Students also identified institutional racism and Whiteness as property as sources of their internalized racism, including conflicted feelings of shame and the desire to be proud of Hmong culture, language, families, and communities.

Hmong American students utilized this developing critical race consciousness to understand the ongoing racial microaggressions discussed above and engage these experiences in productive ways. One Hmong American student, for example, discussed how important it has been for her to have the vocabulary to validate her experiences, particularly when the subtlety of racism usually results in invalidation of her experiences by others:

> Those terms really helped, being able to . . . like, the definition being offered about racism, where it wasn't just "hate" but a system of privilege and advantage and disadvantage. That made a lot of sense to me. Like, if you feel something but you can't make any sense of it and it feels like it doesn't make any sense, given what you know, then you feel like it's wrong or invalid. So, being able to have those terms and to understand how I feel in those terms is really helpful because then I feel like my experience is valid. So if someone closes the elevator door before I get to it, knowing that I'm coming to the elevator, like I said, I know that that's a microaggression. Even though she didn't say "I don't want you in the elevator with me."

This student is describing an actual incident in which a White undergraduate student hurried to shut the elevator door before she could enter.

When the Hmong American student shared this experience with other students, many of them Hmong American, she initially received a lot of criticism that she was overreacting or that it was not a racist incident. However, because the student knew that invalidation of a racialized experiences is a racial microaggression itself (Yosso et al., 2009), she trusted her own analysis in the face of others, even other Hmong American students, who minimized race in this situation.

When asked if confronting racism is harder when that racism is in the form of microaggressions, another student discussed this in one of his responses:

> It definitely is harder, even in terms of other minority or other Hmong students . . . I feel like because we have some of the tools to understand it so we can say that it is, whereas other people don't (have those tools) so they don't see it as racist. One of the things, in my own defense, that I feel makes me see it is how you feel, you know. If it makes you feel uncomfortable or if it makes you feel like this because of . . . and you start to wonder why you feel like that and you see patterns. Once you see patterns you can start to say that it's racist. But when, for a lot of students, a lot of minority students, they feel it but they're taught to ignore it and move on because it's not going to do anything even if they confront it.

The posting of a racist sign in the residence hall, discussed above, was widely publicized in local media outlets and received some national coverage in blogs such as *Colorlines* and *Angry Asian Man*. In addition, the Hmong American Student Association[2] and two Hmong American resident assistants connected to the living learning community issued a statement in which they named institutional racism as the cause of racism in the residence halls:

> The writing of these posters is not what is problematic; it is the racist ideologies and practices that were present in the posters that we need to address.

> We need to think critically about where these ideas have stemmed from. We must recognize the institutional contributions to the problem so that we can correct it.

The university ultimately decided on individual punishments for the two White women who wrote the racist sign in the residence hall. However, Hmong American research participants and other student activists who understood these incidents as results of institutionalized racism named Hmong studies as an important part of an institutional response; they recognized the larger systemic issues that led to such individual racist acts and consequently needed to be addressed. In sum, Hmong American student participants consistently illustrated how their development of critical race consciousness was key to their ability to name institutional racism and Whiteness as property in their educational experiences.

CONCLUSION AND RECOMMENDATIONS

Today, ethnic studies programs are increasingly under attack and marginalized at all education levels, including universities (Romero, 2010; Sleeter, 2011). The Hmong American students in this study have had to struggle against their university's attempts to maintain Whiteness. Critical race consciousness empowered students to advocate for their right to be meaningfully represented epistemologically and ontologically within university academic and social life.

Hmong American participant experiences highlight the need for reallocation of power and resources, and illustrate the impact that the politics of racial representation can have on the lived realities of students of color on campus. Herein, I highlight three recommendations that evolved from this research. First, university faculty, staff, and students must recognize the ongoing impact of institutional racism and avoid the assumption that university "diversity" initiatives are connected to the well-being of students of color. Instead, universities should emphasize outcomes for students of color as indicators of well-being, and these outcomes should be identified in equitable collaboration with students and communities of color. This requires substantive decision-making power beyond one or two representatives on a committee.

Second, students of color should be granted the right to approve or veto policies and initiatives implemented in their name. To recognize their full membership within the institution, it is important for students to be able to stop or substantively revise courses that represent Hmong Americans in stereotypical or shallow ways, refuse to allow professors to use student of color organizations as captive research participants for their own gain, and ensure that the university's media self-representation of race and campus climate is accurate.

A final recommendation for practice emerging from this analysis is to provide Hmong American campus community members with resources to "grow their own" faculty and instructors in Hmong American studies if such academics do not exist in the region. Moreover, this provision of resources should be done in a way that does not separate culture from context. In other words, it is important to teach contemporary issues, culture, and language within historical and institutional contexts, as well as to provide students with space to develop their own critical race consciousness as part of their ongoing growth and development. In this way, students will be able to address internalized racism and develop critical race consciousness through the knowledge they gain in these courses.

NOTES

1. The name of the initiative is a pseudonym.
2. This name is a pseudonym.

REFERENCES

Beck, N. (2014, May 7). Backlash: We, too, are UWEC protesters revolt against "microaggression," demand university action. *University of Wisconsin-Eau Claire Spectator.* Retrieved from http://www.spectatornews.com/campus-news/2014/05/07/backlash/

Bernal, D. D. (2002). Critical race theory, Latino critical theory, and critical raced-gendered epistemologies: Recognizing students of color as holders and creators of knowledge. *Qualitative inquiry, 8*(1), 105–126.

Bonilla-Silva, E. (2006). *Racism without racists: Color-blind racism and the persistence of racial inequality in the United States* (2nd ed.). Lanham, MD: Rowman & Littlefield.

Carter Andrews, D. J. (2012). Black achievers' experiences with racial spotlighting and ignoring in a predominantly White High School. *Teachers College Record, 114*(10), n10.

Crenshaw, K. W., Gotanda, N., Peller, G., & Thomas, K. (Eds.). (1995). *Critical race theory: The key writings that formed the movement.* New York, NY: New York University Press.

DeCuir-Gunby, J. T. (2006). "Proving your skin is White, you can have everything": Race, racial identity, and property rights in Whiteness in the Supreme Court case of Josephine DeCuir. In A. D. Dixson & C. K. Rousseau (Eds.), *Critical race theory in education: All God's children got a song* (pp. 89–112). New York, NY: Routledge.

DePouw, C. (2012). When culture implies deficit: Placing race at the center of Hmong American education. *Race, Ethnicity and Education, 15*(2), 223–239.

Dixson, A. and Rousseau, C. (Eds.). (2006). *Critical race theory in education: All God's children got a song.* New York, NY: Taylor & Francis.

Flaherty, C. (2013, November 25). In-class sit-in. *Inside Higher Ed.* Retrieved from http://www.insidehighered.com/news/2013/11/25/ucla-grad-students -stage-sit-during-class-protest-what-they-see-racially-hostile#sthash.nRu-Wdam5.dpbs

Gillborn, D. (2005). Education policy as an act of White supremacy: Whiteness, critical race theory and education reform. *Journal of Education Policy, 20*(4), 485–505.

Harris, C. I. (1993). Whiteness as property. *Harvard Law Review, 106,* 1707–1791.

Hing, J. (2014, February 14). When a hashtag sparks more than a dialogue. *Colorlines: News for action.* Retrieved from http://colorlines.com/archives/2014/02/ bbum_or_when_a_hashtag_sparks_more_than_a_conversation.html

Hylton, K. (2012). Talk the talk, walk the walk: Defining critical race theory in research. *Race, Ethnicity and Education, 15*(1), 23–41.

Kwan, Y. Y. (2015). Microaggressions and Hmong American students. *Bilingual Research Journal, 38*(1), 23–44.

Ladson-Billings, G. (1998). Just what is critical race theory and what's it doing in a *nice* field like education? *International Journal of Qualitative Studies in Education, 11*(1), 7–24.

Ladson-Billings, G., & Tate, W. F., IV. (1995). Toward a critical race theory of education. *Teachers College Record, 97*(1), 47–68.

Lee, S. J. (2009). Behind the model-minority stereotype: Voices of high- and low-achieving Asian American students. *Anthropology & Education Quarterly, 25*(4), 413–429.

Leonardo, Z. (2003). The agony of school reform: Race, class, and the elusive search for social justice. *Educational Researcher, 32*(3), 37–43.

Museus, S. D., & Park, J. J. (2015). The continuing significance of racism in the lives of Asian American college students. *Journal of College Student Development, 56*(6), 551–569.

Nelson, D. D. (1998). *National manhood: Capitalist citizenship and the imagined fraternity of White men.* Durham, NC: Duke University Press.

Ngo, B., & Lee, S. J. (2007). Complicating the image of model minority success: A review of Southeast Asian American education. *Review of Educational Research, 77*(4), 415–453.

Parker, L., & Castro, E. (2013). An introduction to critical race realism: Theoretical and methodological implications for education research. In D. J. Carter Andrews & F. Tuitt (Eds.), *Contesting the myth of a "post racial" era: The continued significance of race in U.S. education* (pp. 50–68). New York, NY: Peter Lang.

Romero, A. F. (2010). At war with the state in order to save the lives of our children: The battle to save ethnic studies in Arizona. *The Black Scholar, 40*(4), 7–15.

Romero, A. F., Arce, S., & Cammarota, J. (2009). A barrio pedagogy: Identity, intellectualism, activism, and academic achievement through the evolution of critically compassionate intellectualism. *Race, Ethnicity, and Education, 12*(2), 217–233.

Rosaldo, R. (1993). *Culture and truth: The remaking of social analysis.* Boston, MA: Beacon Press.

Sanchez-Eppler, K. (1993). *Touching liberty: Abolition, feminism, and the politics of the body.* Berkeley, CA: University of California Press.

Sleeter, C. E. (2011). *The academic and social value of ethnic studies: A research review.* Washington, DC: National Education Association. Retrieved from http://www.nea.org/assets/docs/NBI-2010-3-value-of-ethnic-studies.pdf

Solórzano, D. G., Ceja, M., & Yosso, T. J. (2000). Critical race theory, racial microaggressions, and campus racial climate: The experiences of African American college students. *Journal of Negro Education, 69*(1/2), 60–73.

Solórzano, D. G., & Yosso, T. J. (2002). Critical race methodology: Counter-storytelling as an analytical framework for education research. *Qualitative Inquiry, 8*(1), 23–44.

Stovall, D. O. (2006). Where the rubber hits the road: CRT goes to high school. In A. D. Dixson & C. K. Rousseau (Eds.), *Critical race theory in education: All God's children got a song* (pp. 233–242). New York, NY: Routledge.

Taylor, E., Gillborn, D., & Ladson-Billings, G. (2009). *Foundations of critical race theory in education.* New York, NY: Routledge.

Teranishi, R. T. (2010). *Asians in the ivory tower: Dilemmas of racial inequality in American higher education.* New York, NY: Teachers College Press.

University of Wisconsin System. (2014). *University of Wisconsin System fact book 2013–14: A reference guide to University of Wisconsin System statistics and general information.* Retrieved from https://www.wisconsin.edu/download/publications%282%29/Fact-Book.pdf

University of Wisconsin System Office of Policy Analysis and Research. (2013). *Ten-year headcount reports.* Retrieved from http://www.uwsa.edu/opar/ssb/2012-13/pdf/r_a103_tot.pdf

Xiong, Y. S. (2010). State-mandated language classification: A study of Hmong American students' access to college preparatory curriculum. *AAPI Nexus: Asian Americans & Pacific Islanders Policy, Practice, and Community, 8*(1), 17–42.

Yosso, T. J. (2005). Whose culture has capital? A critical race theory discussion of community cultural wealth. *Race, Ethnicity, and Education, 8*(1), 69–91.

Yosso, T. J. (2006). *Critical race counterstories along the Chicana/Chicano educational pipeline.* New York, NY: Routledge.

Yosso, T. J., Smith, W., Ceja, M., & Solórzano, D. G. (2009). Critical race theory, racial microaggressions, and campus racial climate for Latina/o undergraduates. *Harvard Educational Review, 79*(4), 659–691.

CHAPTER 4

VOICES OF ASIAN AMERICAN AND PACIFIC ISLANDER STUDENTS AND THE POLITICS OF DIVERSITY POLICY

Angela W. Kong

A lot of us knew that this was the moment. We had a moment. And we had to take it, not take it away from Black and Chicano/a students, not even to tack on a list of other demands or anything like that, but to really change how the university could look like and feel like. I don't think we were given the opportunity to be included after all that time and all those conversations... I don't think it happened.

—Filipina first-generation college student

Asian Americans are the fastest-growing racial group in the nation (Pew Research Center, 2012). At the same time, the Native Hawai'ian and Other Pacific Islander (NHPI) population is growing rapidly as well. With the increasing presence of AAPIs across the nation, it is imperative to understand the needs of this population within higher education.

In this chapter, I analyze AAPI students' reflections on their involvement in protests against a series of racist events mocking Black History Month at

Focusing on the Underserved, pages 89–98
Copyright © 2017 by Information Age Publishing
All rights of reproduction in any form reserved.

the University of California, San Diego (UCSD) during February of 2010. Central to this chapter is an analysis of how AAPI student activists struggled to work with other undergraduates of color and within the confines of the university to improve campus diversity policy, while simultaneously fighting for the needs of the numerically represented—yet highly underserved— pan-AAPI group. AAPI undergraduates represented 48% of the total UCSD student population in Fall 2009 (UC San Diego Student Research and Information, 2011). In the following sections, I examine how AAPI students who are committed to improving diversity policies discovered the importance of their voices, needs, and concerns in political efforts to transform the university.

THE CONTEXT

In February of 2010, several incidents sparked tension in the campus racial climate at UCSD. These incidents included a "Compton Cookout" party, a noose found hanging in the university library, a university student-televised show calling Black[1] students "n%#*!rs," and a Ku Klux Klan hood placed on a campus statue.[2] These racist events led to a critical response from AAPIs and other people of color at UCSD.

On February 26, 2010, approximately 300 students, staff, and faculty came together to protest the series of racist incidents by staging a sit-in at the UCSD chancellor's office and submitting a list of demands to Chancellor Marye Anne Fox. The first five policy demands illustrated the ways in which Black student organizers sought to reshape diversity policy. They requested administrators to fund more outreach efforts to hire African-American faculty, more events sponsored by the Black student union, staff and programs that aimed to achieve educational equity, and research-based scholarships for African American students. Many understood the racist events as assaults on underrepresented students and all students at UCSD, while others wanted to support improved conditions for Black students at the university. The sit-in expressed to the administration that it was imperative to take seriously the demands of students. Protestors comprised of a coalition of student organizations—the Asian and Pacific Islander Student Alliance (APSA), Black Student Union (BSU), Movimiento Estudiantil Chican@ de Aztlán (MEChA), Kamalayan Kollective (KK), Native American Student Association (NASA), Queer People of Color (QPOC), and the Students Affirmative Action Committee (SAAC). Other student participants included students from the Cross-Cultural Center, Lesbian Gay Bisexual and Transgender Resource Center, Women's Resource Center, the Department of Ethnic Studies, and the Summer Bridge Program.

The students requested a response to the list of demands by March 4, 2010, coinciding with the national and international Day of Action. On this day, the multi-ethnic student organizations and the UCSD administration signed common goals that concerned increasing diversity in admissions, curriculum, campus culture, faculty, resources, research, and student conduct. Some of the goals demanded (a) resources for the BSU to increase diversity of undergraduates; (b) funding the African American studies minor and Chicano/a Latino/a arts & humanities minor coordinator position; (c) resources to the Campus Climate Council, an advisory council to the chancellor to address campus climate, equity, and inclusion; and (d) the creation of research centers for African American, Chican@, and indigenous communities. Other goals addressed issues of recruitment and retention of underrepresented students and faculty.

While policies would benefit all students at the university, AAPI college students were not considered an underrepresented or indigenous group at UCSD; their needs were not a focal point in the agreed-upon goals. As an example, AAPIs were not invited to be a part of the Campus Climate Council. Instead, it took AAPI students' insistence and ongoing meetings and talks with the Vice Chancellor of Equity, Diversity, and Inclusion before they were invited to join the council three years later in November 2013 (UCSD student, personal communication, December 12, 2013). The racialization of AAPIs as model minority college students shaped their experiences with the administration and non-AAPI peer leaders. Although the AAPI student leaders discussed the need to fund an AAPI Studies minor and an AAPI Resource center, they did not pursue these demands because of their tenuous racial positioning. Not surprisingly, research reveals that, while AAPI students repeatedly demonstrated a need to revamp educational policy at UCSD for decades, the university consistently failed to understand this need and develop policies to adequately serve its AAPI students (Kong, 2014).

RESISTANCE FROM STUDENTS

The February, 2010 events and ensuing student protests made the racial positioning of AAPI students at UCSD visible. In this section, I analyze how AAPI student leaders struggled to work with other students of color to improve campus diversity policies while fighting for pan-AAPI needs. The eight AAPI student leaders—6 female- and 2 male-identified students— whom I interviewed represented a cross-section of undergraduates who self-identified under the pan-Asian category as Black-Filipino, Chinese, Filipino, Pinay (or Filipino American), Filipino-Chinese, Korean, and Vietnamese-Chinese. I conducted four additional interviews with non-AAPI students (2 female- and 2 male-identified students) who were key players in the student actions against the February 2010 events. These additional interviews provided important insights into the goals of the larger student protest. Informal conversations with AAPI and non-AAPI undergraduates were held in classrooms and office hours during the Compton Cookout protests and sit-in, and after the common goals were signed. These informal conversations shaped the interviews that were conducted from April to October 2011, which each averaged 90 minutes in length. The interviews produced three interrelated themes: (a) marginalization of the model minority, (b) an absence of AAPI student organization political orientations, and (c) the role of history in racial consciousness and race relations.

Marginalization of the Model Minority

AAPIs' hyper-visibility as numerically (over)represented model minority students makes invisible the unique struggles that many of them encounter as low-income, queer, and/or first-generation college students. Scott, a first-generation, queer, Chinese American college student recounted the response to when he received the highest grade and set the curve for an organic chemistry course—he was twice threatened by classmates to drop the course, and his mom received strange calls from individuals. Scott elaborated, "Other than that threatening issue, people responded with a lot of mean words, calling me names like 'faggot.'" Furthermore, when he asked his professor if he could postpone a midterm because of the sit-in at the chancellor's office, the professor replied, "No, because it shouldn't impede on your social life. You are [AAPI]. You are Asian folks. You should be able to handle this." Scott's story reveals the complexity of the stereotype of Asian Americans' universal educational "success." As a queer AAPI student, Scott was threatened and mocked by fellow classmates for scoring well on an exam, yet his professor's strident dismissal of his request to postpone his midterm—and his unreasonable expectation that all AAPI students should do well regardless of the circumstances—made it difficult for Scott to balance academics and involvement in political activism on campus.

The misconception of AAPI students as a model minority that does not face racial struggles also led other students of color to view AAPIs with suspicion during the protests. Liz, a Black-Pinay student, explained the politics that surrounded student organizing:

> There is a divide in how the Black student leaders perceive AAPI struggles. Also, their consciousness in being in solidarity when they need the bodies but when it is time for negotiations or time to strategize...AAPI voices tend to be left out.

AAPI student leaders felt frustrated and unwelcomed in meetings, often blaming Black student leaders instead of the administration who controlled the terms of the discussions. Alicia, a student who identified as a queer Korean American, confided that, because the February 2010 events targeted the Black community, it was challenging to push for policy reform to address issues regarding AAPI and queer students:

> I think it's hard because you want to or I want to avoid tacking on the BSU [list] to take on everyone's struggles you know. I think that's kinda what created some of the resentment that BSU didn't represent everyone in the ways they wanted to be represented, because they can't.

Liz and Alicia recognized that while the AAPI and Black groups were sympathetic to each other's struggles, their racialized experiences made it difficult to envision and create a shared platform on diversity initiatives.

Absence of Asian American and Pacific Islander Organization Political Orientations

The way in which AAPI students worked with each other during the February 2010 events represented the fragile nature of student political mobilization in 2010. Activist Diana recalled that prior to the February 2010 events, "Asian American organizations primarily focused on cultural activities . . . I know they would do . . . around new year's they would have cultural festivals . . . " She expressed her frustration that students elected board members who focused on social rather than political education and current political organizing activities.

While the interviewees did not object to the planning of cultural activities, they were dismayed that the student organizations were unaware of important political issues within their communities. Diana conceded, " . . . even if they did address Compton Cookout issues for a little bit, they just went back to 'It's almost new years. It's almost time for culture show.'" Similar to other interviewees, Diana distinguished herself politically from students in AAPI student organizations. "I'm still a person of color and I deal with racism. And [racism against Asian Americans] is never really addressed and often times considered less harmful." Ultimately, her disconnection with AAPI and non-AAPI students created feelings of isolation.

AAPIs struggled to understand the "power" they carried collectively in the way they attempted to organize around a common cause. Some recognized their role in the protests, sit-ins, and meetings with peers and administrators, while many grappled with how to pursue such work within a heterogeneous panethnic group. When I asked about the status of AAPI students on campus before and after the February 2010 events, Michelle, a Pinay student said, "a lot of the student responses from Asian Americans have been confusion. I feel like people were not on the same page in terms of what they wanted to do or say, or even what their roles were, and that's spilled into the aftermath." Like Diana, Michelle noted the difficulty in organizing AAPI students at the university because AAPI organizations appeared to focus primarily on cultural and social activities. Michelle noted the inability for AAPI student organizations to quickly unite together under a common front. The "aftermath" she referred to represented AAPI students' inability to understand what happened during and after the February 2010 events.

The heterogeneity of students made it difficult to pull together under common causes regarding diversity policy at the university. Kevin, a Chinese-Filipino student, spoke to the lack of cohesion within the AAPI community as he posited,

> I think a lot of [AAPI] students have the potential to be really strong activists, be more in the social justice space. It's just that we don't have that outlet to really educate students. We have our [student organizations] and stuff but our orgs can only do so much.

He addressed the difficulty in balancing social and cultural activities with a political education about their histories and experiences.

Role of History in Racial Consciousness and Race Relations

Kevin reflected on the dilemma of working with AAPI students to engage in social justice issues in an AAPI student organization at UCSD:

> Social injustice is something that is very deep and people might be overwhelmed by it. I noticed that too, being involved in APSA when we [have general body meetings] about anything like social justice related, there's lost members because people get overwhelmed and people don't want to talk about that stuff.

He recognized that the a lack of knowledge about AAPI history and political awareness made it difficult to talk about how their experiences connected to educational, political, and social issues.

Educators and student leaders of color assume that AAPIs know their histories upon their arrival to college. However, U.S. History courses seldom include AAPIs as integral and contributing members of American society. AAPI students' inability to politically mobilize is rooted in the lack of education about how their group struggled against discrimination, contributed to the formation of America, and mobilized as a panethnic group to fight for their rights, liberties, and resources. Kevin explained why it was important to learn about AAPI history as a way to build coalitions, partnerships, and connect with each other:

> The thing is that we have these ... all these movements, but if you don't see yourself connected to the movement, you're not going to engage yourself, you're not going to be as outspoken, you're not going to be as involved, you're not going to be in the frontline because you don't know how this works and how that connects to your identity or your struggle.

There is also an absence of historical discourse regarding how AAPI and Black students have worked together toward common social justice causes. Brandon, a BSU leader, demonstrated his knowledge of the cross-cultural activism between AAPI and Black students. When questioned of a divide between Asian American and Black students, he responded:

> I don't [think] there is any clear connection ... cohesion between Black and Asian students I would say ... I think maybe because this campus isn't aware of how historically Asian Americans and Blacks have been linked in terms of organizing ... May Fu [former UCSD graduate, guest speaker, and professor] talked about how the Black Panthers were formed by two Blacks and an Asian American guy. I was like "What?! Are you serious?!" I think if people knew more information about Yuri [Kochiyama] and the guy in the Black Panther Party, I think that would create a space for that.

Brandon points to the need to hear and see more Asian American and Black leaders working together in the struggle for equality and justice. Although an ethnic studies major, the first time he recalled learning about cross-cultural activism was actually *after* the February 2010 events.

The absence of written literature and conversations concerning AAPI struggles and cross-cultural activism at UCSD is extensive. More than 25 years ago, the Asian American campus community waged a battle for a permanent Asian American studies program, which encountered resistance from academic departments and the Committee on Academic Personnel in hiring faculty (Kong, 2014). There is still no AAPI Studies Program at UCSD and, moreover, this story about AAPI campus activism had been sitting in the archives for decades. In class and informal campus settings, course readings and discussions connect the educational equity issues and activist struggles experienced by Black and Chicano/Latino students.[3] Campus organizations also produced diversity reports that addressed African American and Chicano/Latino student experiences.[4] For these AAPI students, the desire to understand unique AAPI experiences in relation to other students of color became a part of who they are and how they felt connected to and rooted in the university community. Without professors, student affairs professionals, and leaders who are aware of and able to teach about AAPI struggles, AAPI participation in student activism, and AAPI stories of political coalition building at UCSD, AAPIS are persistently re-inscribed as caring only about their studies, apathetic to important social justice movements, and perceived as monolithic academic robots.

More than 50 years after the founding of the University of California, San Diego campus, there is now a Cross-Cultural Center, Department of Ethnic Studies, Lesbian Gay Bisexual Transgender Center, Office of Academic Support and Instructional Services (OASIS), Student Promoted Access Center for Education and Service (SPACES), Women's Center, Black Resource Center, Inter-Tribal Resource Center, and Raza Resource Centro. The creation of these campus centers and programs were all based on the demands and needs of students of color. Students expanded and redefined the meaning of diversity that moved beyond the achievement gap; they helped to create safe spaces for all students of color to thrive. Today, Asian American and Pacific Islander students continue to educate the UCSD administration so that they understand these underserved populations' challenges in terms of access, success, campus climate, and intergroup relations. To note, an AAPI resource center still does not exist and AAPI students continue to assume the intellectual burden of educating administrators about their struggles and experiences. The underlying assumption that AAPI students are not a vital part of discussions regarding diversity perpetuates the stereotype that they do not need nor deserve institutional support, help, and student services. The Asian American and Pacific Islander student experience is an unfolding story of multiplicity, negotiation, and struggle.

RECOMMENDATIONS FOR INSTITUTIONAL POLICY

The story told above has several implications for policy at postsecondary institutions. Due to space limitations, I review three recommendations in this section: (a) disaggregate data on AAPIs, (b) institutionalize AAPI studies programs, and (c) implement student organization training through campus community centers.

1. *Disaggregate the Asian American and Pacific Islander category.* The story shared above suggests that colleges and universities must disaggregate data on AAPIs in their research reports to understand their challenges in regard to access, retention, and graduation. Currently, UCSD and many institutions lump all AAPI students into the category of "Asian American and Pacific Islander" or into "Asian

Americans" and "Pacific Islanders." Disaggregated data are necessary to combat overgeneralizations of this community, inform more complex understandings of this population, and effectively inform institutional policies and practices designed to support diverse student populations. Indeed, aggregated data for the panethnic group occludes the underrepresentation of many ethnic groups within the Asian American and Pacific Islander categories in higher education (Museus, 2013).

2. *Institutionalize an Asian American and Pacific Islander studies program.* The absence of AAPIs in the history books, discussed above, warrants the institutionalization of Asian American and Pacific Islander studies programs. It is imperative for students to develop a racial consciousness and understanding of their own communities by educating AAPI and non-AAPI students, staff, faculty, and administrators regarding these communities' histories, the heterogeneity of their experiences, how social and political issues affect them, and the myriad impacts of racism and colonization on the AAPI community. It is also necessary to structure courses that connect the academy to the community in order to train and build future leaders to answer problems such as homelessness, employment, and domestic violence, as well as teach students about cross-cultural activism to combat racism and homophobia.

3. *Implement Asian American and Pacific Islander student organization training through campus community centers.* Campus centers such as the cross-cultural center can partner with AAPI student organizations to train student leaders to facilitate discussions and create programs surrounding cultural, social, and political issues. The training would also delve into topics such as building ally-ships and coalitions, learning about the needs of marginalized communities, and shaping campus diversity initiatives. The training would help student organizations document material to assist future leaders in yearlong student coordinating positions. Other campus centers, such as the women's and LGBT centers, would also contribute in developing themed workshops that address the intersectionality of race with gender and sexuality.

NOTES

1. I use the category of Blacks and African Americans interchangeably. However, I recognize that distinctions within the panethnic group that structures their experiences necessitates further discussion.
2. A heartfelt thanks to students and student interviewees, whose strength in transforming the college campus is extraordinary.

3. A Compton Cookout Teach-Out speaker noted the powerful coalition between Black and Brown students, which referred to Black and Chicano/Latino students.
4. *Do UC us? Campaign to increase numbers of African-American students at the University of California, San Diego* (2009) by UCSD Black Student Union, and *San Diego: A Legacy of Institutional Neglect* (2003) by UCSD Chicano/Latino Concilio.

REFERENCES

Kong, A. W. (2014). *Re-examining diversity policy at University of California, San Diego: The racial politics of Asian Americans* (Unpublished doctoral dissertation). University of California, San Diego.

Museus, S. D. (2013). *Asian American students in higher education.* New York: Routledge.

Pew Research Center. (2012). *The rise of Asian Americans.* Washington, DC: Pew Social & Demographic Trends. Retrieved from http://www.pewsocialtrends.org/2012/06/19/the-rise-of-asian-americans/

University of California, San Diego Student Research and Information. (2011). *Undergraduate Enrollment, Fall 2009.* San Diego, CA: University of California, San Diego Office of Student Research and Information.

University of California, San Diego Black Student Union. (2009). *Do UC us? Campaign to increase numbers of African-American students at the University of California.* San Diego, CA: The Black Student Union of the University of California, San Diego. Retrieved from http://diversity.ucsd.edu/_files/pdf/DoUCus-CampaignReport.pdf

University of California, San Diego Chicano/Latino Concilio. (2003). *Report card on the University of California, San Diego: A legacy of institutional neglect.* San Diego, CA: UCSD Chicano/Latino Concilio. Retrieved from https://academicaffairs.ucsd.edu/_files/aps/reports/uftf/Attachment4.pdf

PART II

ADVANCING RACIALLY CONSCIOUS POLICY AND PRACTICE

CHAPTER 5

UNDOCUMENTED ASIAN AND PACIFIC ISLANDER STUDENTS

A Primer for Developing Critical Awareness and Advocacy Among Educators

Tracy Lachica Buenavista

As undocumented residents, many of the young students
are without full political rights, cannot naturalize, and cannot vote.

—Gonzales, 2008, p. 221)

There are 11.4 million undocumented residents in the United States whose lives are negatively impacted by the absence of formal political rights (Baker & Rytina, 2013). In particular, the lack of legal protection has fostered numerous barriers to education for youth with undocumented status (Abrego 2006). Yet, educators across the nation remain largely unaware and uninformed about the undocumented student population (Gildersleeve & Ranero, 2010; Perez, 2010). Even less is known about undocumented Asian American and Pacific Islander (AAPI) students, whose issues

Focusing on the Underserved, pages 101–119
Copyright © 2017 by Information Age Publishing
101

remain obscured by problematic social perceptions that racialize AAPI students as model minorities (Buenavista, 2013; Buenavista, Chen, & So, 2013; Chan, 2010). In this chapter, I draw from nationally disseminated stories of undocumented AAPI students to describe some of the issues faced by undocumented AAPI students in economic, political, and social contexts. I also share the perspectives of undocumented Asian American students to describe their immigrant and racial marginalization, the financial hardships to which they are subjected, and the surveillance and political disenfranchisement they experience without a viable pathway to citizenship. Their narratives are from a larger project in which I interviewed 15 Asian American immigrants with undocumented status (Buenavista, 2013). Overall, this chapter is a primer to help educators learn and prepare to enter national discussions about how undocumented immigration shapes AAPI student experiences and, subsequently their life chances.

DIVERSE STUDENT CONTEXTS

American news media has been able to capture the diversity of undocumented AAPI student contexts. Arguably one of the most visible activists of the undocumented student movement, Vietnamese American Tam Tran was a graduate of UCLA and doctoral student at Brown University before her untimely passing in 2010 (Wong et al., 2012). Tran, an aspiring scholar and filmmaker, was largely known for her congressional testimony on behalf of her undocumented peers in 2007. Born in Germany and raised in the United States for the majority of her life, Tran was not only undocumented, she was also stateless and without citizenship or nationality. As refugees of the Vietnam War, her family applied for political asylum in the United States, but was denied because they did not emigrate directly from Vietnam as other Southeast Asian refugees did. The ambiguity of her immigration status underscored the limitations of the American immigration system, which continues to lack mechanisms for many individuals to attain legal status.

Unlike Tran, Fita[1] did not grow up in the United States, and her story has received less coverage. In 2006, Fita emigrated from Tonga at 18 years of age (Guzman-Lopez, 2011). Upon her arrival, she enrolled at El Camino Community College in Torrance, California, with aspirations to pursue engineering. As a non-resident student, Fita was charged international student tuition and could not afford to attend school. Although her presence in the country was initially authorized, she eventually overstayed her visa and acquired undocumented status. Fita's experience served as the basis of a news story that featured her work collecting the narratives of undocumented

Pacific Islanders and in which it was reported that an estimated one-third of the Tongan American community was undocumented.

Tran and Fita's stories bring attention to the diversity among undocumented AAPIs and the ways that undocumented immigration has impacted them. AAPI narratives demonstrate how the United States has served as a destination for the politically and economically displaced, yet is a space where undocumented immigrants remain disenfranchised. Similarly, Tran's migration was a consequence of American involvement in the Vietnam War, but her family was unable to attain the political protection that many Southeast Asian refugees sought. Fita's migration is representative of the capitalist disruption of the Tongan economy, which facilitated the Tongan diaspora and migration to places like the United States, Australia, and New Zealand, where many of them have become undocumented (Kinikini, 2005; Lee, 2003). While both of their stories were constructed as the accounts of students on an inextinguishable pursuit of higher education, Tran and Fita had very different educational outcomes.

BARRIERS TO EDUCATION

Within the past decade, scholars have examined the experiences of students like Tran and Fita to understand how undocumented status has shaped the academic trajectories of immigrant students. Researchers have revealed that each year, approximately 50,000 to 65,000 undocumented youth graduate from high school with few opportunities for social, political, and economic mobility because of their status (Gonzales, 2007; Madera et al., 2008; Perez, 2009). Among the most cited scholarship, the themes of economic disenfranchisement, criminalization, and racial marginalization characterize undocumented immigrant experiences and provide educators with general insight regarding the various factors that impact the educational participation of young people without legal status.

Economic Disenfranchisement

Undocumented immigrants have few legal options for employment and are relegated to low-paying jobs, harsh working conditions, and persistent job insecurity (Bernstein & Blazer, 2008). Many undocumented AAPI immigrants work in domestic service and manufacturing industries (Fujiwara, 2008; Parreñas, 2001), although undocumented workers are also heavily concentrated in service, construction, and farming occupations (Passel & Cohn, 2009). Undocumented youth are subjected to these labor disparities; many are also workers and part of families who lack socioeconomic mobility because of limited job options (Abrego & Gonzales, 2010; Bernstein & Blazer, 2008). The median annual income of $36,000 for undocumented families is noticeably less than the median annual income of $50,000 of their U.S.-born counterparts (Passel & Cohn, 2009). Moreover, one-third of children with undocumented parents live in poverty, regardless of their own status. The economic disenfranchisement imposed on undocumented immigrants relegates them to poor and low-income neighborhoods, and such residential segregation has determined the types of schools undocumented youth are able to attend. As a result, undocumented youth are more likely to attend schools that are under-resourced and ill-prepared to mediate the learning of immigrant students (Gildersleeve & Ranero, 2010).

Poverty also deters undocumented students from developing postsecondary aspirations and pursuing higher education (Perez, 2010). Only half of the undocumented immigrants who have completed high school have college experience, which is well below the rate for those who are born in the United States (Passel & Cohn, 2009). College affordability is one of the most serious barriers to higher education for undocumented youth. Undocumented students are ineligible for federal financial aid and, in most states, they are not qualified for state-sponsored financial aid programs (Rincon, 2008). Although many undocumented youth are 1.5-generation youth who have lived and attended school in the United States for the majority of their lives, most states classify these students as out-of-state or international students, which require them to pay exorbitant non-resident tuition and fees (Ruge & Iza, 2005). Even in states that enable some undocumented students to pay in-state tuition, divestment in public higher education has led to unprecedented fee increases and a gross inability for undocumented families to afford college.

Criminalization

While research on undocumented youth often focuses on the impact of poverty, criminalization is at the epicenter of undocumented immigrant realities. For example, "illegal alien" has remained the popular nomenclature to describe immigrants with undocumented status (De Genova, 2004; Ngai, 2004; Simanski & Sapp, 2012). The term "unauthorized immigrant" is also commonly used in literature focused on the undocumented population, including reports produced by government agencies such as the Department of Homeland Security. Such naming is indicative of the negative sentiment toward immigrants with undocumented status. Due to the social stigma associated with undocumented status, many youth have found it difficult to seek support and resources in both school and social contexts (Abrego, 2008; Perez, 2009). For example, undocumented immigrants are concerned with exposing their status and are often prevented from easily accessing public services without required documentation, which has led students to become wary of their ability to pursue opportunities such as college.

Illegality, though socially constructed, has very material consequences. Due to their status and the conceptualization of immigrants as "illegal," many have suffered from relentless policing, detention, and deportation (Hernández, 2008; Ngai, 2004). Policing reflects a prison industrial complex that pervades American society and entails the racial profiling and hyper-surveillance of People of Color, including immigrants (Ray, 2005; Volpp, 2002). The increased policing of communities of color has led to the proliferation of federal, state, municipal, and privately-run detention centers, as well as the subsequent removal of undocumented immigrants from the United States (Hernández, 2008). For example, in 2011, the U.S. Immigration and Customs Enforcement detained 429,000 immigrants, and the Department of Homeland Security deported more than 390,000 individuals (Simanski & Sapp, 2012, p. 1). Although the federal government has granted undocumented youth some legal protection in school contexts[2] and minors are mandated to participate in K–12 public schooling, no federal guidelines actually insist undocumented youth should have equal access to higher education.

Racial Marginalization

Although the plight of undocumented immigrants has garnered increased scholarly attention, AAPI experiences are under-examined; few studies have interrogated the ways in which undocumented AAPI youth have differentially experienced education (Bangalon, Peralta, & Enriquez, 2012; Buenavista, 2013; Buenavista & Chen, 2013; Chan, 2010; Eusebio, 2012). In 2012, 1.3 million undocumented AAPIs comprised 11.4% of the total undocumented immigrant population (Baker & Rytina, 2013). The majority of undocumented AAPIs were from the Philippines, India, Korea, China, and Vietnam, but included individuals from countries such as Bangladesh, Indonesia, and Tonga or regions such as Latin America. The number of undocumented AAPIs compared to their Latino counterparts has often been used to understand undocumented student experiences in postsecondary contexts. For example, the disproportionately high representation of undocumented AAPIs in college relative to their overall representation in the United States[3] has been used to narrow the focus on the lack of college access for undocumented Latino students (Gonzales, 2010) or to stress the need to examine the diversity of undocumented students (Bangalon et al., 2012). Yet, there remain few efforts to truly discern the experiences of undocumented AAPI youth.

In a project focused on undocumented Asian American immigrant youth, I found that while these youths had been subjected to the same financial hardship and criminalization as other undocumented immigrants, the simultaneous racialization of Asian Americans as model minorities led to a complex marginalization that often exacerbated issues related to their immigration status (Buenavista, 2013). For example, during interviews, undocumented Asian Americans stressed how their entry to the United States was initially permissible. Many of the youth explained how they had entered with a temporary visa, but overstayed and acquired undocumented status. The emphasis on overstaying served as a mechanism to downplay the illegality associated with being undocumented. In addition, undocumented Asian American youth had found that, although it was problematic that educators assumed that they were academically talented, such stereotyping inadvertently deterred from their status being detected. In terms of their vulnerable legal status, interview participants also practiced a strategy of non-disclosure in order to avoid suspicion, which subsequently perpetuated the model minority stereotype and the invisibility of their hardships.

FEDERAL AND STATE POLICY EFFORTS

The economic disenfranchisement and criminalization of undocumented immigrants have led to recent policy efforts to alleviate some of the burdens placed on this community. However, the racial marginalization of undocumented AAPIs points to the need to scrutinize the diversity of experiences among undocumented immigrants. In the following sections, the narratives of some undocumented Asian American youth I have worked with poignantly outline and critique contemporary policies at federal, state, and institutional levels that target undocumented youth. In doing so, my goal is to synthesize AAPI student experiences and provide important points for educators to consider as they become more immersed and entrenched in research and practice intended to serve undocumented students.

Federal Development, Relief, and Education for Alien Minors (DREAM) Act

> I have mixed emotions about [the DREAM Act] because I qualify, but my brother doesn't. He didn't finish school and right now he's working. Who's to say that I should get citizenship and he shouldn't? We both grew up here, been through the same struggles. And what about my parents?
>
> —Alfredo

Few legislative efforts exist to create potential pathways to legal status for undocumented immigrants. The proposed federal DREAM Act (S. 952/H.R. 1842, 2011) represents the most robust attempt to offer immigrants a mechanism to change their undocumented status.[4] The federal DREAM Act would position young people to be initially classified as "conditional non-immigrants" in the United States, and eventually legal permanent residents (LPR). To note, while a direct process to naturalization is not outlined in the DREAM Act, under traditional immigration policy, any person with LPR status in the United States can apply for citizenship after fulfilling various residency requirements. The necessity for young people to understand this limitation of the DREAM Act is demonstrated by Alfredo's statement above. Alfredo, a 23-year-old college student with undocumented status, emigrated with his parents from South Korea to the United States when he was 8 years old. Currently, he is enrolled at a large, four-year public institution. While he was cognizant that his status as a college student made him an ideal candidate for the DREAM Act, he articulated a common misunderstanding that the legislation would enable him to naturalize his status to that of American citizen.

The indirect pathway to citizenship is not necessarily the biggest limitation of the proposed legislation. Rather, the overwhelming number of requirements young people must fulfill poses several barriers to completing the pathway to LPR. Alfredo was wary of the fact that if the legislation passed, his other family members would not be beneficiaries. To even be eligible to apply for the DREAM Act, an individual must have entered the country before the age of 15. The age limit of the DREAM Act renders most of the undocumented population ineligible for relief, including Alfredo's parents who arrived in their thirties. DREAM-eligible youth are also marked by their successful attainment of a high school diploma, general education development (GED) certificate, or acceptance into an institution of higher education. Alfredo's brother, who also has undocumented status, would not qualify for the DREAM Act because he would not fulfill the educational prerequisites. Furthermore, Alfredo's brother's experience represents the majority of undocumented youth who are pushed out of the educational pipeline and who lack access to postsecondary education.

A dilemma presents itself even for those who consider the DREAM Act as an educational access initiative—the act simultaneously represents a recruitment strategy for the U.S. Armed Forces (Mariscal, 2007), which is especially problematic for AAPI immigrant communities who have already demonstrated a legacy of military participation (Buenavista, 2012; Buenavista & Gonzales, 2010/2011). Scholars have touted the DREAM Act as a strategic mechanism to meet recruitment goals for the various branches of the military, and have even acknowledged how it is poised to compete with colleges for desirable recruits (Bicksler & Nolan, 2009; Stock, 2009). Youth of color are increasingly targeted for military recruitment, which in many ways can be considered a deterrent to college for many non-traditional students who are eligible for other forms of postsecondary support. Educators must think about how the militarized character of the DREAM Act actually threatens efforts to increase the access and retention of undocumented immigrants in higher education.

It is of the utmost importance for educators to understand that the DREAM Act offers a *pathway* toward naturalization, but not citizenship itself, and represents only the beginning of a long process toward relief for undocumented youth. Further, while educators might be working with undocumented students at various institutions, they are anomalies among their peers, the majority of whom have been shut out of higher education. In this context, educators must use their educational positions to increase awareness regarding the access and retention issues of undocumented youth in higher education beyond those enrolled at their institutions.

State Financial Aid Policies

[California Assembly Bill] 540 is a catch-22. On one hand California says, sure, you can go to school and we'll let you pay in-state fees. But on the other hand, they won't give us any financial aid. Of course, it's better than nothing because I know other places are making laws that are making it even harder for us [undocumented students] to go to school...And don't get me started on the budget cuts! The state keeps cutting our funding and then putting the costs on the students. Hopefully, California will get it together and figure something out.

—Deena

Without a pathway to legal resident status, undocumented students are ineligible for federal financial aid and face insurmountable barriers to college, namely cost (Perez, 2010; Rincon, 2008). At a state level, although many undocumented students have lived the majority of their lives in the United States, they also frequently face difficulties demonstrating they are residents of the state and are sometimes subject to out-of-state or international student fees (Ruge & Iza, 2005). Simultaneously, the insidious trend of state divestment in public higher education has resulted in colleges and universities imposing fee increases onto students and families. The combination of financial aid ineligibility, ambiguous residency, and increasing costs urgently threatens the affordability of college for undocumented students.

At the federal level, the lack of comprehensive immigration reform has forced undocumented youth and families to rely more on state efforts to alleviate burdensome college costs. In response, 12 states have passed legislation that has enabled some undocumented students to be eligible for in-state resident fees (National Immigration Law Center, 2012). In the opening of this section, Deena discussed California Assembly Bill 540 (AB 540), which laid out certain criteria that students could fulfill to be exempt from non-resident state fees. AB 540-eligible students have (a) attended a California high school for three or more years, (b) graduated from a California high school or earned the equivalent of a high school diploma, (c) registered at a public college or university, and (d) filed an affidavit promising to become "lawful permanent residents" at the earliest possible opportunity (AB 540, 2001). A common misperception about AB 540 is that it provides an unfair advantage to undocumented students over "documented" students to avoid paying non-resident fees. However, the reality is that undocumented youth actually comprise the minority of students who have successfully applied for AB 540 designation (UCOP, 2010).

Although AB 540 has been instrumental in lowering postsecondary expenses for undocumented students, Deena also highlighted a major contradiction in such state efforts: no federal financial aid eligibility. AB 540 is not an immigration policy and provides no pathway to residency, nor does it grant undocumented students the ability to receive state-sponsored grants and scholarships. To address financial aid access, some states offer in-state aid to undocumented students. At the time I interviewed Deena, she described AB 540 as a "catch-22," and the California DREAM Act (2011) had not yet been approved. Comprising two different bills—AB 130 and AB 131—the California DREAM Act was signed into law in 2011.[5] AB 130 provided AB 540 students the opportunity to apply for privately funded scholarships and grants made available at public institutions. AB 131 extended financial aid possibilities for undocumented students by granting them eligibility for Cal Grants, the largest source of state financial aid for students enrolled in California public institutions, as well as scholarships and grants from non-privately funded sources. While such policies are an important step to making higher education more affordable to undocumented students, to date California, Texas, and New Mexico are the only states that have passed legislation to make undocumented students eligible for in-state aid. Further, in states such as California, funding is limited to students who qualify under AB 540; these resources benefit only students who have fulfilled all the requirements to acquire the designation.

It is important to note all the states that have passed policies attempting to deny the participation of undocumented immigrants in public education. For example, several states have banned undocumented students from being eligible for in-state tuition, including Arizona, Colorado, Georgia, and

Indiana (Russell, 2011). Arizona also prohibits undocumented students from qualifying for any type of state-sponsored financial aid. While such measures pose barriers to undocumented youth who pursue higher education, states such as Alabama and South Carolina actually prevent them from enrolling in public colleges and universities.

Higher education practitioners, particularly those working in financial aid and student affairs, are central in the information dissemination of undocumented student rights within a postsecondary context. Part of educators' job responsibilities includes becoming familiar with various policy changes that may impact financial aid and enrollment opportunities for undocumented students. Racially conscious educators are in a position to be sympathetic allies who can advocate on behalf of undocumented AAPI students whose issues are exacerbated by their racialization as model minorities and the misperception that they do not suffer from economic difficulties. However, and perhaps more importantly, educators must also call into question the potential power they may be assigned under the auspices of policing and denying undocumented students' access to education in the name of institutional policies that align with nativist state mandates. Educators occupy a complex position when their intentions are to serve all students at their institutions, but might be forced to implement and negotiate policies that hurt some undocumented students due to their immigration status.

Deferred Action for Childhood Arrivals

> Ate,[6] is this policy that everyone's talking about really happening? I want to be excited but I'm so scared the government's going to change their mind again. They still haven't fully given DREAMers a path to citizenship. We can work, I suppose, but we're still unable to travel, to qualify for financial aid . . . Can we please do a quick call later to dialogue about this?
>
> —May

On June 15, 2012, President Barack Obama announced an executive order and then Secretary of Homeland Security Janet Napolitano issued a memorandum for Deferred Action for Childhood Arrivals (DACA).[7] At the center of DACA is the intended prevention of deportation for certain qualified immigrants, namely young people who had entered the United States before the age of 16, had been residing in the United States for at least five years, and were "physically present" on the day the memorandum was issued. To be eligible for DACA, individuals must also be younger than 30 years old, a high school graduate or in possession of a GED or an honorably discharged military veteran, and not have been convicted of felony or "significant" misdemeanor offenses. The benefit of DACA is that young people who are granted deferred action are able to remain in the United States for a period of two years, which is subject to renewal, and can become eligible to apply for work authorization and a driver's license in some states.

DACA outlines criteria intended to protect young undocumented immigrants from being placed into removal proceedings and expedites reviews for individuals already in the removal process. The perplexity with DACA is that it does not guarantee relief to individuals who apply. In fact, the memorandum clearly states, "[The Department of Homeland Security] cannot provide any assurance that relief will be granted in all cases" (Napolitano, 2012, p. 2). Rather, DACA only encourages federal entities—U.S. Immigration and Customs Enforcement (ICE), U.S. Customs and Border Protection (CBP), U.S. Citizenship and Immigration Services (USCIS), and others—to practice "prosecutorial discretion" for individuals who do not "pose a threat to national security or public safety" (p. 1). The logic of prosecutorial discretion is to assess immigrant removal on a case-by-case basis and to provide relief to "low-risk" individuals who would otherwise be subjected to deportation without attention to the circumstances surrounding their arrival and subsequent experiences in the United States.

While relief is not guaranteed, there are further limitations of DACA, namely those identified above by May. May, a 23-year-old, undocumented Filipino college student, migrated with her parents more than a decade ago. Her experience has been characterized by financial burdens that have led her to work in the informal economy to pay for school and help sustain her family. Upon the announcement of DACA, she immediately contacted me with her concerns, including the reality that the administrative order did not (a) provide a pathway to citizenship, (b) alleviate all travel constraints, or (c) provide financial aid eligibility for undocumented youth. Also significant was her fear of the impermanence of DACA, which is not law and can be revoked at any time.

May's overt skepticism and her quick outreach efforts to me represent two important points to keep in mind regarding DACA. First, faculty and other educational practitioners have the potential to serve as important sources of support for undocumented youth. May's communication with me occurred following the formal announcement of DACA on national news media, which did not provide her any sort of relief in context of her status and instead only facilitated confusion and the desire to process with someone her thoughts on DACA. However, it is salient to note that her ability to contact me was grounded in a strong collegial relationship—developed over several years—during which we nurtured a high level of mutual trust and respect. Second, May's concerns highlighted the importance of educators to be informed with the most recent developments and policies that shape the status of undocumented students, and how such policies may impact their postsecondary experiences.

The need for educators to stay abreast with such policies is not so that they are equipped to provide any legal advice. Instead, it is to prepare them to demonstrate to students that they are reliable institutional allies to whom they could turn with their concerns, as well as to direct students to the appropriate professional and community-based resources to responsibly address their questions. Educators can serve as integral liaisons between colleges and universities, community-based resources, and undocumented students. This role is especially important in the context of policies such as DACA, which directly impact an individual's deportability, one of the biggest stressors imposed upon undocumented youth.

RECOMMENDATIONS FOR COLLEGE EDUCATORS

> Because of the backlash that undocumented students face, for many of them, it feels safer not to expose one's immigration status. But this means, never opening up and asking for help. (Chan, 2010, p. 31)

The prevailing mechanism for student services is one in which the onus of assistance is placed onto students: Students must seek help to receive it. However, if they recognize and understand that students with an undocumented status are survivors of both a broken immigration system and a police state that render their transition to possessing legal status nearly impossible, the student-facilitated approach to support services within an educational context must inevitably change. Rather than expect undocumented students to learn help-seeking behaviors, educators must combat a nativist culture of fear that permeates campuses and creates critical spaces and opportunities for undocumented students to pursue education. In the following, I offer recommendations with regard to how educators can become allies and help to transform education to better serve undocumented students.

Develop and Practice a Critical College-Going Pedagogy That Centralizes Undocumented Immigrant Experiences

Whereas institutional agents would like to imagine that they have played an active role in the recruitment and retention of undocumented students in college, for the most part, few examples of institutional efforts have been developed with undocumented students in mind. Gildersleeve and Ranero (2010) argue that educators could learn and teach a critical "college-going pedagogy" to enhance postsecondary opportunities for undocumented youth (p. 21). This might include community-based outreach programs that are held in the neighborhoods and schools where undocumented students and families are located, and culturally-relevant advising sessions and programs that centrally address the ways in which undocumented immigrant status might impact admissions, enrollment, and/or financial aid.

However, such potential efforts only touch the surface in addressing the marginalization of undocumented AAPI youth. Educators must be able to speak to the fears of undocumented students and families. Apprehension, detention, and deportation are likely occurrences within migrant communities. Only when educators acknowledge and accept this reality will they be able to strategize with undocumented youth to maximize students' resources. Academic enrollment has been one way for undocumented youth to access resources often unavailable to most other undocumented immigrants, such as peer networks, workshops on changing immigration policies, school-based health insurance, and other student-centered programs and services that do not require traditional forms of identification other than a student I.D. Furthermore, education has opened up the network of support for undocumented students, who have often received formal and informal assistance—from teachers, professors, administrators, and staff, and social networks—with issues that affect their daily lives. For example, educators are often asked to provide character statements and letters of support for undocumented students who need to explain complexities with their status for employment and scholarship purposes. Developing and practicing a college-going pedagogy with undocumented students in mind requires educators to view their professional responsibilities in more creative ways.

Assert an Ally Position on Undocumented Immigration

While concrete actions lead to social change, representation is also important in forwarding a pro-migrant agenda in higher education. The vast majority of immigrants with undocumented status are Latina/o, which has resulted in the proliferation of support from programs and organizations that have a strong Latina/o constituent, including scholarship foundations and outreach programs (Bangalon et al., 2012; Gildersleeve & Ranero, 2010). However, the mere presence of other individuals who explicitly represent diverse experiences often challenges prevailing assumptions that undocumented immigration is solely a Latina/o issue. For example, in one story, the prominent Filipino journalist Jose Antonio Vargas (2011) literally changed the face of undocumented immigration when his *New York Times Magazine* feature revealed to the nation that he was in fact without legal status. Vargas' admission serves as an important example of how public figures and educators across diverse backgrounds can potentially position themselves as allies to assert the relevance of undocumented immigration to larger audiences, both within and outside of their institutions.

It is important to emphasize the *different* ways in which AAPI students experience being undocumented. For example, while some undocumented Asian Americans might fly under the radar due to racial stereotypes that suggest that they are model minorities, the criminalization of Pacific Islanders might actually perpetuate the policing of these students. When educators are informed—formally or experientially—about the diversity of undocumented student experiences, they can empathetically inform their networks about how the intersections of immigration and race shape students' lives. However, to assert a critical race position in the larger discourse on undocumented immigration is not meant to overshadow student-initiated efforts or be a divisive strategy to shift resources from Latina/o programs to AAPI college students. Instead, it is a strategy of initiating broad-based coalition building across racial and ethnic lines, in hopes of garnering increased access to institutional resources for immigrant students at large.

Challenge the Culture of Fear and Create Spaces of Change

Education practitioners are often gatekeepers to their institutions. As described throughout the analyses of federal, state, and institutional policies, educators sometimes passively perpetuate anti-undocumented immigrant sentiment when they conduct *business as usual*. Many educators are uninformed, or ill informed, of shifting legislation that can open up or shut out undocumented students from education. In other instances, educators take a hands-off approach in finding creative ways to interpret potentially anti-immigrant policies.[8] Whether one lacks the knowledge or simply accepts changing policies without regard to the impact on undocumented students, educators sometimes participate in maintaining a racist and nativist culture of fear that characterizes undocumented student experiences. Thus, it is essential for educators to be more proactive in the creation of spaces within their institutions where undocumented students and allies can organize.

One key effort integral in the empowerment of undocumented youth throughout the country has been the development of the DREAM Resource Center (DRC), a project of the UCLA Labor Center.[9] The main objective of the DRC is to provide an infrastructure to develop educational resources and materials, and foster leadership development and a large network of support for undocumented youth and their allies. While the driving force behind the DRC has been the undocumented student organizers and allies, educators cannot overlook the central role that Kent Wong, the director of the UCLA

Labor Center, has had in carving out a physical space for undocumented youth. With areas of expertise in labor studies and Asian American studies, he has fostered a transformative space where undocumented youth have become empowered and "unafraid." The DRC was officially established in 2011, but aspects of the DRC had been ongoing projects hosted out of the UCLA Labor Center, including the publication of two largely student-authored books, *Underground Undergrads: UCLA Undocumented Immigrant Students Speak Out* (Madera et al., 2008) and *Undocumented and Unafraid: Tam Tran, Cinthya Felix, and the Immigrant Youth Movement* (Wong et al., 2012).

In the broader undocumented narrative, AAPI immigrant experiences are significant and should be included in a national research agenda on undocumented student education. Historically, AAPIs along with Latina/o immigrants were at the center of formal and informal efforts that delineated some migrants as "illegal" in the United States (Ngai, 2004). Today, AAPIs have played key roles in awakening the American consciousness regarding the plight of undocumented immigrants. As student activists, institutional allies, and community representatives, AAPIs have challenged misperceptions of the undocumented immigrant community and have brought attention to the contradictions of the American education and immigration systems. Educators' roles are not only to conduct research and develop practices that may better serve undocumented students. It is also their responsibility to assert their work as both deeply political and a matter of social and economic sustainability for undocumented students and the communities from which they come.

NOTES

1. For confidentiality purposes, only Fita's first name was used in the story.
2. There is a contradiction in the United States regarding the educational rights of undocumented students. In the case Plyler v. Doe (1982), the U.S. Supreme Court determined that public K–12 education is a fundamental right for children regardless of their immigration status. There is no federal equivalent that mandates states to provide access to higher education for undocumented students.
3. Researchers often cite data from a series of University of California annual reports regarding tuition exemptions that show almost 50% of the potentially undocumented student population in the UC system are Asian, which is disproportionately higher than their overall representation in the United States. The most recent report available at the time this chapter was written reveals that over a ten-year period, Asians and Latinos comprised 45% and 48%, respectively, of potentially undocumented students in the UC system (University of California Office of the President, 2013).
4. At the time that this manuscript was written, provisions of the DREAM Act (S. 952/H.R. 1842, 2011) were included in the Comprehensive Immigration

Reform proposal presented to Congress. I reference the DREAM Act as a stand-alone entity to contextualize the statements of the participants.

5. The California DREAM Act of 2011 is comprised of AB 130 and AB 131, and was sponsored by California Assembly member, Gil Cedillo. Although signed into law in 2011, AB 130 was not implemented until January 2012. AB 131 went into effect in January 2013.

6. *Ate* is the Tagalog (Philippine language) word for older sister.

7. For the memorandum regarding Deferred Action for Childhood Arrivals, please see: http://www.dhs.gov/xlibrary/assets/s1-exercising-prosecutorial-discretion-individuals-who-came-to-us-as-children.pdf. Further, in 2014 the Obama administration announced Deferred Action for Parents of Americans and Lawful Permanent Residents (DAPA), which would have given three-year work permits to undocumented immigrants whose children have legal status in the United States, as well as expanded the 2012 DACA program to include more undocumented immigrants. Legal challenges prevented program implementation and was affirmed by a deadlocked Supreme Court in United States v. Texas, 579 U.S., 2016.

8. Accounts in which student affairs professionals and administrators have come up with creative strategies to challenge the inadequacy of institutional policies have been documented. For example, in a story, "The Right Thing to Do," published in the *Journal of College Admission,* administrator Arnaldo Rodriguez (2010) recalled how the admissions committee at Pitzer College developed guidelines to provide scholarships to undocumented 1.5-generation immigrants accepted into the university.

9. For more information on the DREAM Resource Center, see: www.dreamresourcecenter.org.

REFERENCES

Abrego, L. J. (2006). "I can't go to college because I don't have papers": Incorporation patterns of Latino undocumented youth. *Latino Studies, 4*(3), 212–231.

Abrego, L. J. (2008). Legitimacy, social identity, and the mobilization of law: The effects of Assembly Bill 540 on undocumented students in California. *Law & Social Inquiry, 33*(3), 709–734.

Abrego, L. J., & Gonzales, R. G. (2010). Blocked paths, uncertain futures: The postsecondary education and labor market prospects of undocumented Latino students. *Journal of Education for Students Placed at Risk, 15*(1/2), 144–157.

Baker, B., & Rytina, N. (2013, March). *Estimates of the unauthorized immigrant population residing in the United States: January 2012.* Washington, DC: Department of Homeland Security Office of Immigration Statistics.

Bangalon, A., Peralta, M., & Enriquez, L. E. (2012). Different experiences, similar fears: Asian Pacific Islander and Latina/o undocumented student experiences. In K. Wong, J. Shadduck-Hernández, F. Inzunza, J. Monroe, V. Narro, & A. Valenzuela, Jr. (Eds.), *Undocumented and unafraid: Tam Tran, Cinthya Felix, and the immigrant youth movement* (pp. 99–103). Los Angeles, CA: UCLA Center for Labor Research and Education.

Bernstein, J., & Blazer, J. (2008). Legalizing undocumented immigrants: An essential tool in fighting poverty. *Journal of Poverty Law and Policy, 42*(7–8), 408–415.

Bicksler, B. A., & Nolan, L. G. (2009). *Recruiting an all-volunteer force: The need for sustained investment in recruiting resources—An update.* Washington, DC: Strategic Analysis.

Buenavista, T. L. (2012). Citizenship at a cost: Undocumented Asian youth perceptions and the militarization of immigration. *AAPI Nexus: Policy, Practice and Community, 10*(1), 101–124.

Buenavista, T. L. (2013). Overstaying our welcome: Undocumented Asian immigrant experiences with racial microaggressions in research and education. In R. Endo & X. L. Rong (Eds.), *Educating Asian Americans: Achievement, schooling, and identities* (pp. 103–128). Charlotte, NC: Information Age.

Buenavista, T. L., & Chen, A. C. (2013). Intersections and crossroads: A counter-story of an undocumented Asian American college student. In S. D. Museus, D. C. Maramba, & R. T. Teranishi (Eds.), *The misrepresented minority: New insights on Asian Americans and Pacific Islanders, and the implications for higher education* (pp. 198–212). Sterling, VA: Stylus.

Buenavista, T. L., Chen, A., & So, M. (2013). *A minority among minorities: The role of Asian and Pacific Islanders in the development of a culture receptive to undocumented students.* NASPA Knowledge Communities. Retrieved from http://www.naspa.org/images/uploads/main/2013_NASPAKC_Fall_Publications.pdf.

Buenavista, T. L., & Gonzales, J. B. (2010/2011). DREAMs deterred: Filipino experiences and an anti-militarization critique of the Development, Relief, and Education for Alien Minors Act. *Asian American Policy Review, 21*, 29–37.

California DREAM (Development, Relief, and Education for Alien Minors) Act, California A.B. 130/A.B. 131, 2011.

Chan, B. (2010). Not just a Latino issue: Undocumented students in higher education. *Journal of College Admission, 206*, 29–31.

De Genova, N. P. (2004). The legal production of Mexican/migrant "illegality." *Latino Studies, 2*(2), 160–185.

Eusebio, C. (2012). Asian American, undocumented, and unafraid. In K. Wong, J. Shadduck-Hernández, F. Inzunza, J. Monore, V. Narro, & A. Valenzuela, Jr. (Eds.), *Undocumented and unafraid: Tam Tran, Cinthya Felix, and the immigrant youth movement* (pp. 96–98). Los Angeles, CA: UCLA Center for Labor Research and Education.

Fujiwara, L. (2008). *Mothers without citizenship: Asian immigrant families and the consequences of welfare reform.* Minneapolis, MN: University of Minnesota Press.

Gildersleeve R. E., & Ranero, J. J. (2010). Precollege contexts of undocumented students: Implications for student affairs professionals. *New Directions for Student Services, 131*, 19–33.

Gonzales, R. G. (2007). Wasted talent and broken dreams: The lost potential of undocumented students. *Immigration Policy in Focus, 5*(13), 1–11.

Gonzales, R. G. (2008). Left out but not shut down: Political activism and the undocumented student movement. *Northwestern Journal of Law and Social Policy, 3*, 219–239.

Gonzales, R. G. (2010). On the wrong side of the tracks: Understanding the effects of school structure and social capital in the educational pursuits of undocumented immigrant students. *Peabody Journal of Education*, *85*(4), 469–485.

Guzman-Lopez, A. (2011, October 17). Undocumented Tongan gives voice to community's concerns. *Southern California Public Radio*. Retrieved from http://www.scpr.org/news/2011/10/17/29433/undocumented-tongan-gives-voice-others/

Hernández, D. M. (2008). Pursuant to deportation: Latinos and immigrant detention. *Latino Studies*, *6*, 35–63.

Kinikini, L. L. (2005). *Narrative survival in the Tongan diaspora: The case of the American deportees* (Unpublished master's thesis). Honolulu, HI: University of Hawaii.

Lee, H. M. (2003). *Tongans overseas: Between two shores*. Honolulu, HI: University of Hawaii Press.

Madera, G., Mathay, A. A., Najafi, A. M., Saldivar, H., Solis, S., Titong, A., & Tran, T. (2008). *Underground undergrads: UCLA undocumented immigrant students speak out*. Los Angeles, CA: UCLA Center for Labor Research and Education.

Mariscal, J. (2007). Immigration and military enlistment: The Pentagon's push for the DREAM Act heats up. *Latino Studies*, *5*, 358–363.

Napolitano, J. (2012, June 15). *Exercising prosecutorial discretion with respect to individuals who came to the United States as children*. Washington, DC: Department of Homeland Security. Retrieved from http://www.dhs.gov/xlibrary/assets/s1-exercising-prosecutorial-discretion-individuals-who-came-to-us-as-children.pdf

National Immigration Law Center. (2012, January). *Basic facts about in-state tuition for undocumented immigrant students*. Retrieved from http://www.nilc.org/basic-facts-instate.html

Ngai, M. (2004). *Impossible subjects: Illegal aliens and the making of modern America*. Princeton, NJ: Princeton University Press.

Parreñas, R. S. (2001). *Servants of globalization: Women, migration, and domestic work*. Stanford, CA: Stanford University Press.

Passel, J. S., & Cohn, D. (2009). *A portrait of undocumented immigrants in the United States*. Washington, DC: Pew Hispanic Center. Retrieved from http://www.pewhispanic.org/files/reports/107.pdf

Perez, W. (2009). *We ARE Americans: Undocumented students pursuing the American dream*. Sterling, VA: Stylus.

Perez, P. A. (2010). College choice process of Latino undocumented students: Implications for recruitment and retention. *Journal of College Admission*, *206*, 21–25.

Plyler v. Doe, 457 U.S. 202 (1982).

Ray, M. (2005). "Can I see your papers?" Local police enforcement of federal immigration law post 9/11 and Asian American permanent foreignness. *Washington & Lee Race & Ethnic Anc. Law Journal*, *11*(1), 197–218. Retrieved from http://scholarlycommons.law.wlu.edu/crsj/vol11/iss1/8

Rincon, A. (2008). *Undocumented immigrants and higher education: Si se puede!* New York, NY: LFB Scholarly.

Rodriguez, A. (2010). The right thing to do. *Journal of College Admission*, *206*, 19.

Ruge, T. R., & Iza, A. D. (2005). Higher education for undocumented students: The case for open admission and in-state tuition rates for students without lawful immigration status. *Indiana International & Comparative Law Review*, *15*(2), 1–22.

Russell, A. (2011, March). State policies regarding undocumented college students: A narrative of unresolved issues, ongoing debate and missed opportunities.

American Association of State Colleges and Universities Policy Matters. Retrieved from: http://www.aascu.org/uploadedFiles/AASCU/Content/Root/PolicyAndAdvocacy/PolicyPublications/PM_UndocumentedStudents-March2011.pdf

Simanski, J., & Sapp, L. M. (2012). *Immigration enforcement actions: 2011.* Washington, DC: Office of Immigration Statistics. Retrieved from http://www.dhs.gov/sites/default/files/publications/immigration-statistics/enforcement_ar_2011.pdf

Stock, M. D. (2009). *Essential to the fight: Immigrants in the military eight years after 9/11.* Washington, DC: Immigration Policy Center.

University of California Office of the President Student Financial Support. (2013). *Annual report on AB 540 tuition exemptions: 2011–12 academic year.* Oakland, CA: University of California Office of the President. Retrieved from http://www.ucop.edu/student-affairs/_files/ab540_annualrpt_2012.pdf.

United States v. Texas, 579 U.S. (2016).

Vargas, J. A. (2011, June 22). My life as an undocumented immigrant. *New York Times Magazine.* Retrieved from http://www.nytimes.com/2011/06/26/magazine/my-life-as-an-undocumented-immigrant.html?pagewanted=all

Volpp, L. (2002). Critical race studies: The citizen and the terrorist. *UCLA Law Review, 49,* 1575–1599.

Wong, K., Shadduck-Hernández, J., Inzunza, F., Monore, J., Narro, V., & Valenzuela, A., Jr. (Eds.). (2012). *Undocumented and unafraid: Tam Tran, Cinthya Felix, and the immigrant youth movement.* Los Angeles, CA: UCLA Center for Labor Research and Education.

CHAPTER 6

PACIFIC ISLANDER EDUCATION AND RETENTION

The Development of a Student-Initiated, Student-Run Outreach Program for Pacific Islanders

**Natasha Saelua, Erin Kahunawaika'ala Wright,
Keali'i Troy Kukahiko,[1] Meg Malpaya Thornton,
and Iosefa (Sefa) Aina**

So at the beginning of the three-day retreat, I guess your defenses are up, you don't know anyone, but by the end of that retreat, everything's let down, tears have been shed...you leave with this sense of satisfaction like, "I know I can do it." I guess that's what PIER retreats do for you; they allow you to bridge that gap between your culture and your academics...allowing students to have that for themselves. It's kind of beautiful and heartbreaking to know that other students don't see themselves or perceive themselves as intelligent. All they see [is how they] are compared to trash. Just to know that by the end of the workshops they [say to] themselves, "I can do this, and I can accomplish anything as long as I keep my mind focused."

Focusing on the Underserved, pages 121–137
Copyright © 2017 by Information Age Publishing
All rights of reproduction in any form reserved.

121

Mia,[2] a student at Carson High School in Carson, California, participated in the Pacific Islanders Education and Retention (PIER) project throughout her entire four years in high school. In the reflection above, she reveals how PIER's year-end leadership retreat offers an empowering space to confront the stereotypes, oppression, and disconnections that prevent many of her peers from doing well academically, as well as to think about the possibility of higher education. This retreat, in concert with PIER's year-round activities focused on youth empowerment and cultural relevance in higher education, address the alarming educational disparities that characterize the Pacific Islander community in the United States.

PIER is a student-initiated, student-run outreach project that was conceived by, and created for, Pacific Islanders. This chapter purposefully sheds light on the experiences of Native Hawai'ian and Pacific Islander undergraduate students in navigating higher education. More specifically, we consider the processes, practices, and strategies that led to the creation of the PIER project. To provide broader context for our discussion, we begin with a demographic overview of the Pacific Islander population that includes a focused discussion on educational attainment in the University of California system. Next, we review the sparse literature on Pacific Islander access to higher education, noting some of the major gaps that persist. We rely on tribal critical race theory (Brayboy, 2006) as a conceptual framework for understanding Pacific Islander college students' community engagement through PIER. Following this, we consider the development of the PIER project, focusing on how curricular opportunities, cross-cultural collaboration, and proactive support collectively contributed to the creation of PIER. The voices of PIER high school students such as Mia offer powerful insights into the project's influence on their educational trajectory. We conclude by providing recommendations for practice and research aimed at strengthening access to, and retention in, higher education for Pacific Islanders.

Our hope is that this story speaks to multiple audiences. Although our chapter focuses on experiences of Pacific Islander students on one campus, we believe that this story can speak to the realities of Pacific Islanders on college campuses across the country. We offer a counternarrative (Ladson-Billings & Tate, 1995) to deficit perspectives of the educational experiences of Pacific people, and show how student activism serves as a fulcrum for institutional change. Moreover, this chapter offers rare insight on student engagement and cultural community service activities from the distance of 15 years. Hindsight affords us a sharper perspective on the work we—who have since pursued opportunities as administrators and researchers in the field of higher education—did and continue to do.

DEMOGRAPHIC OVERVIEW

According to the 2010 Census, more than 1.2 million Native Hawaiʻians and Pacific Islanders[3] live in the United States, comprising about 0.4 percent of the nation's total population (EPIC, 2014). Pacific Islanders are the third fastest-growing populations in the United States, expanding by 40% between 2000 and 2010, close to the rate of population growth of Asian Americans (46%) and Latinos (43%). Pacific Islanders are an aggregation of more than 20 ethnic groups, including Native Hawaiʻians (indigenous people of Hawaiʻi), Samoans, Chamorro (indigenous people of Guam), Tongan, Marshallese, Palauan, Chuukese, and many others. The Los Angeles Combined Statistical Area (CSA)[4] has the largest number of Pacific Islanders of any CSA in the continental United States (105,348); the largest number of Native Hawaiʻians, Chamorro, and Samoans on the continent reside in the Los Angeles CSA (EPIC, 2014, p. 40).

Pacific Islanders in California face significant challenges in K–12 education. According to a report released in 2008 by the University of California Asian American and Pacific Islander Policy Multicampus Research Program (Education Work Group), Pacific Islanders' dropout rates are much higher than their Asian American (7.9%) and White (11.5%) peers—more than one-fifth of Pacific Islanders drop out of school between grades 9 and 12 (Chang et al., 2010). In October 2013, fewer than 40% of Pacific Islanders who took the California High School Exit Exam, a mandated test for high school graduation, were able to pass either the mathematics or English-language arts sections of the test (California Department of Education, 2014). In 2012, of the 2,585 Pacific Islander seniors who graduated from high school, only 820 (31.7%) completed all courses required for entrance into the University of California (UC) or California State University (CSU). Together, these data reveal that a significant number of Pacific Islander students do not move through the K–12 system in California. For those who do, moreover, very few are eligible to matriculate directly into a four-year college upon graduation.

College access has been, and remains, an urgent policy issue for Pacific Islander community advocates. In fact, disaggregated data on ethnic groups offered by the University of California Office of the President verify this gap. In 2011, the admissions rates for Pacific Islander freshmen and transfers were the lowest among underrepresented groups. Of the 820 students statewide who had completed UC/CSU coursework, only 379 Pacific Islander students applied for Fall 2012 admission to the University of California, Los Angeles (UCLA) (EPIC, 2014). Moreover, Pacific Islander applicants had a lower-than-average admission rate. For example, Fijian (8%) and Samoan (11%) students were admitted to UCLA at rates lower than any racial group. Pathways to higher education for this community reveal barriers at every step, from graduating high school, completing the necessary coursework, applying to university, and being admitted. It is no surprise that, according to the 2010 U.S. Census, only 18% of Pacific Islander adults (age 25 and older) hold a bachelor's degree, a rate lower than the national average (28%) and identical to African Americans. Samoan and Tongan Americans have the lowest rates of bachelor's degree attainment (11% and 19%, respectively) for the population age 25 and older among Pacific Islander ethnic groups.

Unfortunately, statistics of this nature have characterized the Pacific Islander community for many decades. The data underscore the critical need to examine and understand the structural factors influencing educational attainment for this population. In the following section, we review the literature on Pacific Islanders in education to examine how scholars have shed light on this issue.

THE PAUCITY OF RESEARCH ON PACIFIC ISLANDERS IN HIGHER EDUCATION

At first glance, the literature on Pacific Islanders and their experiences in higher education is very sparse, which has prompted calls for further research by several scholars studying the Asian American and Pacific Islander communities (Benham, 2006; Museus, 2013; Wright & Balutski, 2013). Part of this paucity can be attributed to the conflation of Pacific Islanders within the "Asian American and Pacific Islander" racial group, which has resulted in masking the wide range of ethnic, political, cultural, socioeconomic, linguistic, and generational diversity under that umbrella. Racialization of Pacific Islanders as "Asian Americans," "Asian Pacific Islanders," or "Asian Pacific Americans" by policy makers and researchers has empowered both discourse and methodology that "lump" data on Asian groups (Chinese, Japanese, Filipino) with data on Pacific Islander groups (Native Hawai'ian, Samoan, Marshallese). Consequently, the educational experiences of Pacific Islanders are rarely included in educational research on Asian Americans and, more often than not, subsumed by larger Asian American populations.

The literature that does exist on Pacific Islanders offers a stark landscape, noting achievement gaps, limited access to resources, and the need for more culturally relevant material (Ah Sam & Robinson, 1998; EPIC, 2014; Hune & Yeo, 2010; Kawakami, 1990; UCLA Asian American Studies Center, 2006; Takeuchi & Hune, 2008; Tran et al., 2010; Tsutsumoto, 1998; Vakalahi, 2009). For example, through individual interviews and focus groups, Tran et al. (2010) asked Pacific Islander high school and college students in Southern California about their educational experiences. They found that socioeconomic status, lack of social support or educational resources, and stereotypes made it challenging for those students to prioritize higher education. Their findings corroborated existing research about Pacific Islanders (Ah Sam & Robinson, 1998; Kawakami, 1990).

Interestingly, our literature review revealed a major research gap that we discuss later in the chapter—more research focuses on the experiences of Native Hawaiʻian undergraduates in Hawaiʻi (Hagedorn, Lester, Moon, & Tibbetts, 2006; Hokoana & Oliveira, 2012; Ichiyama, McQuarrie, & Ching, 1996; Makuakane-Drechsel & Hagedorn, 2000; Ogata, Sheehey, & Noonan, 2006) than other Pacific Islander ethnic groups. Hokoana and Oliveira (2012), for example, offer their perspectives on working with Native Hawaiʻian students by integrating cultural values into student programming. Early in the chapter, the authors share their experience in a leadership development program for Hawaiʻian students, as well as its impact on their own journey through higher education. By drawing a specific relationship between leadership and retention, the article provides an important framework to build on in this chapter.

As participants in the Pacific Islands' Students Association (PISA), we considered ourselves student leaders and activists, drawing strength from the proud history of Asian American and Pacific Islander student activism on our campus. Indeed, a growing body of scholarship on this history and legacy reveals how AAPI college students have been at the forefront of state- and nation-wide social movements (Aguirre Jr. & Lio, 2008; Omatsu, 1994; Ryoo & Ho, 2013; Umemoto, 1989). Ryoo and Ho (2013), for example, offered a compelling analysis of how Asian American students at UCLA were able to make the rough transition into college through involvement in activism and community service. Several of the students in their study articulated how the combination of activism and Asian American studies coursework had a positive influence on their sense of belonging at the UCLA campus, as well as tie their experience to their cultural communities. This important scholarship reveals the value of campus activism and culturally relevant courses for first-generation students who have traveled significant cultural, socioeconomic, and even geographic distances to enter their campuses.

It is critical that higher education scholars build on the literature above so that postsecondary education leaders can gain a greater awareness of this community and increase support to Pacific Islanders in higher education. Throughout this chapter, we argue that access to leadership development programs, exposure to student activism, and connection with supportive staff provided a transformative environment for Pacific Islander students to build the Pacific Islander Education and Retention project. However, at this point, we make a critical departure from existing paradigms and instead utilize racial *and* indigenous frameworks to depict Pacific Islander student activism at UCLA.

TRIBAL CRITICAL RACE THEORY

Our review of the literature indicates that Pacific Islanders have been characterized within the *umbrella terms of* Asian Americans and Pacific Islanders, Asian Pacific Americans, Asian Pacific Islanders, and Asian and Pacific Islander Americans—all of which are commonly used by researchers, community organizations, and media—and as indigenous or native people (Akee & Yazzie-Mintz, 2011; Cook, 1983; Wright & Balutski, 2013). For this chapter, we employ both critical race theory and tribal critical race theory, weaving our narrative back and forth between the two conceptual frameworks. This is an important strategy for us because of compounding ways that both racism and imperialism set the context for Pacific Islanders accessing higher education.

Introduced by legal scholars in the 1980s, critical race theory (CRT) has been a highly effective analytical tool to theorize race in education and educational inequities (Ladson-Billings & Tate, 1995). For example, CRT has been used to examine and analyze the experiences of African Americans in education within the United States (Ladson-Billings, 2006). Among its seminal tenets, CRT asserts that racism is: (a) endemic in U. S. society, (b) an everyday experience for people of color, and (c) not a historical concept that ended with the Civil Rights Movement or the election of a Black President of the United States. Furthermore, CRT asserts that the United States was founded on the basis that property rights supersede human rights, a fact exemplified in a history of slavery, genocide of the indigenous populations, and violent seizure of Native lands.

Brayboy (2005) expanded CRT to examine how racialization has impacted indigenous communities—in particular American Indians—and advanced CRT to include indigenous peoples with tribal critical race theory (TribalCrit). Mirroring the tenets of CRT, Brayboy outlines nine core tenets of TribalCrit, including: (a) that colonization is endemic to society; (b) U.S. policies toward indigenous people are rooted in imperialism, White supremacy, and a desire for material gain; (c) indigenous people occupy a liminal space that accounts for both the political and racialized natures of their identities; and (d) the concepts of culture, knowledge, and power take on new meaning when examined through an indigenous lens (Brayboy, 2005).

From a Pacific Islander perspective, TribalCrit would suggest that the history of colonization, economic imperialism, and militarization in the Pacific have created undesirable circumstances in Pacific Islander communities, including low educational attainment (Brayboy 2005; Labrador & Wright, 2011; Wright & Balutski, 2013). The history of colonization has put Pacific Islanders at a disadvantage, benefitting dominant groups that have had a head start in the accumulation of social capital. Subordinate groups have since suffered from symptoms of poverty—higher rates of unemployment, higher rates of health problems, decreased lifetime earning potential, and reduced levels of education among future generations (Baum, Ma, & Payea, 2010).

Employing TribalCrit allows a full exploration of Pacific Islanders' experiences as "liminal" beings (Brayboy, 2005), and provides a counter-narrative of our position as raced, indigenous people struggling to succeed in Western institutions of higher education. With this framework, we shift our focus to the creation of the PIER project, focusing first on the historical context of PISA's outreach and the events leading up to our engagement with Carson High School. Following that, we hone in on three critical elements that led us to coalesce around the project, examining each through the lens of TribalCrit: (a) curricular opportunities for leadership development through the Asian American Studies Center; (b) opportunities to interact with other students of color around the creation of the Student Initiated Outreach Committee (SIOC); and (c) the presence of a supportive institutional agent.

CREATION OF THE PACIFIC ISLANDERS EDUCATION AND RETENTION (PIER) PROJECT

For the PISA students at UCLA, community outreach was a central focus since 1992. When Iosefa (Sefa) Aina came to UCLA that year, PISA already had an identity as an overtly political organization. Sefa recalls that in his very first PISA meeting, the organization's members voted to sign on to a resolution to develop Chicano Studies. He acknowledges the influence of several graduate students, including Sepa Sete, Lua Maynard, and especially Erin Kahunawaikaʻala Wright, who urged the organization to have critical conversations—especially about our community and our youth—and were instrumental in forging PISA's political commitments.

As a result, in the early 1990s PISA shifted away from its past activities of hosting lūʻau or concerts featuring Pacific Islanders simply as performers. Instead, PISA focused on a mission of outreach to high schools even with a group of fewer than 10 core members. The most popular outreach activity, "Day in the Life," featured PISA hosting Pacific Islander high school students for half-day field trip visits to the UCLA campus. Eventually, these field trips developed into a more extensive day-long conference with keynote speakers, workshops, campus tours, and other activities. Since high school students were the target audience, the event quickly became known as the "high school conference." Through the 1990s, PISA's annual high school conference grew in size and reputation, eventually hosting as many as 600 high school students from Southern California high schools. This outreach activity demonstrated PISA's early interventions to address higher education access challenges in the Pacific Islander community.

The high school conference was the primary outreach vehicle for PISA until May 1997, when the event inadvertently became a site of conflict between student participants from different regions, partially motivated by gang affiliations and caused by non-conference attendees. The conflict quickly escalated and, in a gross over-reaction to the situation by the campus administration, both the UCLA Police Department and the Los Angeles Police Department's Riot Squad were summoned. While the incident did not deter PISA's engagement in high school outreach, it did prompt serious discussion by PISA's leadership and advisors about making a long-term impact in schools. With the large high school conference, some PISA members felt that they had failed to connect personally with any of the visiting students. Amidst these conversations, an important turning point occurred when PISA chairperson Sefa Aina graduated and was hired to work in a staff position with Meg Thornton at the Asian American Studies Center in the Student/Community Projects division in Campbell Hall.

ASIAN PACIFIC AMERICAN
LEADERSHIP DEVELOPMENT PROGRAM (APALDP)

Despite the overwhelming size of the UCLA campus, small pockets exist where students of color congregate, and Campbell Hall has always been one of those places. Home to the Academic Advancement Program, the American Indian Studies Center, the Center for Community College Partnerships, and the Asian American Studies Center, on any given day you could find racially diverse students streaming in and out of the building. In 1998, PISA meetings took place in a small, second-floor conference room opposite from Sefa's office. In addition to working with Meg as an academic advisor for Asian American studies majors, Sefa also served as an organizational advisor for the Asian American, Southeast Asian American, and Pacific Islander student groups. Most importantly, Sefa was the facilitator for the APALDP (pronounced *apple-dap*). The APALDP, a two-quarter "student community leadership course, was designed to promote leadership and activism in the Asian/Pacific Islander communities among undergraduate students" (Asian American Studies, 2004). In the first quarter, students were introduced to various leadership concepts and models, politics of individual identity and community empowerment, contemporary community issues, and approaches to campus community building. During the second quarter, students were required to participate in field studies where they volunteered in a community-based organization for a minimum of five hours weekly. Although participation in the class was open to all students, Meg and Sefa explicitly made an effort to recruit the leadership of the Asian American, Southeast Asian American, and Pacific Islander student groups.

Sefa began teaching the APALDP class in the fall quarter of 1997. Troy Lau, a PISA member and APALDP student, used the class to focus on the issue of Pacific Islanders and educational attainment. He initiated a weekly after-school program for the Pacific Islander students at Carson High School, sponsored by the Los Angeles Unified School District's Asian Pacific American Commission (LAUSD, 1998). Troy was a tireless advocate for the youth; his energy inspired other undergraduate students to join him at Carson High School for tutoring and mentoring sessions. In particular, he took the time to establish relationships with Carson High School's administration, athletics personnel, community members, counselors, and teachers. Troy's leadership cultivated a high level of personal investment in the program among other PISA students, who continued the outreach project after he left the university to pursue other interests. Natasha, who joined APALDP in 1999, took over Troy's outreach project, earning academic credit for her work while assuming leadership of PISA as chairperson.

Sefa, Meg, and Erin (at the time, a graduate student in the Higher Education and Organizational Change program at UCLA's Graduate School of Education and Information Sciences) worked with Troy and Natasha to rebuild PISA after a difficult time of strife and drama. Although we were of different cultural backgrounds, we united through our self-identification with the term "Pacific Islander," a term that none of us had heard—much less identified with—before our arrival at UCLA. Yet, as we came together and learned about our shared cultural values, we were empowered by the possibilities that this racial term afforded us. We forged a collective identity which offered a way to break beyond the stereotypes about our people, unravel the negative and hostile discourse about our communities, and tell new stories about our people's survival from, and resistance to, imperialism. In doing so, we became an embodiment of the fourth tenet of TribalCrit: "Indigenous people have a desire to obtain and forge tribal sovereignty, self-determination, and self-identification" (Brayboy, 2006, p. 429).

CROSS-CULTURAL COLLABORATION

UCLA students have struggled to maintain their voice in, and control over, programs and services that impact them. Organizations such as the Afrikan Student Union (ASU), the American Indian Student Association (AISA), and Movimiento Estudiantil Chicano de Aztlán (MEChA) were founded during the social and political upheaval of the 1960s to advocate for their community's needs (Maldonado, 2010). In 1997, these organizations began to pressure the University of California Office of the President to allocate resources for the creation of a funding source for student-initiated, student-run outreach programs at all UC campuses.

PISA's activism around outreach grew as a result of our daily exposure to Carson High School and our perceived gaps in university-sponsored outreach programs. In 1999, Carson High School students had to attain a minimum 3.5 grade point average to be eligible for UCLA's Early Academic Outreach Program (EAOP). Very few Pacific Islanders met the grade requirement to participate in EAOP or similar programs. Surrounded by like-minded students of color, PISA students envisioned an intervention that would offer college resources and information to youth from their community. As a result, PISA joined the students of color in pressuring UCLA administration to support our efforts.

In 1999, the Student Initiated Outreach Committee (SIOC) was created on the UCLA campus. The SIOC solidified a permanent coalition (Maldonado, 2010) between six organizations around student-initiated outreach: the Afrikan Student Union, American Indian Student Association, PISA, MEChA, Samahang Pilipino, and the Vietnamese Student Union. PISA's exposure to the students of color coalition had a powerful impact on the way we thought about, and enacted, our effort in the community. Working with other communities that understood the permanent nature of racism and colonization—also known as TribalCrit tenet one—galvanized us to ask critical questions about the root causes of the education gap: Why were the schools with high populations of Pacific Islanders so under resourced? Why were there gang problems in urban, low-income areas? Where did these stereotypes about our young people come from? And, why didn't anyone else seem to care about this community?

Posing and centering these kinds of questions in our programming were acts of resistance for many of us. Instead of sharing our families' feelings of pride in our accomplishments as college students in a prestigious university, we often felt alienated and unable to connect to the institution. Therefore, by channeling our access to the resources of the campus back to our community, we were empowered by our ability to capitalize on our access to knowledge and resources at UCLA to benefit our community. The fact that we did this hand-in-hand with students from other cultures that were going through a similarly painful, liberating process—acting out TribalCrit tenet five—transforms the meaning of culture, knowledge, and power at UCLA. *Our* cultures were valued, *our* epistemologies guided the work, and *our* power as students bent the university to our will.

PROACTIVE SUPPORT

By invoking our cultural values as a source of strength, we opened up our organizational potential to serve our community while educating our peers. Although we were all at different stages in this process, PISA was fortunate to have proactive support from Meg Thornton at the Asian American Studies Center, as well as staff at the Community Programs Office and Center for Student Programming. Meg's background in community organizing as director of Search to Involve Pilipino Americans (SIPA) gave her the opportunity to work alongside the Office of Samoan Affairs and other Pacific Islander community leaders. She understood the complexities and pitfalls of the "Asian Pacific American" rubric, and felt at times that it was a contradiction, particularly in the lack of representation for the "Pacific"—and even Filipino—half of the equation. She channeled that perspective into her work as a student affairs officer, visualizing her work on campus as an organizer who could bring people together and work toward a common goal. In doing so, she recognized the need to actualize the "Asian Pacific Islander" label through authentic collaboration with Pacific Islanders on the UCLA campus. More importantly, she regarded the Pacific Islanders on campus as a natural extension of the Southern California Pacific Islander community, and found ways to connect PISA students to the elders in the region who could provide us with additional support, mentorship, and love.

Because of her perspective, Meg became a trusted ally and friend to PISA, helping us to develop as professional, community-minded people. Her support was active, guided by her knowledge of the cultures from which we came. She knew that PISA was not just a mechanism for us to engage with the campus or get involved; PISA was a family and an extension of our home communities to the UCLA campus. Meg pushed us, too. She asked the tough questions and guided our activism intellectually and holistically. For example, whenever a PISA student expressed an idea, Meg would ask us to articulate how that idea would benefit our community or campus. She helped us actualize the final tenet of TribalCrit, connecting theory and practice in working for social justice (Brayboy, 2005). PISA's activism to dismantle structural inequality and combat oppression took form through PIER. As students, we felt safe to try new and different activities because of Meg's work in creating a supportive, safe environment for us. By validating our cultural heritage and offering proactive support, while at the same time ensuring that the Asian American Studies Center was responsive to the needs of our community, she helped transform the campus, our organization, and our community.

INFLUENCE ON PACIFIC ISLANDER
HIGH SCHOOL STUDENTS

In her research for her Master's thesis about PIER in 2012, Natasha interviewed seven former PIER students to understand how they thought PIER had influenced their educational trajectories. The students articulated that PIER transformed a negative educational environment into one that validated the lives and histories of Pacific Islander youth (Saelua, 2012) and shared their appreciation for a space that was created by, and for, Pacific Islanders. When asked to compare better-known outreach programs with PIER, such as UCLA's Early Academic Outreach Program or Upward Bound, students immediately pointed out the importance of a racially-specific focus. Both TribalCrit and CRT speak of the importance of counternarratives and counter-spaces, and PIER became a space for the high school students to talk about their daily experiences with racism, stereotyping by teachers, living in an urban environment, being subjected to difficult or dangerous situations, and frustration with the people around them who did not support their academic aspirations. They expressed gratitude and profound relief for the presence of their mentors, who acted as role models, tutors, facilitators, dance partners, program coordinators, workshop facilitators, cooks, interpreters, chauffeurs, shoulders to cry on, or mediators, depending on what the students needed. In this way, UCLA students both supported and enhanced the educational mission of the high schools, providing culturally relevant support for this population.

As mentioned earlier, the fourth tenet of TribalCrit states that "Indigenous peoples have a desire to obtain and forge tribal sovereignty, tribal autonomy, self-determination, and self identification..." (Brayboy, 2006, 429). Mia shared the following memory of her time as a PIER student:

> I would walk into a room and I would see all my friends doing their homework and they were being helped by other Pacific Islanders, and I thought, "This is pretty awesome, I guess I'll stay here." And the biggest thing for me wasn't that I was being helped with my academics, but that I was comfortable, and I knew these people, and I knew that what they wanted to do was to help me, and that's why I stayed involved in PIER throughout high school as well, because bottom line was that those were my people, and they were helping me, for the betterment of our people. (Saelua, 2012)

Mia found PIER to be a supportive and affirming environment where she could focus exclusively on her cultural communities, have access to a female Pacific Islander college student who served as an accessible, consistent role model, and learn more about the higher education process. In this way, PIER ejected the negative environment and offered students an empowering space where they were acknowledged openly and joyfully as intelligent

Pacific people. The work of Pacific Islander college students breathed new life to the "Pacific" identity, constructed a meaningful connection for high school students to their homeland, and provided them the space to proudly claim their Pacific culture and Indigenous heritage.

DISCUSSION AND RECOMMENDATIONS

How does our story matter to higher education faculty, staff, researchers, or practitioners? In our conversations about this chapter, the authors recounted how the experience of working with PIER changed our lives. We were all so passionate about the work that, even when most of us left UCLA, we found ways to stay involved in the struggle to open up access to higher education for our community. Anecdotally, we know that this is true for many of the students who have worked with PIER over the last 16 years.

For educators who work with Pacific Islander students, we offer three suggestions to begin initiating counter-narratives and counter-spaces. First, provide courses—especially those with service-learning components—that actively and meaningfully engage students' cultural identity. Help students make connections to their off-campus community by building a network with diverse community-based organizations and tapping into that network when students seek to engage in community work. Or have students invite those community networks to the classroom as expert resources for your classes. Pacific Islander students will be more inclined to engage in activities that feature opportunities to meet and work with local Pacific Islander community leaders.

Second, find opportunities to make Pacific Islanders more visible on campus, beyond a *lū'au* or multicultural/diversity days. Transform physical spaces with Pacific Islander art, images of Pacific Islander scholars, and people. Ask Pacific Islander students to bring their families to campus for events. Invite Pacific Islander scholars, activists, community organizers, and entrepreneurs to campus for informal or formal talks. Offer to host high school Pacific Islander clubs for campus tours or "day-in-the-life" activities so that they can observe and sit in on college classes.

Most importantly, educate yourself and your colleagues about existing Pacific Islander stereotypes, the political connections between various Pacific Islands and the United States, and pressing issues facing Pacific Islander communities; and seek Pacific Islander students, staff, and faculty to help generate these conversations with you.

For researchers, it remains urgent that institutions disaggregate data on Asian Americans and Pacific Islanders, pursuant to the Federal Office of Management and Budget Directive 15 (OMB 15). OMB 15 separated the

Asian American and Pacific Islander racial category, creating a separate "Native Hawai'ian and Other Pacific Islander" category.

Furthermore, we echo earlier calls for researchers to add to the limited existing knowledge about the experiences of Pacific Islanders in higher education. What prevents and what facilitates Pacific Islander students' access, retention, and persistence? What can be done to increase the number of Pacific Islanders in graduate programs? What are the structural barriers to success that must be eliminated, and what are the strategies of successful individuals and programs from which we can learn? Finally, we need research that studies the influence of institutionalized counter-spaces on student success, such as cultural centers, and on the institution's cultural environment.

CONCLUSION

In the late 1990s, three key elements existed at UCLA that led to the creation of the Pacific Islander Education and Retention project: (a) curricular opportunities for leadership development through the Asian Pacific American Leadership Development Project; (b) opportunities for cross-cultural interaction; and (c) holistic, proactive support from an institutional agent. We believe that this story is instructive for how institutions, academic units, student affairs professionals, and, most importantly, the students themselves can be engaged in creating an empowering campus environment and increase access to higher education for Pacific Islanders in high school. Over a decade after the events described in this chapter, the PIER project continues to serve Pacific Islander students. The authors are grateful for all of the PISA students over the years that believed in the work of the PIER project and continue to serve Pacific Islander youth and communities.

ACKNOWLEDGEMENTS

The authors thank past and present UCLA faculty and staff who provided support, advice, and encouragement to PISA students and PIER staff: Keith Camacho, Carri Fierro, Kris Kaupalolo, Tim Ngubeni, Antonio Sandoval, Asena Taione-Filihia, and Melissa Veluz-Abraham.

NOTES

1. Formerly known as Troy Keali'i Lau.

2. Pseudonym used by Saelua for Master's thesis, "PIER Through a Critical Lens: Evaluation of a Student Initiated, Student Run Outreach Project."
3. We use the term "Pacific Islanders" and "Native Hawai'ians and Pacific Islanders" interchangeably in this chapter.
4. Los Angeles Combined Statistical Area includes Los Angeles, Orange, Riverside, San Bernardino, and Ventura Counties.

REFERENCES

Aguirre, A., Jr., & Lio, S. (2008). Spaces of mobilization: The Asian American/Pacific Islander struggle for social justice. *Social Justice, 35*(2), 1–17.

Ah Sam, A. L. F., & Robinson, N. B. (1998). Pacific Islanders in higher education: Barriers to recruitment and retention. *Pacific Educational Research Journal, 9*(1), 39–49.

Akee, R. Q., & Yazzie-Mintz, T. (2011). "Counting experience" among the least counted: The role of cultural and community engagement on educational outcomes for American Indian, Alaska Native, and Native Hawaiian students. *American Indian Culture and Research Journal, 35*(3), 119–150.

Asian American Studies. (2004). *Syllabus, Asian American Studies 187B section 2: Student community leadership.* Los Angeles, CA: University of California, Los Angeles.

Benham, M. K. P. (2006). A challenge to Native Hawaiian and Pacific Islander scholars: What the research literature teaches us about our work. *Race, Ethnicity, and Education, 9*(1), 29–50.

Baum, S., Ma, J., & Payea, K. (2010). *Education pays 2010: The benefits of higher education for individuals and society.* New York, NY: The College Board.

Brayboy, B. (2006). Toward a tribal critical race theory in education. *The Urban Review 37*(1), 425–446.

California Department of Education (2014). *School summary, dropouts by grade and ethnic group, Carson Senior High School, 1997–98.* Retrieved from http://data1.cde.ca.gov/dataquest/

Chang, M., Fung, G., Nakanishi, D., Ogawa, R., Takahashi, L., Um, K., ... Russ, L. (2010). *The state of higher education in California: Asian Americans, Native Hawaiians, and Pacific Islanders.* Los Angeles, CA: The Campaign for College Opportunity.

Cook, T. (1983). Research, program development and the education of Native Hawaiians: A conversation with Myron Thompson. *American Psychologist, 38*(9), 1015–1021.

Empowering Pacific Islander Communities (EPIC) & Asian Americans Advancing Justice. (2014). *A community of contrasts: Native Hawaiians and Pacific Islanders in the United States, 2014.* Los Angeles, CA: Asian Americans Advancing Justice.

Hagedorn, L. S., Lester, J., Moon, H. S., & Tibbetts, K. (2006). Native Hawaiian community college students: What happens? *Community College Journal of Research and Practice, 30*(1), 21–39.

Hokoana, L., & Oliveira, J. (2012). Factors related to native Hawaiian student success in college. In D. M. Ching & A. Agbayani (Eds.), *Asian Americans and*

Pacific Islanders in higher education: Research and perspectives on identity, leadership, and success (pp. 195–212). Washington, DC: National Association of Student Personnel Administrators.

Hune, S., & Yeo, J. (2010). How do Pacific Islanders fare in U.S. education? A look inside Washington state public schools with a focus on Samoans. *AAPI Nexus: Asian Americans & Pacific Islanders Policy, Practice, and Community, 8*(1), 1–16.

Ichiyama, M., McQuarrie, E., & Ching, K. (1996). Contextual influences on ethnic identity among Hawaiian Students in the mainland United States. *Journal of Cross-Cultural Psychology, 27*(4), 458–475.

Kawakami, A. J. (1990). *Young children and education in the Pacific: A look at the research.* Honolulu, HI: Pacific Region Educational Laboratory.

Ladson-Billings, G. J. (2006, October). From the achievement gap to the education debt: Understanding achievement in U.S. schools. *Educational Researcher, 35*(7), 3–12.

Ladson-Billings, G., & Tate, W. F., IV. (1995). Toward a critical race theory of education. *Teachers College Record, 97*(1), 47–68.

Los Angeles Unified School District (LAUSD). (1998). *Augmented cities, county, and community relations committee meeting notes.* Retrieved at: http://www.lausd.k12.ca.us/lausd/board/secretary/html/committees/ccc/cccr01-08-98.html

Maldonado, D. (2010). *Toward a student-initiated retention organization methodology: A political history of retention at UCLA* (Unpublished doctoral dissertation). University of California, Los Angeles.

Makuakane-Drechsel, T., & Hagedorn, L. S. (2000). Correlates of retention among Asian Pacific Americans in community colleges: The case for Hawaiian students. *Community College Journal of Research and Practice, 24*(80), 639–655.

Museus, S. (2013). Asian Americans and Pacific Islanders: A national portrait of growth, diversity, and inequality. In S. D. Museus, D. C. Maramba, & R. T. Teranishi (Eds.), *The misrepresented minority: New insights on Asian Americans and Pacific Islanders, and the implications for higher education* (pp. 11–41). Sterling, VA: Stylus.

Ogata, V. F., Sheehey, P. H., & Noonan, M. J. (2006). Rural Native Hawaiian perspectives on special education. *Rural Special Education Quarterly, 25*(1), 7–15.

Omatsu, G. (1994). The "Four Prisons" and the movements of liberation: Asian American activism from the 1960s to the 1990s. In K. Aguilar-San Juan (Ed.), *The state of Asian America: Activism and resistance in the 1990s* (pp. 19–70). Boston, MA: South End Press.

Ryoo, J. J., & Ho, R. (2013). Living the legacy of '68: The perspectives and experiences of Asian American student activism. In S. D. Museus, D. C. Maramba, & R. T. Teranishi (Eds.), *The misrepresented minority: New insights on Asian Americans and Pacific Islanders, and the implications for higher education* (pp. 213–226). Sterling, VA: Stylus.

Saelua, N. (2012). *PIER through a critical lens: Evaluation of a student-initiated, student-run outreach project* (Unpublished master's thesis). University of California, Los Angeles.

Takeuchi, D., & Hune, S. (2008). *Growing presence, emerging voices: Pacific Islanders & academic achievement in Washington.* A report submitted to The Washington

State Commission on Asian Pacific American Affairs. Seattle, WA: University of Washington.

Tran, J. H., Wong, M., Wright, E. K., Fa'avae, J., Cheri, A., Wat, E., ... Foo, M. A. (2010). Understanding a Pacific Islander young adult perspective on access to higher education. *California Journal of Health Promotions, 8,* 23–38.

Tsutsumoto, T. S. (1998). *Higher educational perspectives: Through the narratives of Samoan college students* (Unpublished master's thesis). University of California, Los Angeles.

UCLA Asian American Studies Center—Census Information Center. (2006). *Pacific Islanders lagging behind in higher educational attainment: Analytical brief of new census data.* Los Angeles, CA: UC AAPI Policy Initiative.

Umemoto, K. (1989). "On Strike!" San Francisco State College strike, 1968–1969: The role of Asian American students. *Amerasia Journal, 15*(1), 3–41.

Vakalahi, H. F. O. (2009). Pacific Islander American students: Caught between a rock and a hard place. *Children and Youth Services Review, 31*(12), 1258–1263.

Wright, E. K., & Balutski, B. J. N. (2013). *The role of context, critical theory, and education* (pp. 163–184). Sterling, VA: Stylus.

CHAPTER 7

ASIAN AMERICAN AND PACIFIC ISLANDER STORYTELLING AND SOCIAL BIOGRAPHY AS PEDAGOGY IN HIGHER EDUCATION

Jeffrey Tangonan Acido, Jennifer Farrales Custodio, and Gordon Lee

This chapter introduces social biography as a pedagogical framework centered on the use of stories that evoke, provoke, and explore the intersections of the personal and the collective. In this chapter, we explore the concept of *social biography*, which refers to the practice of situating the histories of the individual into larger historical, collective narratives to counter dominant hegemonic paradigms, conventions, and assumptions. The chapter concludes with recommendations and implications for incorporating and developing social biography as pedagogy in higher education.

Focusing on the Underserved, pages 139–149
Copyright © 2017 by Information Age Publishing

ASIAN AMERICAN PACIFIC ISLANDER STORIES AND STORYTELLING

Stories are made and told. Stories are narratives about people and the world that surrounds them. In many societies, stories are passed from one generation to the next. This is how history, tradition, culture, and values are transmitted and retained. Our view and deployment of stories and storytelling are grounded in critical race theory (CRT)—a conceptual lens to study how dominant systems of racial oppression shape the lives of Asian Americans and other people of color (Museus, 2014). CRT allows us to re-center the Asian American and Pacific Islander (AAPI) identity journey, with AAPIs as the primary negotiators of their identities (Accapadi, 2012). AAPI communities, including Native Hawai'ians and Filipinos, are built on oral and aural traditions and appreciate stories and storytelling as important vehicles of teaching, learning, and disseminating cultural values, traditions, and norms. They also often view stories and storytelling as, in part, a process of self-discovery.

SOCIAL BIOGRAPHY AS PEDAGOGY

In higher education, AAPI students are more likely to encounter dominant institutional cultures that differ from their respective community's traditions, beliefs, and experiences (Museus, 2014). We argue that AAPI students need to be engaged in pedagogy that centers and does not essentialize their personal stories and experiences, while using their cultural knowledge to challenge dominant Western values and ideologies. Our experiences teaching AAPI students compel us to propose a pedagogical shift away from privileging heavily text-based reading and learning of history toward a pedagogy of social biography.

Social biography (re)affirms the agency of AAPI students through (re) claiming their personal and community stories that are not always lifted and highlighted in higher education curricula. In our earlier works, we state, "Everything begins with our story" (Acido & Lee, 2012, p. 5). Social biography, as a method, delineates stories as intersecting and intertwining with other(ed) stories as part of learning and discovering oneself as part of higher education.

Social biography in higher education incorporates a holistic approach to learning through our personal stories, our histories, and our understanding of how our collective stories are intricately woven and connected. The approach of social biography brings AAPI students directly to the source of their own experiences, discoursing their pains and struggles, and coming to redemptive understanding of who they are and who they want to become.

Since AAPI students come from communities that ontologically transmit their traditional cultures and history through acts of storytelling, we need to engage pedagogical practices, such as social biography, to allow them to share their own personal stories and experiences and learn from others as well. Although higher education institutions construct spaces for AAPI students to explore their culture and identity, these spaces are not always easy to find (Museus, 2014). Indeed, what is inherent in the pedagogy of social biography is its critique of spaces that do not allow for multiple ways of understanding and shaping history.

PHILOSOPHIES OF SOCIAL BIOGRAPHY

Over the past several years, we have come to realize that the one constant practice we engage in our daily lives is the exchange of stories and storytelling. In the Hawai'ian Islands, there are many iterations of the act of storytelling, including *talk-story, moolelo,* and *pakasaritaan.*[1] Any gathering or significant rite and ritual usually involves storytelling. Although these stories are not written in text, they are occasionally summoned through memories.

To many people in Hawai'i, stories are not *just* stories. They believe individual stories, when strung together, make up narratives that define our past and define and refine how we live our lives. To AAPIs and other oppressed groups, who have had no fair and affirmative historical representation, the act of telling stories becomes political and social by bringing private stories into public spaces to challenge hegemonic stories. These hegemonic stories were generated colonial encounters and often privilege White, Western Anglo-Saxon ruling class experiences, at the expense of silencing and erasing the history of colonized peoples, including AAPIs.

We claim that social biography, with its use of storytelling and stories—when coupled with political, historical, economic, and social consciousness—is a liberatory and critical method of understanding history, as well as the intricacy, complexity, and profundity of our lives. In addition, in our work with Native Hawai'ians, Filipinos, and other AAPIs who are from the working classes in the California Bay area, Philippines, and Islands of Hawai'i, we hear stories and witness the act of storytelling as central to the process of a liberatory education.

Given the way hegemonic history has silenced stories from marginalized groups, these experiences are not often read or taught in the everyday discourse of formal education. Where AAPI and other marginalized communities (e.g., working class, indigenous, and LGBTQ communities) have limited access to resources and tools of production, telling their stories is an act that can subvert and challenge hegemonic narratives. To tell one's story is to reflect and discern history, and the act of telling one's story is essentially the writing of one's story. DeSalvo (1999) describes stories and the writing process as the following:

> So changing our stories...can change our personal history, can change us. Through writing, we revisit our past and review and revise it. What we thought happened, what we believed happened to us, shifts and changes as we discover deeper and more complex truths. It isn't that we use our writing to deny what we've experienced. Rather, we use it to shift our perspective. (p. 11)

Telling stories, like writing our stories, allows people to shift their own perspectives and the perspectives of other people and institutions. However, the summoning of stories is not an easy process, and summoning a story can often be very challenging and often results in unearthing deeply buried traumatic histories and memories.

In the case of Hawai'i, Native Hawai'ians and other AAPIs are intertwined in their shared history of colonization and imperialism and are channeled into subservient plantation lives, domestic work, tourism industry, and military roles that often do not require certification of higher education. Thus, stories articulated by these communities may not reflect affirmative narratives. Complex colonial relationships have warped the way these marginalized populations tell stories of themselves. For example, Filipino and Filipino American students in classes that we have taught at the University of Hawai'i at Mānoa (UHM) have ingrained in themselves stories about the Philippines being poor and dirty, where everyone is clamoring to come to America, and where Filipinos want to come to America for a better life. Their sentiments, whether they are born in the Philippines or in the diaspora, are always situated in a colonial binary, where the Philippines assumes the lesser, more negative condition from which people escape, and America is the land of promise and the place of hope. This is the hegemonic narrative that has been handed down for many generations, and it is a story that is often repeated and assumed as true for everyone.

We assert that social biography does not assume that our stories are either true or false, but suggest that these stories are instead a reflection of how people have experienced their own realities. The stories are true in the sense that people describe the meaning of their experiences, but they are false in the sense that these individuals only understand their own experience in the context of colonial domination and discrimination. They are conditioned to believe that unjust realities are and have always been the norm. The history that they have learned about themselves has been framed through a Western and colonial reading. In other words, they have been naturalized to accept an un-natural understanding of themselves. This reality is the context in which social biography asserts people's lived-history.

Social biography allows marginalized people to tell their narrative from their own definitions and words. By telling their stories, these individuals can unravel the illusory narratives that veil them from realizing their own agency in the context of their own history of oppression. Only when they place suffering in the context of struggle, can they see a redemptive and liberatory history. In this way, social biography becomes a site for knowledge production and, at the same time, an engaged pedagogy and critical praxis.

Utilizing social biography can help people realize that their identity as AAPIs and condition of being underrepresented in higher education is not an accident. Framing their stories within a political, historical, economic, and social context, they can recognize that their stories are still in the process of being written and re-written. Viewing their stories through a liberatory frame, they can acknowledge that they have forms of agency, consciously or unconsciously, to address the needs of their community and that they are more than who they thought they were.

SOCIAL BIOGRAPHY IN HIGHER EDUCATION

In our use of social biography, we have incorporated rituals, field trips, pilgrimages, and other pedagogical tools that facilitate and bring out stories that can be weaved as central components into the educational process. We emphasize that the activities and rituals described below are always grounded in the place, people, and practices of a particular community. Therefore, it should not be seen as a blue print, but rather a guiding example of what is possible for educators, community members, and other practitioners. In the following sections, we offer only a vignette or snapshot of what the practices that we have developed through our work in the islands of Hawaiʻi, the Philippines, and the California Bay area.

Developing Social Biography Curriculum

The higher education curriculum can play an instrumental role in the dissemination and practice of social biography. Though we have developed this pedagogy in recent years in the traditional classroom setting, we realize that social biography has its roots in community-oriented projects, including visits and pilgrimages to significant landmarks and sacred sites in which the community of learners reside. We seek to expand the walls of the "classroom" to include places in which participants grew up, including the streets, playgrounds, homes, and other places that have shaped who they are today. Thus, this kind of pedagogy and curriculum not only allows one to discover, but also closes the gaps between and among their individual stories and mends fragmented stories in collective journey and with the community by way of (re)telling and remembering their stories in this social fabric of reality (Acido & Lee, 2012). In addition to expanding and redefining the definitions of the classroom, we allow every student to be a teacher and every teacher to be a student. Each time one tells a story, one becomes the teacher.

Social Biography in Praxis

In the courses we have taught in the past years, we begin and end our sessions with protocols that allow one to speak authentically and intentionally. We attempt to create a safe space for our AAPI students and community members to, without hesitation or judgment, (re)tell and remember their life histories, stories of trauma and oppression, and stories of selfhood, self-discovery, and self-consciousness. Conducive to creating a sacred space is gathering in a circle so that participants can see and acknowledge one another, re-orient and minimize the power relations and hierarchies in the classroom, and see each other as equals in the learning environment (Duldulao, 2012). This type of space and structure constructs a sense of belonging and community. The intention is to transform the classroom into a communal, a transformative space, and an essential component for learning and teaching.

At the beginning of each session, in a moment of silence, participants call attention to be physically and spiritually present in the sacred space. Then, they introduce themselves each time class begins by sharing their names, their homes, and names of ancestors whom they want to invite with them into this space. This act of naming helps to bring mind, body, and soul to be physically present, and prepares participants mentally and emotionally to open themselves into a space of (re)learning and recovering their stories. Most importantly, this act of naming affirms their identity and purpose, and recognizes that they are not alone in this process of storytelling as they remember those who came before them.

We are aware that the act of naming can be a subversive act. Reflecting on colonial histories, participants realize that the process of colonization has not allowed them to name their realities. In social biography, they intentionally try to recall their personal names, names of the land, and names of how their bodies are feeling. The act of individuals naming themselves is an act of self-becoming—the process of knowing one's self as an agent of change that continues to change while realizing one's self as an extension and creative participant of history. To realize one's self-becoming is to acknowledge that one has every right to exist and thrive with dignity and become always open to the potential affirmative possibilities. In addition, to summon one's historical self-hood means that one's identity is formed by the struggle of one's community past while living out the tensions of the present.

Windows of Relationality

We frame stories using the four components of the windows of relationality: political, economic, social, and historical. We use these components of the frame to analyze and understand stories and view them in multiple ways. Stories allow participants to peer into different windows to understand episodes and phenomena in their everyday lives and experiences, including the past that shaped them and the present that continues to mold them (Duldulao, 2012).

In order to see stories not merely as "anecdotes," but as types of connections to each other, participants tease out the political, economic, social, and historical aspects of their stories. When they realize that their story both emerges and is created out of these four dimensions, they begin to realize their agency. In other words, they can look back and see that they have always existed in history and that their stories are always consequential. When they examine their story and incorporate these four dimensions, they can proclaim that they are not an accident.

Stations of Kalihi as an Example of Placed-Based Social Biography in Praxis

The *Stations of Kalihi* is one of the social praxis tools we created to help our students share their stories and is a full day of stories and storytelling from our students and members of the community in Kalihi, Hawai'i. This particular component of the social biography curriculum entails urban crawls and site visits to ordinary and sacred places in local communities. Students map out and make sense of the phenomena and occurrences that molded and continue to shape their lives in order to have a better grasp of the world around them. The goal here is to weave students' social biography into the historical biography of the places and spaces that the students selected. At each station, the students take turns telling their personal stories and the histories of the place they have selected, oftentimes engaging the community by interactive participation and short dialogue. Through this process, students tell their stories of struggle, stories of being, stories of redemption, and the event becomes the community-based and place-based learning experience for all participants. This is where students learn not only about themselves, but also about the community where they have rooted their sense of identity. The goal is to weave their personal stories, for example, with the larger AAPI, Filipino, and Hawai'i community stories in their chosen site.

In many instances, the students visit their selected site more than once to become familiar with and get a better sense of their station. Ultimately, the

Stations of Kalihi is a vehicle for one to intertwine their story with the story of the community and land that they find most resonant. Through this process, students begin to expand their personal story to collective narrative, moving from a provincial to a broader reading of history. The incorporation of their story into the collective story allows them to see their bodies through the window of relationality—to see their bodies and stories as a source of connection to the larger community of bodies and stories. The window of relationality is a lens to see more than the physical features of ourselves and to see that our body as well as our story is connected through a historical umbilical cord to the community that we represent. In the final analysis, the social praxis of stations in Kalihi allows them to tell a story that does not pathologize their experience, but sheds light on who they were and who they want to become.

In the weeks following the *Stations of Kalihi* event, participants spend most of their time reflecting on and discerning what happened at the stations. Participants gather their thoughts and reactions, and remember how students felt after the event, and how they were transformed or not transformed, with what they did and what took place. In a reflexive class discussion, participants probe and delve into deeper issues and feelings with which they are dealing. To heighten the reflections, select members of the community who participated in the *Stations of Kalihi* are invited to talk about what they experienced and witnessed and to reflect on the impact that the students made on their own lives. Pedagogically, the community's input and reflection are an invaluable part of students' learning experience. The community reflection is a necessary process to give a deeper affirmative meaning to the project. The community refracts its own understanding of the story-telling rituals performed by the students, informing them of their own understanding and allowing the students to synthesize the wisdom offered by the community and within their own lives and experiences.

After their collective and individual contemplations, students write their personal reflections as their final project in class. At the same time, we call on community members for their reflections and thoughts. The culmination of the *Stations of Kalihi* and student and community reflections was an anthology, *On the Edge of Hope and Healing: Flipping the Scripts of Filipinos in Hawai'i*. Their stories and reflections became powerful tools of codifying their history, and the writing and codifying of their history and lived experiences are an invaluable tool for students to reflect on their purpose and their being an important part of the social fabric of reality (Acido & Lee, 2012). In essence, through their writings, both the students and the larger community become the "textbook" that allows them to have a dialogical conversation with their own past in order to inform their present.

IMPLICATIONS FOR POLICIES, PROGRAMS, AND CURRICULUM

AAPI students are heterogenous, and so are their educational needs and ways of learning (Hune, 2002). They differ in cultural background and experience. Therefore, as educators and practitioners, we need to recognize and excavate their diverse personal stories and histories. The recommendations below provide further thought and discussion on integrating social biography in our curriculum and pedagogy in higher education.

In the time of this writing, amidst budget cuts, standardized curricula and technological innovation are becoming the dominant focus of formal education, and the nation is undergoing a shift away from community-based education that engages the community as the vehicle for learning and understanding the social and political problems of our time, as sites of knowledge production. The push for science, technology, engineering, and mathematics (STEM) related fields has created a binary of opposition and (un)consciously marginalized community-based departments such as ethnic studies, educational foundations, and other departments that focus on bridging community related issues with their respective academic disciplines. Institutions of higher education must expand policies and concepts of research and importance beyond the STEM fields and in the lives and respective communities of their students. Through our community-based pedagogy, we advocate for policies that address students' social reality and support community participation, with community engagement as part of the education that institutions of higher learning provide. We believe policies must enable, not disable, the student from seeking knowledge outside of the structure of institutions of higher education to affirm that colleges and universities do not have, and should not have, a monopoly on wisdom.

The larger educational trajectory for which we aim regarding the use of the pedagogy of social biography in higher education is one that points toward a curriculum that seeks social change. In the midst of higher education's granting certificates and degrees, we are beginning to see our students become technocrats who are highly skilled at what they are doing, but do not understand what they are doing in the larger system of social relations. In other words, they are able to gather information but do not understand what the information is and what to do with it. We have witnessed numerous times in our teaching and advising of students in the university their inability to decide for themselves their own future. Questions that always arise from our students include, "Can you tell me the answer?" or "Can you tell me what to do?" or "How does this help me get an "A"?" These questions are a reflection of a technocratic education geared toward certification and finding employment, rather than the process of learning.

The curriculum in higher education plays an instrumental role in creating an educated citizenry. Therefore, we believe that part of the problematic effects of today's dominant curriculum is the production of a technocratic education. In incorporating social biography in the higher education curriculum, the practice of stories, story telling, and the ethos in which stories are seen as constitutive of educational practice can humanize the community of learners and begin to develop a citizenry who are conscious of themselves and the society in which they live. What this all means is to render our educational institutions as spaces in which one can develop and affirm their identity. For AAPIs, this inevitably means an invocation of both the people and history of AAPI communities in education. This step toward a holistic curriculum brings in a myriad of implications with regard to historical trauma, restorative justice, indigenous and community education, affirmation of multiple epistemologies and intelligences, and opening up to pedagogies that address colonization and promote a democratic education. In the end, a curriculum that addresses these issues and promotes an ethos of holistic worldview is a step toward education as a practice for social change.

CONCLUSION

The effects of our visioning of curriculum on such policies have the potential to create a thriving higher education culture that (re)affirms multiple ways of learning. Moreover, it affirms the communities from which AAPI students come and allows them to engage their own stories and communities as sites of knowledge production. We firmly believe that pedagogies and policies that promote affirmative explorations of the AAPI students' identity will aid in their recruitment and retention and garner community support outside of the particular institution of higher education. Indeed, more than ever, we cannot afford to separate and fragment the student from their community. In the final analysis, policies that enable community-based pedagogies will create learning outcomes that are holistic and propel assessments to include the personal stories and community participation and engagement. It is our hope that, through utilizing practices like social biography, higher education addresses the rich and complicated ways in which AAPI students and communities can and do shape education.

NOTE

1. *Talk-story* is a colloquial term used by locals in Hawai'i, while the word *moolelo* in Native Hawai'ian language loosely translated means *history* and *pakasaritaan* in Ilokano language means *history* as well.

REFERENCES

Accapadi, M. M. (2012). Asian American identity consciousness: A polycultural model. In D. M. Ching & A. Agbayani (Eds.), *Asian Americans and Pacific Islanders in higher education: Research and perspectives on identity, leadership, and success* (pp. 57–94). Washington, DC: National Association of Student Personnel Administrators.

Acido, J., & Lee, G. (2012). *On the edge of hope and healing: Flipping the script of Filipinos in Hawaii.* Honolulu, Hawai'i: TMI Global Press.

DeSalvo, L. (1999). *Writing as a way of healing: How telling our stories transforms our lives.* Boston, MA: Beacon Press.

Duldulao, G. A. (2012). Forgotten pains. In J. T. Acido & G. D. Lee (Eds.), *On the edge of hope and healing: Flipping the script of Filipinos in Hawaii* (pp. 117–119). Honolulu, Hawai'i: TMI Global Press.

Hune, S. (2002). Demographics and diversity of Asian American college students. *New Directions for Student Services, 97,* 11–20.

Museus, S. D. (2014). *Asian American students in higher education.* New York, NY: Routledge.

CHAPTER 8

FACILITATING COLLEGE ACCESS FOR HMONG STUDENTS

Challenges and Opportunities

**William Collins, Anna Chiang,
Joshua Fisher, and Marie P. Ting**

Asian Americans and Pacific Islanders (AAPIs) have often been aggregated into one homogenous group (Teranishi, Ceja, Antonio, Allen, & McDonough, 2004; Wing, 2007). However, data from the 2010 U.S. Census Bureau suggest that the AAPI racial category consists of more than 48 different ethnic groups that occupy positions along the full range of the socioeconomic spectrum, from the poor and under-privileged, to the affluent and highly-skilled (Cepeda 2011; National Commission on Asian American and Pacific Islander Education [CARE], 2011). However, despite such stratification, the successes of certain AAPI subgroups are often generalized and applied to AAPIs as a whole, which obscures the distinctions and challenges that exist within the larger racial group.

Focusing on the Underserved, pages 151–162
Copyright © 2017 by Information Age Publishing

The "model minority" myth suggests that AAPIs have universally succeeded and no concern needs to be given to this group because of such success (Li & Wang, 2008; Peterson, 1966; Suzuki, 1977). The basis for this view is that certain groups of AAPIs—notably those of Taiwanese, Japanese, or Chinese ancestry—have excelled academically and socio-economically relative to the overall United States population (Museus, 2014). Yet other groups of AAPIs, particularly Southeast Asians (SEAs) and Pacific Islanders, have not experienced the same levels of success. Indeed, Museus, Maramba, and Teranishi (2013) has detailed educational and economic inequalities among AAPIs as well as a need for disaggregated data on AAPIs that disrupts, rather than reflects, the mythical "model minority" Asian American monolith. He calls for a focus on underserved populations, such as the Hmong, in order to better understand the needs of such groups.

SOUTHEAST ASIAN AMERICAN COLLEGE ACCESS

Higher educational attainment has long been recognized as a pathway to upward mobility and economic security. In recent years, this truism has become even more apparent as the income gap between college graduates and non-graduates has widened. Baum, Ma, and Payea (2013) show that college graduates, in comparison to those with only a high school diploma, have greater wealth, more security, better health, closer families, and stronger communities.

Educational attainment bestows a variety of benefits to those fortunate enough to complete college. As a result, interest in college attendance has continued to spike throughout the last century. For example, over the last decade, undergraduate college enrollment increased from 13.2 million to more than 18 million students in 2012 (Aud et al., 2012). Yet, access to college is not equally distributed across racial groups. For example, Whites and AAPIs are more likely to attend college, while Black and Hispanics are less likely to attend (National Center for Education Statistics [NCES], 2012; Pew Research Center, 2012). In fact, as a single aggregated group, AAPIs attend college at the highest rate of all racial groups. Yet, among Asian American ethnic groups, glaring differences persist in both educational attainment and economic status. In particular, Southeast Asians, which include people from Vietnam, Laos, and Cambodia, attend college at lower rates and come from families with lower incomes (Museus, 2013).

This chapter sheds light on the experiences of the Hmong, one such group whose college attendance rates are among the lowest of all racial and ethnic groups in the nation. We illuminate the challenges facing a group of Hmong American students as they consider pursuing higher education. While illuminating the struggles related to higher education attainment for this group of high school students, the chapter also offers some interventions that may be helpful to promote college access to this underserved community.

CULTURAL AND ECONOMIC CHALLENGES FACED BY SOUTHEAST ASIAN AMERICANS

As Southeast Asians, the Hmong are one of the most impoverished ethnic groups in the United States. The 2000 U.S. Census shows that 49% of Southeast Asians live in poverty, compared to less than 10% of Japanese and Chinese Americans (Teranishi, 2004). Hmong American per capita income and educational attainment percentages are exceedingly low in comparison to other AAPI populations as well as other racial groups in the United States.

Generally, Hmong came to the United States as refugees from Laos as a consequence of their involvement in the Vietnam War. In the United States, many Hmong settled in warmer climates, such as California, but significant numbers settled in urban centers of the Midwest, such as Minneapolis, Minnesota (Kitano & Daniels, 1987). Several thousand Hmong also reside in the Detroit, Michigan area. Hmong often encountered problems that are common to new immigrant groups, including language barriers, lack of fit between their skills and labor market needs, discrimination, generational differences, conflict between family expectations and educational aspirations, and general culture shock as they adjust to a new socio-cultural milieu (Museus, 2013).

EXPERIENCES OF HMONG AMERICAN HIGH SCHOOL STUDENTS

Generally, focus group interviews provide insight into how people interpret and understand complex relationships as well as how current behavior may be influenced by past decisions or incidents. The central goal of focus group interviews is to understand how informants think (Bogdan & Biklen, 1992), and in our case, how Hmong American students think about going to higher education. We used the focus group format because it allowed for an in-depth exploration of topics and yielded rich detail about the students' experiences (Rubin & Rubin, 2005).

In order to better understand the lived experiences of Hmong American high school students and the factors that influence their perspectives about college, we conducted field interviews with a group of these students who live in a major urban city in the Midwest. The students with whom we spoke participated in the Aspire Project (a pseudonym), a community-based

grassroots organization that works with Hmong American students at Castle-
mont Academy (a pseudonym) on a weekly basis, offering additional support, educational workshops, and a space for community building among
these students. We conducted a focus group with seven Hmong American
students—six females and one male participant—which represented 44% of
the 16 students in the after-school program. The seven students who participated in our study are from lower socio-economic status families and all reside in the same neighborhood of an urban community noted for its high in-
cidence of poverty and characterized by high crime rates. Four of the student
participants were in eleventh grade, two were tenth graders, and one was in
ninth grade. We sought to understand the factors that impact these students'
desire, perception, and ability to pursue higher education. In exploring the
factors that influence the decisions that the students make regarding their
pursuit of higher education, four particularly salient categories emerged: (a)
attitudes about college, (b) lack of college knowledge, (c) family stresses, and
(d) the presence of programs that address unique cultural factors impacting
the students' decisions about college.

CONFLICTING ATTITUDES ABOUT COLLEGE

Overall, the students in our study acknowledged that a postsecondary degree is important for social mobility. Pa confided, "I want to do the things
that none of my family did yet . . . not even my oldest brother has finished
college yet, so I want to be the first in my family to finish . . . you know, live a
successful life." Similarly, Lee elaborated, "I definitely want to go to college
and, if I do pursue college, I want to make sure what I do in college I'm very
passionate about."

Although students believe that a higher education degree is important,
college also seemed like an unrealistic, foreign concept. Lee explained:

> I feel as if our whole life, we set that goal of going to "college," but then,
> what about college? I take so much into consideration that, you know, there's
> money wise, there is no guarantee for a job afterwards . . . We are not even
> sure ourselves of what to do, and so, I feel like college is nothing but an empty
> word to me, because I feel like I don't even know what to do, like what am I
> even going to do when I get there.

Like many first-generation students, Lee could not visualize going to college and seemed confused about the whole college-going process. The
foreignness of college compounded the fact that students in this study
knew very few people within their community who had attained a higher
education degree. Yang shared, " . . . half of the people I know either got
married or are working right now because I don't think college is the

first thing on their mind right now." Xiong expressed a similar concern, observing, "I know a few Hmong college students...but there is not a lot...I just know a few. I know more Hmong people who are in their early 20s and are not in college. I know more people like that than I do people who go to college." Pang added, "Well I really don't see any people going to college. To me, it's just about getting married or, you know, getting a job, getting the quick money."

Many of these students lacked immediate Hmong role models with college experience and accessible points of information about the benefits of higher education. Students indicated that they know more members of their community who do not go to college—going to college after high school is viewed as out of the norm and not a priority.

Lack of College Knowledge

In regard to the college-going process, the students in this study felt that, within their schools, there was little substantive guidance or encouragement related to attaining a higher education from their counselors or teachers. Pa assessed, "My counselor, well she really isn't dependable but she does teach us a little about college, but not really—just a fieldtrip and other stuff about college." While Vue also noted a lack of support for students who wish to pursue higher education, he attributed this more to lack of available resources and opportunities than students in wealthier school districts can access to advance their post-secondary opportunities:

> I just, sometimes, I look at my school and I feel like "oh man, the suburban schools they are doing much better [than ours]...because they have more programs and stuff. We have school problems. We lack in funding and stuff like that. We don't have enough money for all these things.

Perhaps equally challenging is the struggle that students face when trying to obtain college-going information within their homes. Vue offered, "Most of us come from families where our parents never finished high school/ They don't know English...They don't understand English...They don't have like a college education...They don't have like the best jobs either."

The parents of students in this study have difficulty supporting students academically not only because they do not understand English, but also because they lack formal education. As a result, these parents do not have the experience necessary to help their students navigate the education system, assist with homework, or provide guidance about college. Lee commented, "Our Hmong parents here...they don't really know how to...get us academically ready...They are not too sure how to approach us. They are not too sure how to make sure we study."

Nevertheless, it is important to note that parents expressed interest in their students' schoolwork and tried to be supportive of their children's academic pursuits. Pa asserted, "My parents express their support, in a way, by taking you to school every day. And, they always tell me to do my homework and get my work done." Although Pa's parents may not be able to assist with homework, they demonstrated their care about her academic achievement through other means. Other students shared a similar sentiment about parents encouraging their academics. For example, Lee illustrated this point when he recalled, "My parents was...telling me 'Get A's, go to college, and get a job...Don't go to college and come back and just stay home,' you know, so I'm thinking a lot [about] what should I go into..."

Poverty and Family Obligations

Although students described parents who encouraged their higher education aspirations, family obligations often seemed to supersede that encouragement. Yang elaborated:

> For me, like, I love my parents a lot, and I don't want to be like spending time in college, when I could just work and get that money, like quick money, to just come and you know help them out with bills and stuff, cuz I wouldn't want them to like work and stuff.

This sentiment depicts the kind of dilemma many Hmong students faced in regard to their feelings about going to college versus the obligation that they feel toward their families. Often, the students' grave concerns about their families' financial stability profoundly impacted their desires to pursue higher education. The limited financial resources within these families not only influenced students' goals, but also their ability to achieve academically, as some must work to supplement the family income. Yang described her struggle to balance homework, college search, and work obligations:

> We only share one computer and my brother is always using it for his homework and stuff. So, I can't really just log onto the computer and try and look up colleges and stuff, like I don't have that much time, because I gotta work, and I'm hardly home because I have school and then, in the afternoon, I go to work and I don't come back until night.

The limited financial resources available at home, combined with the obligations for work after school, impeded Yang's opportunity to explore postsecondary options. Indeed, as students fixate on their immediate priorities, their thoughts about the future and the role that college may play in their lives can be pushed out of their minds. Vue spoke about how his family's financial experience affected his sibling's pursuit of college:

> We don't have enough money to go to college. My sister didn't go to college right after high school because, at that time, we were struggling with money and she didn't want to put pressure on my parents' shoulders. My parents were disappointed that she didn't go to college, but they didn't really understand the reason why she decided not to go to college. My sister didn't want to put more debt in my parents' hands.

For Vue and her Hmong peers, money for college is an important factor to consider when thinking about the plausibility of attending college. It is also evident that children and parents persistently face challenges in communication when it involves postsecondary education planning. In Vue's situation, he understood the poor financial situation of the parents, but hid this awareness to avoid contributing to stress in the family. Similarly, Vang had concerns about parents and college costs:

> Money is a really big issue, like everybody has their own way of doing things— for example, some people, they want to work first to earn that money, so that their parents don't have to pay for them, so they choose to work first so they can pay their own college fees and stuff.

These first-generation Hmong American students had been raised in poverty and, as a consequence, often consider full-time working as a priority in their post-high school plan; they would rather contribute to their family's economic stability than pursue a post-secondary degree.

Positive Impact of Pre-College Preparation Programs

The interviews revealed a common desire among the students to pursue college. However, they all had reservations about the plausibility of attending college because they had received minimal guidance, support, and college knowledge. One way they were able to access these resources was through pre-college preparation programs that served as a network of support for these students. Vue spoke about how the influential Aspire Project had impacted his desire to go to college:

> Before I was like involved in youth organizations and stuff like that, I didn't really care at all. All that was on my mind was that okay, yeah, I have to finish college, get a job . . . And that's the way of life. But, you know, being involved

with this program, they really add more meaning to why I should go to college ... not just to get a job, but to make friends, have fun, discover yourself.

Being in a support program enabled Vue to be exposed to college and
helped him find a purpose behind pursuing a college education. Like many
students from similar backgrounds, Vue leveraged intervention programs
to increase college knowledge, as well as awareness of opportunities beyond
high school.

Participants also discussed the importance of being involved in pre-college programs that address challenges surrounding students' ethnic identity. For students in this study, this became particularly important given the
dwindling numerical Hmong population in the city in which they live. For
example, Yang recalled:

We used to have this really big Hmong population in [our city], but I guess
because of the bad environment that we are surrounded by ... abandoned
houses, and a lot of criminal cases and stuff ... I guess everybody just pretty
much moved out.

The loss of large numbers of Hmong in the city limited opportunities
for the students to have a strong and supportive social network. Support
networks were also critical when students articulated the racism-related
struggles that they faced. Vue shared one instance:

I used to walk home with my friends, and like there was like these ... kids
from our school, same grade, different class though. And, they used to
come ... mock us ... not mock us ... try and mock us ... like "*ching chong*" you
know ... call us Chinese even though we are not and I went home ... I used to
be so mess-up. I went home, and I told my sisters about it, and they told me
that was racism. Like what is that?

In the absence of other perspectives, Hmong students had internalized
other people's negative views of their ethnic community. Due to such situations, ethnic specific pre-college programs are essential, as program mentors can offer varying perspectives about the Hmong identity to the students.
Vang explained how he found his community to be invisible in school curricula and how the Aspire Project had significantly supported him:

As a kid, I was like, "Well, maybe this is what I am supposed to learn. Maybe
there is no Hmong leaders and stuff." But, you know what? Especially being
involved in the [Aspire Project], I was exposed to like a lot of different Asian
American leaders ... like Hmong ... people who are like good role models.

This program provided information about leaders in the Hmong community. In doing so, it exposed students to Hmong role models that were otherwise invisible in mainstream curricula.

PROMOTING COLLEGE ACCESS FOR HMONG AMERICAN HIGH SCHOOL STUDENTS

The primary objective of this chapter is to shed light on challenges related to college access for a group that has been underrepresented in higher education. While much research places AAPI students next to and sometimes ahead of White students in terms of academic success, such research seems to limit understandings of the AAPI student experience. Analyses of the experiences of AAPI subgroups that are underserved and underrepresented in higher education are a vital step toward combatting stereotypes and filling gaps in information.

Our data demonstrated that Hmong students face numerous challenges and obstacles to their upward mobility. Our research with Hmong American students reveals that many aspire to educational attainment beyond high school. Our analysis illuminates Hmong American students: (a) are largely unfamiliar with the college application process; (b) are generally uninformed about financial aid opportunities; (c) are relatively unaware of the career options that are available to college graduates; and (d) have parents who are generally not college-educated and are ill-equipped to provide advice and guidance about college choices. These obstacles are consistent with those reported by researchers who have studied other underserved populations (Cabrera & La Nasa, 2000; Hoxby & Avery, 2013; Tierney, Corwin, & Colyar, 2005). Yet, our participants remained optimistic about their futures, whether they planned to work or continue education after high school. Furthermore, their voices overwhelmingly indicated that intervention programs were beneficial for building a support network of their peers and accessing information about the college-going process that they would be unlikely to receive otherwise.

Knowledge of such obstacles provides a basis for developing interventions to address them. For example, it is likely that the Hmong American students we interviewed and other similarly situated students would benefit from interventions and programs that: (a) inform them about the college application process and financial aid; (b) provide them with exposure to college campuses; (c) expose them to college students with similar backgrounds and experiences; (d) advise and re-assure parents about the feasibility of meeting college costs; (e) educate them about career options; and (f) promote their identity development, self-efficacy, and resilience.

Similarly, institutions of higher education can play a role in building authentic partnerships with under-resourced communities to ensure that students from these communities enroll in colleges that are the best fit. Colleges and universities can sponsor faculty and staff to visit schools and community centers to talk about appropriate academic preparation, review study and career opportunities, and discuss research experiences and recent discoveries. Institutions of higher education can also host Hmong students on campus so that they can observe campus facilities first-hand and make connections between pre-college academic work and the kind of experience they can expect to have in college. Doing so will give Hmong students a basis for developing realistic expectations about the college experience.

Another avenue for promoting a college-going culture is for colleges and universities to share resources and strategies that equip educators and community organization leaders to serve this population. For example, a valuable contribution in Hmong communities would be workshops about holistic approaches to designing programs that actively facilitate pathways to higher education for Hmong youth. Such interventions might incorporate academic, social, and cultural elements in after-school or extra-curricular activities. Such an effort is most likely to be successful if operated as a true partnership between colleges or universities and local community-based organizations.

This analysis results in a number of other implications for promoting college access among Hmong and other similarly situated students, which then suggests that educators who seek to advocate for Hmong American students consider the following:

1. Identify Hmong American students' strengths or obstacles to higher education attainment. In particular, programs should seek to incorporate relevant Hmong American history, language, and customs that often are missing from typical school experiences.

2. Provide Hmong Americans with access to college knowledge, rather than assume that students are familiar with the application process, financial requirements and forms (such as the *Free Application for Federal Student Aid* [FAFSA]), and knowledge of different institutional types. High school guidance counselors are often overburdened with excessive numbers of students and, therefore, may not have adequate time to devote to college knowledge matters.

3. Offer academic preparation, mentoring by peers and adults with similar backgrounds, college campus visits, and interactions with like-minded academically oriented Hmong students from other communities in order to reinforce positive academic attitudes.

4. Encourage colleges and universities to sponsor workshops for school personnel and community organization staff so they can learn about Hmong American history, culture, or language.
5. Persuade institutions of higher education and schools to partner with community-based organizations, such as "Aspire Project," to build relationships between educational institutions and the Hmong American community and Hmong students. Colleges and schools can work with and provide resources to these community-based organizations so that they can deliver messages that promote academic success and higher education attainment in their day-to-day work with students.
6. Encourage institutions of higher education to re-examine data collection and reporting practices related to AAPI populations, and explore ways in which data collected on AAPI populations can be disaggregated and better highlight the needs within certain subgroups, such as Hmong American students.
7. Provide mentoring from "near-peers" who are close in age and already in college and who can speak frankly about challenges and opportunities of attending college.
8. Offer direct exposure to college campuses, faculty, and research facilities can help students realize the opportunities available, but they also need to be able to see themselves actually on the campus and in the careers promised by college degree attainment.
9. Provide tutoring and standardized test preparation to build the confidence needed to navigate successfully the college application, enrollment, and achievement process.

College degree attainment is increasingly important for financial stability and access to a middle-class lifestyle. Hmong Americans continually face significant barriers to educational attainment and upward mobility. Strategic interventions informed by relevant research can contribute to progress for Hmong American populations.

REFERENCES

Aud, S., Hussar, W., Johnson, F., Kena, G., Roth, E., Manning, E.,...Zhang, J. (2012). *The condition of education 2012.* Washington, DC: U.S. Department of Education, National Center for Education Statistics. Retrieved from http://nces.ed.gov/pubsearch

Baum, S., Ma, J., & Payea, K. (2013). *Education pays: The benefits of higher education to individuals and society.* New York, NY: The College Board.

Bogdan, R. C., & Biklen, S. K. (1992). *Qualitative research for education: An introduction to theories and methods* (2nd ed.). Boston, MA: Allyn & Bacon.

Cabrera, A. F., & La Nasa, S. M. (Eds.). (2000). Understanding the college choice of disadvantaged students [Special issue]. *New Directions for Institutional Research, 107.*

National Commission on Asian American and Pacific Islander Research in Education (CARE). (2011). *The relevance of Asian Americans & Pacific Islanders in the college completion agenda.* Washington, DC: National Commission on Asian American and Pacific Islander Research in Education.

Cepeda, E. (2011, August 3). The needs of diverse Asian-American students often overlooked. *Contra Costa Times,* p. A12.

Hoxby, C. M., & Avery, C. (2013). *The missing "one-offs": The hidden supply of high-achieving, low-income students.* Washington, DC: The Brookings Institute.

Kitano, H. H. L., & Daniels, R. (1987). *Asian Americans: Emerging minorities.* Englewood Cliffs, NJ: Prentice Hall.

Li, G., & Wang, L. (Eds.). (2008). *Model minority myth revisited: An interdisciplinary approach to demystifying Asian American educational experiences.* Charlotte, NC: Information Age.

Museus, S. D. (2014). *Asian American students in higher education.* New York, NY: Routledge.

Museus, S. D., Maramba, D. C., & Teranishi, R. T. (2013). *The misrepresented minority: New insights on Asian Americans and Pacific Islanders, and their implications for higher education.* Sterling, VA: Stylus.

National Center for Educational Statistics [NCES]. (2012). *The condition of education.* Retrieved from http://nces.ed.gov/programs/coe/indicator_caa.asp

Peterson, W. (1966, January 9). Success stories, Japanese American style. *The New York Times Magazine,* p. 21.

Pew Research Center. (2012). *The rise of Asian Americans.* Retrieved from http://www.pewsocialtrends.org/2012/06/19/the-rise-of-asian-americans/

Rubin, H. J., & Rubin, I. S. (2005). *Qualitative interviewing: The art of hearing data.* Thousand Oaks, CA: Sage.

Suzuki, B. H. (1977). Education and socialization of Asian Americans: A revisionist analysis of the "model minority" thesis. *Amerasia Journal, 4*(2), 23–51.

Tierney, W. G., Corwin, Z. B., & Colyar, J. E. (2005). *Preparing for college: Nine elements of effective outreach.* Albany, NY: State University of New York Press.

Teranishi, R. (2004). Yellow and "Brown": Emerging Asian American immigrant populations and residential segregation. *Equity and Excellence in Education, 37*(3), 255–263.

Teranishi, R. T., Ceja, M., Antonio, A. L., Allen, W. R., & McDonough, P. M. (2004). The college-choice process for Asian Pacific Americans: Ethnicity and socioeconomic class in context. *The Review of Higher Education, 27*(4), 527–551.

Wing, J. Y. (2007). Beyond black and white: The model minority myth and the invisibility of Asian American students. *The Urban Review, 39*(4), 455–487.

CHAPTER 9

JOURNEY TO SUCCESS

A University-Community Partnership to Improve College Access and Success Among Cambodian American Students

Mary Ann Takemoto, Simon Kim, Karen Nakai, and Karen Quintiliani

Asian Americans are seldom considered an "underrepresented" group in higher education, or a group that needs any support from federal funding agencies and institutions of higher education. However, not all Asian Americans experience higher education the same. There are tremendous discrepancies in student achievement and degree attainment across Asian American and Pacific Islander (AAPI) ethnic groups (Museus, 2013). Many Southeast Asian Americans (e.g., Cambodian Americans, Vietnamese Americans, Hmong Americans, and Lao Americans) came to the United States as refugees, rather than as voluntary immigrants, and consequently exhibit higher levels of poverty and lower levels of education compared to other Asian American ethnic groups.

For example, more than one-third of Cambodian Americans live in poverty (Takei & Sakamoto, 2011), and 35% of Cambodian Americans do not

Focusing on the Underserved, pages 163–173
Copyright © 2017 by Information Age Publishing

163

complete high school (United States Census Bureau, 2011). Furthermore, 66% of Cambodian adults have never enrolled in, let alone completed, any postsecondary education. It is critical that educators recognize that access to higher education remains a significant challenge for Cambodian Americans and other underserved AAPIs.

The purpose of this chapter is to provide an overview of a program that a public university system has implemented to address the educational challenges that Cambodian American students face. While scholars have conducted research on Southeast Asian American students to inform educational policies (Museus, 2013), there is still limited understanding of how to address the aforementioned challenges. Accordingly, in this chapter we discuss strategies to improve college access and success among Cambodian American students.

Dating back to the 1950s, California State University, Long Beach (CSULB) has a long history of serving Cambodian students. In this chapter, we present a case study describing how the California State University (CSU) system[1] addressed challenges faced by Cambodian American students through the Journey to Success (JTS) initiative. We then utilize this case study as a mechanism to understand ways in which public universities can work with communities to promote college access and success among Southeast Asian American students.

CAMBODIAN IMMIGRATION HISTORY

It is important to understand the context of Cambodian immigration history. Cambodian Americans are in the United States because of one of the most savage regimes of the twentieth century. In April 1975, the radical communist group known as the Khmer Rouge took control of Cambodia's government. Determined to revert the country to a time before European contact, they cut off all communication with Western nations, dismantled the country's infrastructure, and forcibly moved people out of the cities into the countryside in segregated work camps (Chandler, 1991). City dwellers, ethnic minorities, government workers, teachers, artists, and all resisting the Khmer Rouge's totalitarian rule were deemed enemies, tortured, and killed en masse. Schools, libraries, and Buddhist temples were destroyed. Families, the central social unit of society, were divided for population control.

By the time the Vietnamese military invaded Cambodia and defeated the Khmer Rouge in 1979, nearly two million Cambodians had died from murder, starvation, or disease. Thousands of Cambodians fled to refugee camps along the Thai border to escape terror and reunite with family. Many

Cambodians languished in refugee camps for several years and resettled in Australia, Canada, France, and the United States (Becker, 1998).

Around 4,500 Cambodians escaped before the Khmer Rouge gained control of the country (Coleman, 1987). While early arrivals migrated to the United States directly from Cambodia, later immigrants came from other parts of the world where they had conducted business, attended school, or served in the Cambodian military or embassies (Coleman, 1987; Needham & Quintiliani, 2007). Since many Cambodian refugees already spoke English or French, these linguistic skills contributed to their ability to adjust to the new cultural context (Cheng & Yang, 1996; Needham & Quintiliani, 2007). Nevertheless, Cambodian refugees still faced significant challenges in the United States upon their arrival (Haines, 1996; Hein, 2006; Rumbaut, 2006).

The Cambodian refugees who came to the United States after 1979 were considerably different from the first arrivals in terms of educational and occupational backgrounds, and war experiences. More than half of these refugees were agriculturalists from villages in the Cambodian countryside (Rumbaut, 1996). Although usually multilingual in the regional languages, they had little or no exposure to Western languages. While nearly all the men in this group had a 4th grade education, most of the women had received no formal education (Needham & Quintiliani, 2007). Because of their lack of familiarity with the language, educational system, and occupational expectations in the United States, these families struggled to raise their children and to make a living, thereby challenging the model minority myth of universal success.

Today Cambodian Americans live with the legacy of war trauma. Many first- and 1.5- generation Cambodian American refugees—those who came to the United States as children or early teens from Cambodia or a refugee camp—continue to suffer high rates of debilitating mental health conditions, including post-traumatic stress disorder and depression, due to their past exposure to violence and starvation as survivors of the Khmer Rouge regime (Blair, 2000; Kinzie, Fredrickson, Ben, Fleck, & Karls, 1984; Marshall, Schell, Elliott, Berthold, & Chun, 2005; Mollica et al., 1990). The majority of Cambodian Americans in the United States reside in urban, predominantly minority, working-class neighborhoods where poverty and violence exacerbate feelings of fear and uncertainty (Quintiliani, 2009). Furthermore, many Cambodian American refugees and their children have witnessed or experienced community violence in their inner city neighborhoods, which contributed to the prevalence of mental health issues (Berthold, 1999, 2000; Marshall et al., 2005).

During the 1980s, the largest number of Cambodian refugees entered the United States and resettled in Long Beach, located just south of Los Angeles in Southern California, which became the center of the Cambodian diaspora and home to the largest Cambodian community in the United States (Chan, 2004; Needham & Quintiliani, 2007). Despite federal resettlement policy that aimed to disperse Cambodian refugees around the country to prevent the emergence of ethnic enclaves, Cambodians Americans gravitated to Southern California. This migration partly resulted from many Cambodian refugees being drawn to the moderate year-round weather and access to jobs and Asian goods through the Long Beach and Los Angeles Ports (Needham & Quintiliani, 2007). However, another major reason for this migration to Southern California was that several educated Cambodians who had attended universities in Southern California during the 1960s and 1970s, including CSU Long Beach, were then on the forefront of creating local and national responses to refugee resettlement through social service agencies and cultural institutions (Needham & Quintiliani, 2007, 2008).[2]

The United States Census Bureau (2010a, 2010b) reports that approximately 18,000 Cambodian Americans reside in Long Beach; this figure is likely an underestimation of the actual population.[3] Many Cambodians who live in neighboring cities participate in the Long Beach economy and cultural events, and can be considered part of the Long Beach community (Needham & Quintiliani, 2007). Despite many struggles and few resources, Cambodian Americans gained enough political clout in 2007 to have a section of Long Beach named Cambodia Town, the first cultural designation of its kind in the United States (Quintiliani & Needham, 2014). As we discuss in the next sections, an understanding of this immigration and local history of Cambodian Americans played an important role in JTS.

A CULTURALLY DISTINCT APPROACH TO CSU INITIATIVES FOR UNDERSERVED ETHNIC GROUPS

The CSU—the largest and most diverse university system in the country with 23 campuses and more than 437,000 students—has worked to increase underserved students' access to higher education for the past decade. A hallmark of the CSU initiative is the culturally distinct approach taken to serve each ethnic community. Non-traditional partnerships have developed with various community-based, educational, and corporate organizations to expand the pipeline of college-ready high school graduates.

JTS identified underserved AAPI ethnic groups based on the Early Assessment Test that measures high school students' college readiness in English and mathematics. The initiative targeted ethnic subgroups that scored low and failed to meet proficiency, and were considered underprepared for college. In 2010, the CSU Chancellor of California convened a meeting of AAPI community leaders and representatives from PreK–16 educational institutions throughout the state of California to explore ways to provide AAPI students and parents with information about how to prepare for, gain admission to, and finance college. These discussions and the resulting recommendations led to the development of the JTS Initiative. Four CSU campuses, including CSULB, were selected to be a part of the JTS based on their AAPI student demographics. Each campus was required to develop a unique outreach strategy that was culturally relevant to the AAPI ethnic subgroup that they targeted. CSU Long Beach, with their large local Cambodian American population, chose to partner with Cambodian American community-based organizations, community colleges, and local school districts to reach out to local Cambodian American secondary school students and their parents to address their college access needs.

Planning and Implementation

The composition of CSULB's JTS Advisory Board reflected its commitment to an equitable partnership with Cambodian American students and their families, the Long Beach Cambodian American Community, and the three educational systems that constitute PreK–16 education in Long Beach. Experience and expertise were drawn from each sector to develop and coordinate educational outreach events and activities for middle and high school students that were different and distinct from existing programs in culturally relevant ways.

It was determined that Cambodian American personnel and students within the university and school district, leaders of cultural community organizations, and Cambodian American professionals would assume leadership roles in all JTS activities as event volunteers, presenters, and panelists. In the first year of the initiative, the CSULB JTS advisory committee developed a one-day JTS College Fair at CSULB for middle and high school Cambodian American students and their parents to improve college access and achievement for Cambodian and other underserved AAPI students. The larger CSU JTS Initiative, CSULB, and local educational partners, including the Long Beach Unified School District (LBUSD) and Long Beach City College (LBCC), funded the college fair.

LBUSD Cambodian American faculty and staff served on our advisory board, presented a JTS workshops for parents and students, translated program information into Khmer for distribution, and served as interpreters at program events. LBUSD and JTS shared online information on the "How to Get to College" workshops with parents of Cambodian American students and at K–12 schools and district meetings. CSULB Cambodian American student leaders and advisory board members also spoke about the college fair in high schools and staff information tables on school campuses to publicize the event and encourage students to attend.

On September 29, 2011, the JTS College Fair attracted more than 200 middle and high school students, parents, and community members. Representatives of the Chancellor, the university, local school district, and the Cambodian American community welcomed attendees. Since many participants had never been on a college campus before, CSULB provided students and their parents with round-trip bus transportation from the local high school to the university. Participants attended presentations by Cambodian American parents, students, and professionals who testified on how college had impacted their lives. Resource materials were provided in Khmer and in English and interpreters were available for key sessions.

In sum, the JTS College Fair provided valuable information on college opportunities for Cambodian American students and families, and it offered them opportunities to explore a college campus and participate in panel discussions of Cambodian American role models. Equally important, the JTS College Fair collectively mobilized supporters of Cambodian American student success throughout the region. College students and faculty were crucial in developing the advisory board's understanding of the cultural context of Cambodian community and the challenges that Cambodian American students face related to college access.

Sustained Community Partnerships

A series of grassroots AAPI activities followed the JTS College Fair, demonstrating the CSU and CSULB's ongoing commitment to support college access and success among Cambodian American students. At a follow-up workshop for Cambodian American parents at a local Long Beach high school, CSULB Cambodian alumni and students shared their perspectives and experiences of applying for, attending, and graduating from college. However, despite utilizing community connections for recruitment purposes, success in attracting Cambodian students and parents on a Saturday afternoon was limited. It was suspected that such workshops had to be coupled with cultural community-based events organized by community members.

In response, during the 2013–2014 academic year, the CSULB JTS Advisory Board and Cambodian community-based organizations co-sponsored workshops on college awareness and information in the Long Beach community. A financial aid workshop on how to pay for college was also administered at the United Cambodian Community (UCC) center in partnership with UCC, Khmer Girls in Action (KGA), and Khmer Arts Academy (KAA) for middle and high school students. And, a special event for Cambodian middle and high school students and their families, similar to the JTS event held in 2011, took place at CSULB featuring parent and student panels, workshops, campus tours, and classroom activities.

LESSONS LEARNED
ABOUT SUCCESSFUL COMMUNITY PARTNERSHIPS

A unique aspect of the JTS Initiative was the partnership of campus representatives and community leaders, reinforcing the notion that advocacy efforts on university campuses are most effective when done in collaboration with community members (Alvarez & Liu, 2002; Pendakur & Pendakur, 2012). From the inception of JTS, such partnerships were key to successfully develop, market, and implement programs. Community partnerships take time to develop and nurture. To facilitate community participation and engagement, JTS Advisory Board meetings were held at Cambodian community organizations or at local Cambodian restaurants. University representatives also participated in the Cambodian New Year celebration and other significant community events to learn about the Cambodian community and honor the contributions of its members. Developed over time, these relationships between the university and community have progressively strengthened .

A second important aspect of the JTS Initiative was the Student Ambassador Program. In the second year of the initiative, we recognized that involving student leaders would provide us with important input into our programs and enhance our outreach to the community. AAPI college student leaders were selected to participate in a multi-campus CSU leadership training program, which focused on understanding sociopolitical issues to develop leadership potential, positive self-concept, and racial identity (Liang, Lee, & Ting, 2002).

The initiative discussed herein was led by a campus president and supported by the CSU Chancellor's Office and the Presidents' Council on Underserved Communities. Instrumental support from executive administrators helped move the initiative forward. CSULB has been fortunate to have an advisory committee that includes administrators from the president's office, student services, and the academic affairs office on campus. Campuswide collaboration and support from top administrators have been vital to the success of the CSU JTS Initiative.

IMPLICATIONS FOR POLICY AND PRACTICE

While we do not yet have conclusive data regarding the impact of the JTS program on college access and success, the preceding discussion highlights one way in which institutions of higher education can develop and implement infrastructures to meet the needs of underserved AAPI communities through collaborative community–university partnerships. We offer a few recommendations that can help educational institutions enhance their efforts to serve Cambodian American and other underserved AAPI students.

Target Outreach Efforts Based on Community Needs

Outreach efforts should be targeted to specific underserved AAPI subgroups and culturally relevant to their unique languages, experiences, and challenges. First-generation AAPI college students and their parents benefit from information and support to facilitate college readiness, the college application process, and financial aid acquisition. Translation of information, interpreters to facilitate two-way communication at college information events, and first-generation Cambodian American college students and graduates sharing their personal journeys into, during, and after college can contribute to more culturally responsive programming.

Develop Internal and External Partnerships

Collective efforts of educational institutions and grassroots community-based organizations are essential to continuously identify, outreach to, and support underserved AAPI students. However, community partnerships take time to develop and nurture. They require a sense that participation in them is mutually beneficial to the university and the community. To develop and nurture university-community partnerships requires an alignment of goals and shared responsibility in planning and implementing program activities. An internal campus task force comprised of key faculty, staff, student leaders, and administrators from diverse student affairs programs and services, academic departments, and student organizations can aid in effective program planning and implementation.

Seek Funding to Improve Student Access and Success

Institutional commitment and financial support matter in efforts to improve access and success of underserved AAPI students. Top leadership must provide personnel and financial resources to carry such initiatives forward, enable multiple departments and divisions to work together, and give the initiative credibility with community partners. Limited funds, however, are always a challenge. Federal funds to support Asian American Native

American and Pacific Islander Serving Institutions (AANAPISIs) are one critical source of funding to improve student access and success by building an infrastructure to support student leadership development, provide faculty development, and create a culturally relevant and responsive campus environment. At the present time, however, U.S. Department of Education regulations prohibit campuses that have dual designation as both an AANAPISI and Hispanic Serving Institution (HSI) from receiving federal funding in both categories in many cases. To complicate matters, legislative changes are necessary to adequately support the needs of both groups.

Create a Supportive Campus Environment

Academic, social, and cultural supports are all important factors in facilitating student success in college (Museus, 2014). In addition to traditional student support services, it is important for universities to support ethnic studies programs, ethnic student organizations, and culturally specific programming for racially minoritized populations. Such cultural organizations help students develop a sense of belonging and provide opportunities for academic, social, and cultural development. Creating a positive, empowering, and engaging campus environment for these organizations will facilitate higher levels of AAPI student engagement and success.

NOTES

1. The California State University system consists of 23 campuses in California.
2. See Needham and Quintiliani (2007) for a full discussion of the local, national, and international conditions that led Long Beach to become home to the largest Cambodian population in the United States. Chan (2003, 2004) provides an important overview of Cambodian resettlement and community leaders' experiences in the rebuilding process.
3. The actual population of Cambodians living in the City of Long Beach is closer to 25,000–29,000. See Needham and Quintiliani (2007) and Bunte and Joseph (1992) for a discussion of the social and cultural factors that have led to the Cambodian population being undercounted and the reason for the estimated Cambodian population in Long Beach.

REFERENCES

Alvarez, A. N., & Liu, W. M. (2002). Student affairs and Asian American studies: An integrated perspective. *New Directions for Student Services, 97,* 73–80.

Becker, E. (1998). *When the war was over: Cambodia and the Khmer Rouge revolution.* New York, NY: Public Affairs.

Berthold, S. M. (1999). The effects of exposure to community violence on Khmer refugee adolescents. *Journal of Traumatic Stress, 12*(3), 455–471.

Berthold, S. M. (2000). War traumas and community violence: Psychological, behavioral and academic outcomes among Khmer refugee adolescents. *Journal of Multicultural Social Work, 8*(1/2), 15–46.

Blair, R. G. (2000). Risk factors associated with PTSD and major depression among Cambodian refugees in Utah. *Health and Social Work, 25*(1), 23–30.

Bunte, P. A., & Joseph, R. M. (1992, March). *The Cambodian community of Long Beach: An ethnographic analysis of factors leading to census undercount.* Washington, DC: Center for Survey Methods Research, Bureau of the Census.

Chan, S. (2003). *Not just victims: Conversations with Cambodian community leaders in the United States.* Champaign, IL: University of Illinois Press.

Chan, S. (2004). *Survivors: Cambodian refugees in the United States.* Champaign, IL: University of Illinois Press.

Chandler, D. (1991). *The tragedy of Cambodian history: Politics, war, and revolution since 1945.* New Haven, CT: Yale University Press.

Cheng, L. H., & Yang, P. Q. (1996). Asians: The "model minority" deconstructed. In R. Waldinger & M. Bozorgmehr (Eds.), *Ethnic Los Angeles* (pp. 305–344). New York, NY: Russell Sage Foundation.

Coleman, C. (1987). Cambodians in the United States. In D. A. Ablin & M. Hood (Eds.), *The Cambodian agony* (pp. 354–374). Armonk, NY: M. E. Sharpe.

Haines, D. (Ed.). (1996). *Refugees in America in the 1990s: A reference handbook.* Westport, CT: Greenwood Press.

Hein, J. (2006). *Ethnic origins: The adaptation of Cambodian and Hmong refugees in four American cities.* New York, NY: Russell Sage Foundation.

Kinzie, J. D., Fredrickson, R. H., Ben, R., Fleck, J. & Karls, W. (1984). Post-traumatic stress disorder among survivors of Cambodian concentration camps. *American Journal of Psychiatry, 141*(5), 645–650.

Liang, C. T. H., Lee, S., & Ting, M. P. (2002). Developing Asian American leaders. *New Directions for Student Services,* 81–90.

Marshall, G. N., Schell, T. L., Elliott, M. N., Berthold, S. M., & Chun, C.-A. (2005). Mental health of Cambodian refugees 2 decades after resettlement in the United States. *Journal of the American Medical Association, 294*(5), 571–579.

Mollica, R. F., Wyshak, G., Lavelle, J., Truong, T., Tor, S., & Yang, T. (1990). Assessing symptom change in Southeast Asian refugee survivors of mass violence and torture. *American Journal of Psychiatry, 147*(1), 83–88.

Museus, S. D. (2013). *Asian American students in higher education.* New York, NY: Routledge.

Needham, S., & Quintiliani, K. (2007). Cambodians in Long Beach, California: The making of a community. *Journal of Immigrant & Refugee Studies, 5*(1), 29–53. doi:10.1300/J500v05n01_03

Needham, S., & Quintiliani, K. (2008). *Cambodians in Long Beach.* Mount Pleasant, SC: Arcadia.

Pendakur, S., & Pendakur, V. (2012). Let's get radical: The theory and praxis of being a practitioner-ally for Asian Pacific Islander American college students.

In D. M. Ching & A. Agbayani (Eds.), *Asian Americans and Pacific Islanders in higher education: Research and perspectives on identity, leadership, and success* (pp. 31–50). Washington, DC: National Association of Student Personnel Administrators.

Quintiliani, K. (2009). Cambodian refugee families in the shadows of welfare reform. *Journal of Immigrant & Refugee Studies, 7*(2), 129–158.

Quintiliani, K., & Needham, S. (2013). Three decades of Cambodian American political activism in Long Beach, California. In Y. W. Chan, D. Haines, & J. H. X. Lee, (Eds.), *The age of Asian migration: Continuity, diversity, and susceptibility* (Vol. 1, pp. 268–281), Newcastle: Cambridge Scholars.

Rumbaut, R. G. (1996). A legacy of war: Refugees from Vietnam, Laos, and Cambodia. In S. Pedraza & R. Rumbaut (Eds.), *Origins and destinies: Immigration, race, and ethnicity in America* (pp. 315–333). Belmont, CA: Wadsworth.

Rumbaut, R. G. (2006). Vietnamese, Laotian, and Cambodian Americans. In P. G. Min (Ed.), *Asian Americans: Contemporary trends and issues* (2nd ed., pp. 262–289). Thousand Oaks, CA. Sage.

Takei, I., & Sakamoto, A. (2011). Poverty among Asian Americans in the 21st century. *Sociological Perspectives, 54*(2), 251–276.

United States Census Bureau. (2010a). *2006–2010 American community survey selected population tables.* Retrieved from https://www.census.gov/newsroom/releases/archives/american_community_survey_acs/cb12-94.html

United States Census Bureau. (2010b). *Profile of housing characteristics for Los Angeles County, 2010.* Retrieved from http://factfinder.census.gov/faces/tableservices/jsf/pages/productview.xhtml?pid=ACS_14_5YR_DP04&src=pt

United States Census Bureau. (2011). *2011 American survey 1–year estimates.* Retrieved from http://factfinder.census.gov/faces/affhelp/jsf/pages/geography.xhtml?lang=en&code=050&name=Los%20Angeles%20County,%20California&src=geoAssist&log=t

CHAPTER 10

THE UNIQUE CIRCUMSTANCES OF FILIPINOS IN HAWAI'I PUBLIC HIGHER EDUCATION

Niki Libarios

As the second largest ethnic group in Hawai'i, the Filipino population continues to grow at a rapid pace. However, as an underserved and understudied population, their higher education achievement in Hawai'i remains low and they are among the most socioeconomically disadvantaged groups in the state. Moreover, Filipinos are overrepresented in Hawai'i two-year colleges and underrepresented at the state's flagship campus, the University of Hawai'i at Mānoa. These factors are tied together as the United States Census Bureau continues to emphasize the positive correlation between educational attainment and income (2013).

These Hawai'i demographic conditions starkly contrast that of Filipinos in other geographic areas of the continental United States, where data suggest that they do relatively well compared with other ethnic groups. This highlights the need to examine differences among and within specific Asian American ethnic groups as researchers have called for studies that examine the wide-ranging higher education experiences and outcomes of distinct Asian American communities (Buenavista, Jayakumar, & Misa-Escalante,

Focusing on the Underserved, pages 175–192
Copyright © 2017 by Information Age Publishing
All rights of reproduction in any form reserved.

2009; Museus & Chang, 2009). Research should be expanded to study within group variances taking into account factors such as migration history, geography, and immigrant educational and socioeconomic status background.

Exploring these conditions is important for several reasons. First, researchers are calling for greater attention to scholarship on the role of ethnicity in higher education (Abada, Hou, & Ram, 2009; Grodsky & Jackson, 2009). Second, higher education research that focuses on Asian Americans is sorely lacking and more scholarship on this population is warranted. For example, Museus (2009) found that in general, Asian Americans were a central focus in only 1% of articles published in the five most widely used peer-reviewed academic journals in the past 10 years. Lastly, Asian Americans are often viewed as the "model minority" in higher education under the broad and incorrect misconception that Asian Americans are universally academically successful. However, closer examination demonstrates significant differences within and among the different Asian American groups in higher education (Buenavista et al., 2009; Hune, 2002; Museus & Chang, 2009; Museus & Kiang, 2009; Ngo & Lee, 2007). Several scholars have discussed the reality that disparities exist among Asian American ethnic groups—while some Asian American ethnic subpopulations exhibit very high college success rates, others endure relatively low rates (Museus, 2009; Museus & Kiang, 2009). In addition, as I discuss in this chapter, the same Asian American ethnic groups can have drastically different outcomes across geographic contexts, possibly due to differing immigration patterns.

In particular, Filipinos are an understudied group in higher education. Researchers claim that broader Asian American concerns have often buried the educational issues of Filipinos (Buenavista, 2010), or Filipinos have been discussed in the general ethnic context of the United States rather than in relation to other Filipinos in different parts of the United States (Espiritu, 2003; Okamura, 1998). In response, this chapter will focus on the circumstances of Filipinos in Hawai'i, where they have a long and unique history. Four areas will be discussed, including (a) an overview of the representation of Filipinos in the University Hawai'i system, (b) Filipino immigration and upward social mobility, (c) national demographic comparisons of Filipinos, and (d) the higher education experiences of Filipinos in Hawai'i.

REPRESENTATION OF FILIPINOS
IN THE UNIVERSITY OF HAWAI'I SYSTEM

According to the U.S. Census (2010a, 2010c) in 2010, individuals who identified as part Filipino represented 25.1% of the Hawai'i population and people who identified as full Filipino represented 14.5%. These figures make Filipinos the second largest ethnic group in Hawai'i. Furthermore, the Filipino population is growing at a steady pace. Contributing to the increase are high birth rates and continuing immigration from the Philippines (Hawai'i Department of Business, Economic Development, and Tourism, 1993). In addition, Filipinos are among the most socioeconomically disadvantaged groups in Hawai'i. This reality links their historical migration to Hawai'i, as subordinate immigrant laborers who came from the Philippines to work on the sugar plantations, with their current overrepresentation in low-level service-type jobs of the dominant tourist industry in Hawai'i (Agbayani, 1996; Okamura, 2008).

This overrepresentation in low-income communities influences higher education opportunities. Students from lower-income families are more likely to enroll in lower-selectivity institutions, such as open-access community colleges. Self-described full Filipinos comprised 15.7% of those enrolled in Hawai'i community colleges (Institutional Research Office, 2011b). However, at the University of Hawai'i of Mānoa (UHM), which is the flagship campus of the 10-campus University of Hawai'i system, they represented only 7.7% of all undergraduate and graduate students (Institutional Research Office, 2011a). Furthermore, the disparity between the undergraduate and graduate levels at UHM is startling. Filipinos represented 9.6% of UHM undergraduates, but only 4.6% of graduate students.

In sum, Filipinos are overrepresented in Hawai'i community colleges and underrepresented at UHM. For Filipinos in Hawai'i, being concentrated in institutions that primarily confer associate degrees may limit their socioeconomic mobility and constrict their access to higher paying occupations. Given that Filipinos are the second largest ethnic group in Hawai'i, comprising one-fourth of the population, this condition warrants further attention.

IMMIGRATION AND UPWARD SOCIAL MOBILITY

Over the past several centuries, immigrants have come to the United States to improve their way of life and enhance their chances for upward social mobility. Immigrants are primarily concerned with improving their socioeconomic status with regard to job and income opportunities compared to what is available to them in their home country (Bashi & McDaniel, 1997; Erisman & Looney, 2007). Key to achieving upward social mobility is higher education and the completion of a college degree (Karabel, 1986; Karabel & Astin, 1975; Pascarella & Terenzini, 1991). Immigrants recognize the role of higher education as a means to increase their opportunities for occupational and economic advancement.

Although immigration studies have shown that duration of residence is a key factor in socioeconomic assimilation and mobility (Hirschman, 1983; Massey, 1981; Neidert & Farley, 1985), Filipinos have been in Hawai'i for over a century and they still remain a socioeconomically disadvantaged group. As the last immigrant laborer group brought in to work in the sugar plantations, there was no group to replace Filipinos at the bottom of the hierarchy. Thus, the socioeconomic condition of Filipinos in Hawai'i today is grounded in their social origin as immigrant workers and the corresponding challenges they have faced in striving for upward social mobility, notably in education attainment (Agbayani, 1996; Okamura, 2008).

The limited mobility of Filipinos in Hawai'i directly contrasts the socioeconomic mobility of Filipino immigrants on the mainland United States. The Philippines has sent a large number of occupational immigrants to the continental United States since the 1960s, most of whom were middle-class, college-educated, highly trained, English speaking individuals who seamlessly integrated into the United States (Liu, Ong, & Rosenstein, 1991; Wolf, 1997). Moreover, many of these Filipino immigrants came to the United States with backgrounds in the health professions (Reimers, 1985). A study by Vernez and Abrahamse (1996) on immigrants and United States education notes that Filipinos also immigrated to the United States to pursue higher education more so than some other Asian American ethnic groups, such as refugees from Southeast Asia.

The social origins of Filipinos in Hawai'i versus Filipinos in the continental United States are vastly different and may influence their pursuit of higher education and social mobility. White, Biddlecom, and Guo (1993) argued that the upward social mobility of Asian American immigrants is tied to their experiences and contexts for arrival in the United States. This argument underscores the significance of examining the contexts, demographic, and conditions of Filipinos in Hawai'i separately from those in the continental United States.

NATIONAL DEMOGRAPHIC COMPARISONS OF FILIPINOS

While Filipinos are present in every state, they tend to be clustered in certain geographic areas, particularly in Hawai'i and the western continental United States (Hoeffel, Rastogi, Kim, & Shahid, 2012; U.S. Census Bureau, 2010b). According to the U.S. Census (U.S. Census Bureau, 2003a, 2003b), the top 10 ranked *regions* in the United States with large numbers of Filipinos by geographical grouping are: (a) Los Angeles, Riverside, Orange County in Southern California; (b) San Francisco, San Jose, Oakland in Northern California; (c) Hawai'i; (d) Connecticut, Pennsylvania, New York City, New Jersey, Long Island, New York in the Northeast; (e) San Diego,

California; (f) Chicago, Illinois; Gary, Indiana; Kenosha, Wisconsin in the Midwest; (g) Seattle, Tacoma, Bremerton, Washington in the Northwest; (h) Baltimore, Maryland; Virginia; West Virginia; Washington, DC; (i) Arizona; Las Vegas, Nevada in the Southwest; and (j) Sacramento and Yolo, California.

Although the first two California regions have greater actual numbers of Filipinos than the Hawai'i region, the Hawai'i region has the greatest concentrated representation of Filipinos in its population, about 23% of the population. The California regions of San Francisco and San Diego have the next highest percentages, with Filipinos representing only about 5% of the population in each of these regions. In this section, I provide an overview of Filipinos in the Hawai'i region relative to the other regions in terms of *education attainment, occupations, income,* and *poverty level.*

The Hawai'i region had the highest percentage of Filipinos with no high school diploma—23.9% among Filipinos 25 years or older compared to other regions (U.S. Census Bureau, 2003a, 2003b). The Hawai'i region also had the lowest percentages of baccalaureate and graduate degrees among Filipinos 25 years or older at 14.1% and 2.8%, respectively. Nationally, the Filipino average for the same levels of education were 12.6% (for those with no high school diploma), 33.9% (for those with baccalaureate degree), and 7.8% (for those with a graduate degree). These percentages are roughly twice the education attainment percentages of Filipinos in the Hawai'i region. Table 10.1 summarizes the percentage share of Filipino education attainment for those 25 years or older.

Low- to moderate-income occupations—such as sales, construction, and service-related jobs in the tourism industry—generally do not require baccalaureate degrees. In these types of occupational categories in Hawai'i, Filipino men comprised the highest percentage, 69.8%, and second highest percentage of women, 45.2% (U.S. Census Bureau, 2003b). Nationally, Filipino men and women are employed in these occupational categories at 47.4% and 33.4%, respectively. In contrast, the regions with the least percentage of Filipinos in these occupational categories were the Washington,

TABLE 10.1 Percentage Share of Filipino Education Attainment for Those 25 Years or Older

	Filipinos in Hawai'i	Filipinos in the United States	Filipinos in the Highest Region in the Continental United States
No H.S. Diploma	23.9%	12.6%	New York = 5.9%
BA/BS Degree	14.1%	33.9%	New York = 51.9%
Graduate Degree	2.8%	7.8%	New York = 13.7%

Source: U.S. Census, 2003a, 2003b)

TABLE 10.2 Percentage Share of Filipino Occupational Concentrations in Low and Moderate Income Professions by Gender

Filipinos in Hawai'i	Filipinos in the United States	Filipinos in the Highest Region in the Continental United States
69.8% men	47.4% men	Washington, DC = 32% men
45.2% women	33.4% women	New York = 18.5% women

Source: U.S. Census, 2000b)

DC region at 32% for men and the New York region at 18.5% for women (see Table 10.2).

Professional and managerial-type occupations usually require at least a baccalaureate degree or higher. These types of occupations include teachers, engineers, and business executives. In these occupational categories, Filipinos in the Hawai'i region had the lowest percentages for men (30.2%) and women (54.9%). Nationwide, Filipinos fared better at 52.5% for men and 68.3% for women. The highest regions for Filipinos in professional and managerial-type categories were Washington, DC at 68% for men and New York at 81.1% for women. Table 10.3 summarizes the percentage share of Filipino occupational concentration in managerial and high income professions by gender.

The occupational illustration of Filipinos in Hawai'i and across the U.S. is reflected in the per capita income earned by Filipinos (U.S. Census Bureau, 2003a, 2003b). Among the 10 regions, Filipinos in the Hawai'i region had the lowest per capita income at $14,545, while the U.S. average for all Filipinos was $19,259. The per capita income of Filipinos in the New York region was $26,587. Thus, the per capita income of Filipinos nationally is about one-fourth higher than Filipinos in the Hawai'i region. Also, the per capita income of Filipinos in the New York region is almost double that of Filipinos in Hawai'i. Table 10.4 summarizes the per capita income of Filipinos.

In summary, Filipinos in the Hawai'i region are not faring well relative to Filipinos in other U.S. regions in terms of education attainment, occupational status, and income. In particular, Filipinos in the Hawai'i region contrast starkly with Filipinos in the East Coast regions of New York and

TABLE 10.3 Percentage Share of Filipino Occupational Concentrations in Managerial and High Income Professions by Gender

Filipinos in Hawai'i	Filipinos in the United States	Filipinos in the Highest Region in the Continental United States
30.2% men	52.5% men	Washington, DC = 68% men
54.9% women	68.3% women	New York = 81.1% women

Source: U.S. Census, 2000b

TABLE 10.4 Per Capita Income of Filipinos		
Filipinos in Hawai'i	Filipinos in the United States	Filipinos in the Highest Region in the Continental United States
$14,545	$19,259	New York = $26,587

Source: U.S. Census, 2003a, 2003b)

Washington, DC. While Filipinos in the Hawai'i region occupy the lower level socioeconomic landscape, Filipinos on the East Coast appear to be educationally and socioeconomically well established. Compounding the situation of Filipinos in the Hawai'i region is that they constitute a vastly greater percentage of the population than in any other region.

An understanding of historical events can provide some insight on the causes of demographic differences and inequalities between Filipinos in Hawai'i and Filipinos on the mainland. These historical events include *formal* policies between the United States and the Philippines and immigration patterns. The following is a discussion of these possible explanations from a post-1965 perspective and differing immigration patterns.

POST-1965 PERSPECTIVE

In 1965, the United States (U.S.) updated its immigration law regulating its recruitment of immigrant laborers from other countries, including the Philippines (Chua, 2009). The 1965 Immigration and Naturalization Act became a formal mechanism to rank the occupational needs of the United States based on demands of corporate America. Given the shortage of health care practitioners in the United States, this allowed many Filipino nurses and other health care providers to enter the United States based on occupational preference (Chua, 2009). This also permitted many migrant Filipino families to reunite, which was another primary goal of this act (Liu et al., 1991).

Another event that influenced Filipino immigration to the United States since 1965 was the institution of the Labor Export Program in 1974 by then Philippine President Ferdinand Marcos. Ostensibly, this program intended to bolster efforts to export Filipino laborers and professionals to seek occupations in other countries. The underlying intent of this program, moreover, was that these workers would then send money back to their families in the Philippines which, in turn, would help support the economy of the Philippines (Chua, 2009).

The impact of the 1965 Immigration and Naturalization Act and the 1974 Labor Export Program on Filipino immigration to the United States were significant. First, since the 1960s the Philippines had sent the second-largest number of immigrant workers to the United States, trailing only Mexico (Espiritu, 2003). More so, many of these Filipino immigrants were college-educated, highly trained, and professionally qualified workers (Liu et al., 1991; Wolf, 1997), including many in the health related professions (Reimers, 1985). Second, this allowed many Filipinos to reunite with other family members who had immigrated earlier to the United States. Thus, post-1965 Filipino immigrants to the United States can be generalized as being middle-class, college-educated, and English speaking individuals who were provided occupational and family reunification opportunities to help ease their assimilation into the United States (Wolf, 1997).

DIFFERENT IMMIGRATION PATTERNS

A study by Liu et al. (1991) posits that Filipino immigrants tend to be of similar backgrounds of their family sponsors. Moreover, the pursuit of upward social mobility by Asian Americans is often linked to their experiences and contexts for departure from their home country as well as their context for arrival in the United States (Mizokawa & Ryckman, 1990; White et al., 1993). This suggests that different demographic conditions of Filipinos in the Hawai'i region and on the mainland, specifically the East Coast regions, are influenced by immigration patterns and characteristics of these Filipino immigrants.

Many Filipinos in the Hawai'i region have ties to immigrant laborers brought to Hawai'i from the Philippines to work in the sugar cane industry (Alcantra, 1981). Many of these laborers had little or no formal education and came from poor backgrounds (Nordyke, 1989), and this continues to influence the educational and socioeconomic condition of Filipinos today (Agbayani, 1996). Since the backgrounds of Filipino immigrants are likely to be congruent to that of their family sponsors (Liu et al., 1991), this generally suggests that Filipinos who recently immigrated to Hawai'i also have low education attainment and low socioeconomic status, similar to their Hawai'i family members. This phenomenon may be a contributing obstacle to the upward social mobility of Filipinos in Hawai'i as a group.

On the other hand, the continental United States regions, notably those in the East Coast, paint a different picture. Under the same premise that Filipino immigrants tend to be of similar backgrounds as their family sponsors, many of the educated and professionally trained post-1965 Filipinos who immigrated to the United States went and are continuing to go to the continental United States, especially the East Coast. In contrast to Filipinos in Hawai'i, the sponsorship of educated and professional family members can serve to advance the upward social mobility of Filipinos in the East Coast as a group.

There are clear demographic differences between Filipinos in the Hawai'i region and Filipinos on the continental United States, particularly the East Coast. Post-1965 immigration patterns indicate that Hawai'i continues to attract service-type immigrants with limited formal education backgrounds, while the East Coast attracts college educated and highly trained professionals. Filipino immigrants may see the East Coast of the continental United States as having greater social mobility opportunities than in Hawai'i. Or they may be influenced by the positive and negative socioeconomic stereotypes by family members in these different regions. Perhaps they see a more attractive lifestyle in the East Coast than in Hawai'i. From an educational and socioeconomic point of view, though, the discrete populations groups of Filipinos in the Hawai'i region and in the East Coast regions are polar opposites. Demographics suggest that momentum is likely in place for continued upward social mobility of East Coast region Filipinos, while upward social mobility for Filipinos in the Hawai'i region is likely to remain stagnant.

HIGHER EDUCATION EXPERIENCES
OF FILIPINOS IN HAWAI'I

As noted earlier, the socioeconomic condition of Filipinos in Hawai'i is poor and appears to be rooted in the relationship between their educational attainment, occupational status, and earnings. In Hawai'i public higher education, they are overrepresented at community college levels while vastly underrepresented at the more selective University of Hawai'i at Mānoa (Institutional Research Office, 2011a, 2011b). Since educational attainment is linked to future occupational and earning opportunities, an examination of the Filipino educational experience in Hawai'i is necessary. Researchers are calling for higher education institutions to recognize and create campus cultures that effectively serve racially diverse student populations (Chang, Chang, & Ledesma, 2005; Jayakumar & Museus, 2012) such as Filipinos at the University of Hawai'i. Thus, this section will discuss the higher education experience of Filipinos in Hawai'i in terms of their views of higher education and the challenges they face.

VIEWS OF HIGHER EDUCATION

Family and Parental Influence

In Hawai'i, parents of Filipinos have a strong influence on their children's higher education experiences. In a study done by Castillo and Minamishan (1991) on Filipinos at UHM, parents were rated as the persons who most influenced them to enroll in college. In the same study, participants returned extremely low ratings for "lack of family encouragement" as an obstacle. Bachini (2011) also found that family support was a significant factor in the higher education persistence of Filipinos, which is similar to experiences of Filipinos in higher education in the continental United States. A study by Azores (1986/1987) on high school Filipino students reported that the expectations of one's parents influence a Filipino student's educational aspirations. This is supported by a study by Maramba (2008) who found that parents were the most influential factor for Filipina American women's decisions to enroll in college as well as their choice of colleges.

Economic Issues

Many Filipinos recognize that education is a means to improve their economic opportunities and social status (Church & Katigbak, 1992). Filipino parents see education as a way for their children to have more opportunities and a more financially secure lifestyle than their own. Interestingly, Andres (1981) posits that education is valued by many Filipinos for these types of reasons, rather than for knowledge per se. Recognizing the economic benefits of a college education regardless of their own schooling, Filipino parents are highly influential in convincing their children to enroll in higher education (Castillo & Minamishin, 1991). At the same time, Filipino college students often recognize economic struggles and sacrifices their parents are going through to send them to college. According to Maramba (2008), Filipina college students, in particular, feel a sense of debt to finish college so that they can financially help their parents.

Respect for Teachers

Filipino students need strong support while in college (Azores, 1986/1987). This can be provided by teachers who interact with students on an everyday basis and who are often viewed as parents or elders in the school setting (Chattergy & Ongteco, 1991). People in these positions are viewed as authority figures and are highly respected by Filipinos (Church & Katigbak, 1992). The relationship between the Filipino student and his/her teacher is important because of cultural norms that influence the behavior of the Filipino students. For example, in terms of seeking assistance, a cultural norm for Filipinos is to: (a) speak only when spoken to, (b) not ask many questions, and (c) listen and *do as I say*. This starkly contrasts several school norms for students to: (a) volunteer responses; (b) learn by discussing, asking, and verbalizing; and (c) contribute to discussions (Chattergy & Ongteco, 1991).

CHALLENGES

Financial Concerns

Socioeconomic challenges for Filipinos in Hawai'i, coupled with tuition costs and college affordability, influence their public higher education enrollment and the institutions they attend. This may shed some light on their overrepresentation at the community colleges and underenrollment at UHM. Researchers have found that educational achievement and college destinations are influenced by socioeconomic background as lower-income students are more responsive to tuition costs than higher-income students (Hearn, 1991; Jencks, Crouse, & Mueser, 1983; Paulsen & St. John, 2002). This is affirmed for Filipinos in Hawai'i in a study by Castillo and Minamishin (1991) on Filipino student recruitment to UHM, which found that financial need was the greatest obstacle identified in attending college. Furthermore, a study by Bachini (2011) found financial concerns were a significant factor in the higher education persistence of Filipinos. In addition, Okamura's (2008) book *Ethnicity and Inequality in Hawai'i* describes how the tuition increases in the University of Hawai'i system in the late 1990s resulted in a downward spiral of Filipino enrollment at UHM for six consecutive years.

Filipinos may also feel discouraged to take out loans to enroll in more costly four-year colleges and universities such as UHM versus much less expensive community colleges. Mumper (1996) explains that the size of the monthly payments and/or the total amount of post-college debt may deter students from low-income backgrounds from borrowing money to attend college. In sum, Okamura (2008) posits that the socioeconomic status of Filipinos in Hawai'i mirrors their representation in the educational levels of the University of Hawai'i system.

Social Influences

Social influences may also impact the educational experience of Filipinos in Hawai'i public higher education. Hurn (1978) purports that educational expectations are shaped by socialization. Other researchers have found that the educational aspirations of Filipinos are strongly influenced by their peers (Azores, 1986/1987; Maramba, 2008) who often rely on their social network of other Filipinos for academic and social support (Bachini, 2011; Banaria, 2004). These may be factors in explaining the representation of Filipinos in Hawai'i public higher education. For example, the large percentage of Filipinos in the community colleges may attract and provide social support for other Filipinos to enroll in the community colleges, while the reverse may be true for enrolling in UHM given the relatively low percentage of Filipino students on the Mānoa campus. This concept is supported by Harris and Nettles (1996) who maintain that the attraction to a particular college destination for minority students is strongly influenced by the existing percentage of minority students at that campus.

The representation of Filipino faculty at UHM may be a related social influence on the higher education experience of Filipinos in Hawai'i. In 2013, Filipinos represented only 2.2% of the full-time faculty at UHM and 6% of the faculty in the UH community colleges (Institutional Research Office, 2013). As mentioned in the previous section, Filipino students have a strong respect for teachers who serve as role models and sources of support. Thus, potentially detrimental to educational experiences of Filipinos is the lack of visible role models throughout the University of Hawai'i system, especially at the UHM campus. Similar to other ethnically underrepresented or marginalized groups, Azores (1986/1987) noted that Filipino students need ample support during college, yet often did not receive adequate encouragement or guidance due to the lack of Filipino faculty at American universities.

Location and Logistical Concerns

The location of the community colleges relative to UHM and logistical concerns may play a role in the educational experience of Filipinos in Hawai'i. UHM is located in an urban district, which has higher concentrations of Caucasian, Chinese, and Japanese ethnic groups compared to Filipinos. On the other hand, many of the community colleges in Hawai'i are located in areas with high percentages of Filipinos. For example, on the island of Oahu, the communities of Waipahu and Kalihi are well known for their dense population of Filipinos. These are also the locations of Leeward Community College and Honolulu Community College, which have Filipino student representation at 21.6% and 19.6%, respectively (Institutional Research Office, 2011b). The same holds true for the islands of Kauai and Maui, which are heavily populated by Filipinos who enroll at their community college campuses at 19.3% and 18.3%, respectively (Institutional Research Office, 2011b).

For many Filipinos, enrolling in a community college in their home community and living at home can provide convenience and cost savings versus attending UHM or another four-year college campus. From this geographical point of view, enrolling in UHM adds additional burdens such as transportation, parking, housing, and food in addition to the tuition cost differences of attending a community college. Similar to the situation in Hawai'i, many Filipinos in California are encouraged by their parents to enroll in a college close to home because it lessens the family financial burden (Maramba, 2008). Additionally, Paulsen and St. John (2002) assert that low-income students choose their colleges so that they will be able to control their living costs.

POLICY AND PRACTICE RECOMMENDATIONS

Given the circumstances of Filipinos in Hawai'i, the following policy and practice recommendations are primarily intended for the UH system. However, these recommendations may also apply to other higher education institutions where there are representation discrepancies between community colleges and four-year universities of certain ethnic groups. This may include African Americans, Native Hawai'ians, Samoans, and other diverse sub-populations of the Asian American and Pacific Islander community.

First, resources need to be provided for support policies and programs that help qualified Filipino students enroll directly from high schools into four-year universities. Studies continue to indicate that students who enter higher education via the community colleges face numerous barriers in the transfer process to four-year universities and baccalaureate degree completion (Bensimon & Dowd, 2009; Laanan, 2007; Libarios Jr., 2013). Conversely, a study by Libarios Jr. (2013) indicates that Filipinos who enroll in four-year universities are more likely to complete baccalaureate degrees than those who enroll at two-year colleges. Outreach programs that assist in the direct entry into four-year universities should identify Filipino high school students with strong academic potential and provide them workshops to prepare for college entrance exams and the college application process. This would be timely and in accordance with the rise of "early college"-type programs throughout higher education where high school students can take actual course work to begin earning college credits.

Second, four-year universities and community colleges must establish and support strong "transfer bridge" type programs to assist Filipino students in transferring. Beyond the responsibility of the community colleges to "move forward" students to the university level, four-year universities need to partner in the responsibility and "reach out" to students in the community colleges. This shared obligation should be reflected in collaborative practices and programs which include opportunities for community college students to have regular campus visits at four-year universities, active interactions with Filipino students established at the four-year university levels, and venues to meet with faculty and staff at the four-year universities who understand and relate to their cultural background.

Third, university systems should provide adequate financial aid and scholarship support for Filipino students. Studies continue to indicate that higher education attainment of students is often related to their socioeconomic status, higher education affordability, and access to financial aid (Chen & DesJardins, 2010; Tierney & Venegas, 2009), while the ability to pay for college is a concern for Filipinos in Hawai'i (Castillo & Minamishin, 1991). This condition is illustrated in a study by Okamura (2008) who reported a negative correlation between tuition increases in the late 1900s at University of Hawai'i of Mānoa and decreases in Filipino enrollment for six straight years. Additional financial aid and scholarship opportunities for Filipinos in Hawai'i will not only help them in actual costs, but also provide more study time because they may not need to work (or can work fewer hours) to pay for their education.

Last, attention is needed to enhance policies that assist students in transferring from the community college to the university level. Research has shown that universities have not formed sound transfer policies to balance the diversity of their student populations in spite of community colleges having high representations of low income and ethnically underrepresented students (Anderson, Sun, & Alfonso, 2006; Dowd, Cheslock, & Melguizo, 2008; Dowd & Melguizo, 2008). Again in collaboration with four-year universities, transfer policy revisions should target improved outcomes such as simplified application processes, early registration, consistent course equivalencies, and program articulation agreements for students matriculating from community colleges to four-year universities. Improving transfer policies will open up the college success pathway to four-year universities for all community college students and be especially helpful in cases where the community colleges make up a large contingent of underrepresented students, namely Filipinos in the UH community colleges.

CONCLUSION

This chapter explained the representation of Filipinos in the University of Hawai'i system, discussed immigration and upward social mobility, presented national demographic comparisons of Filipinos, commented on the higher education experiences of Filipinos in Hawai'i, and offered policy and program recommendations to improve the higher education achievement of Filipinos in Hawai'i. Filipinos have a rich and distinct history in Hawai'i and represent a major portion of the population. Yet, their continued presence in the lower stratum of Hawai'i public higher education, their comparatively lower socioeconomic status, and their differences compared to Filipinos in other parts of the United States are causes for concern.

While this analysis focused on Filipinos in Hawai'i, future studies might expand this research by including campuses from other parts of the continental United States where Filipino students typically attend and a corresponding analysis of Filipino demographics and academic achievement at these institutions. Perhaps similar studies of Filipino students from other campuses would offer valuable insights into how Filipino higher education achievement is manifested in other socio-demographic contexts. In sum, this chapter presents a clear example of the need to focus attention not only on Asian American groups, but also variances within specific Asian American populations in other parts of the continental United States.

REFERENCES

Abada, T., Hou, F., & Ram, B. (2009). Ethnic differences in eduational attainment among the children of Canadian immigrants. *Canadian Journal of Sociology, 34*(1), 1–28.

Agbayani, A. (1996). The education of Filipinos in Hawaii. *Social Process in Hawaii, 37*, 147–160.

Alcantra, R. R. (1981). *Sakada: Filipino adaptation in Hawaii.* Washington, DC: University Press of America.

Anderson, G., Sun, J. C., & Alfonso, M. (2006). Effectiveness of statewide articulation agreements on the probability of transfer: A preliminary policy analysis. *Review of Higher Education, 29*(3), 261–291.

Andres, T. D. (1981). *Understanding Filipino values: A management approach.* Quezon City, Philippines: New Day.

Azores, T. (1986/1987). Education attainment and upward mobility: Prospects of Filipino Americans. *Amerasia Journal, 13*(1), 39–52.

Bachini, R. C. (2011). *An intercultural perspective on Filipina/o American persistence: Implications for college success* (Unpublished doctoral dissertation). University of Hawai'i, Manoa, Hawaii.

Banaria, J. S. (2004). *Social networking among college students: The impact on the quality of the college experience* (Unpublished doctoral dissertation). University of Hawai'i, Manoa, Hawaii.

Bashi, V., & McDaniel, A. (1997). A theory of immigration and racial stratification. *Journal of Black Studies, 27*(5), 668–682.

Bensimon, E. M., & Dowd, A. (2009). Dimensions of the transfer choice gap: Experiences of Latina and Latino students who navigated transfer pathways. *Harvard Educational Review, 79*(4), 632–658.

Buenavista, T. L. (2010). Issues affecting U.S. Filipino student access to postsecondary education: A critical race theory perspective. *Journal of Education for Students Placed at Risk, 15*(1/2), 114–126. doi: 10.1080/10824661003635093

Buenavista, T. L., Jayakumar, U. M., & Misa-Escalante, K. (2009). Contextualizing Asian American education through critical race theory: An example of U.S. Pilipino college student experiences. *New Directions for Institutional Research, 142*, 69–81.

Castillo, C. A., & Minamishin, S. B. (1991). Filipino recruitment and retention at the University of Hawaii at Manoa. *Social Process in Hawaii, 33*, 130–141.

Chang, M. J., Chang, J. C., & Ledesma, M. C. (2005). Beyond magical thinking: Doing the real work of diversifying our institutions. *About Campus, 10*(2), 9–16.

Chattergy, V., & Ongteco, B. C. (1991). Educational needs of Filipino immigrant students. *Social Process in Hawaii, 33*, 142–152.

Chen, R., & DesJardins, S. L. (2010). Investigating the impact of financial aid on student dropout risks: Racial and ethnic differences. *Journal of Higher Education, 81*(2), 179–208.

Chua, P. (2009). *Ating: Kalagayan: The social and economic profile of U.S. Filipinos.* Woodside, N.Y.: National Bolosan Center.

Church, A. T., & Katigbak, M. (1992). The cultural context of academic motives: A comparison of Filipino and American college students. *Journal of Cross-Cultural Psychology, 23*(1), 40–58.

Dowd, A. C., Cheslock, J. J., & Melguizo, T. (2008). Transfer access from community colleges and the distribution of elite higher education. *The Journal of Higher Education, 79*(4), 442–472.

Dowd, A. C., & Melguizo, T. (2008). Socioeconomic stratification of community college transfer access in the 1980s and 1990s: Evidence from HS&B and NELS. *The Review of Higher Education, 31*(4), 377–400.

Erisman, W., & Looney, S. (2007). *Opening the door to the American dream: Increasing higher education access and success for immigrants.* Washington, DC: The Institute for Higher Education Policy.

Espiritu, Y. L. (2003). *Home bound: Filipinos American lives across cultures, communities, and countries.* Berkeley, CA: University of California Press.

Grodsky, E., & Jackson, E. (2009). Social stratification in higher education. *Teachers College Record, 111*(10), 2347–2384.

Harris, S. M., & Nettles, M. (1996). Ensuring campus climates that embrace diversity. In L. I. Rendon & R. O. Hope (Eds.), *Educating a new majority: Transforming America's educational system* (pp. 330–371). San Francisco, CA: Jossey-Bass.

Hawaii Department of Business, Economic Development, and Tourism. (1993). *The state of Hawaii data book.* Honolulu, HI: Department of Business, Economic Development and Tourism.

Hearn, J. C. (1991). Academic and nonacademic influences on the college destinations of 1980 high school graduates. *Sociology of Education, 64*(3), 158–171.

Hirschman, C. (1983). America's melting pot reconsidered. *American Sociological Review, 9*, 397–423.

Hoeffel, E. M., Rastogi, S., Kim, M. O., & Shahid, H. (2012). The Asian population: 2010. In *2010 Census Briefs.* Washington, DC: United States Census Bureau.

Hune, S. (2002). Demographics and diversity of Asian American college students. *New Directions for Student Services, 97*, 11–20.

Hurn, C. J. (1978). *The limits and possibilities of schooling: An introduction to the sociology of education.* Boston, MA: Allyn and Bacon.

Institutional Research Office. (2011a). *Fall enrollment report, University of Hawaii at Manoa, Fall 2010.* Honolulu, HI: University of Hawaii.

Institutional Research Office. (2011b). *Fall enrollment report, University of Hawaii, Community Colleges, Fall 2010.* Honolulu, HI: University of Hawaii.

Institutional Research Office. (2013). *Fall enrollment report, University of Hawaii, Fall 2013.* Honolulu, HI: University of Hawaii.

Jayakumar, U. M., & Museus, S. D. (2012). Mapping the intersection of campus cultures and equitable outcomes among racially diverse student populations.

In S. D. Museus & U. M. Jayakumar (Eds.), *Creating campus cultures: Fostering success among racially diverse student populations* (pp. 1–27). New York, NY: Routledge.

Jencks, C., Crouse, J., & Mueser, P. (1983). The Wisconsin model of status attainment: A national replication with improved measures of ability and aspiration. *Sociology of Education, 56*(1), 3–19.

Karabel, J. (1986). Community colleges and social stratification in the 1980s. *New Directions for Community Colleges, 54,* 13–30.

Karabel, J., & Astin, A. W. (1975). Social class, academic ability, and college "quality." *Social Forces, 53*(3), 381–398.

Laanan, F. S. (2007). Studying transfer students: Part II: Dimensions of transfer students' adjustment. *Community College Journal of Research and Practice, 31*(1), 37–59.

Libarios, E. N. D., Jr. (2013). *Social stratification and higher education outcomes: The case of Filipinos in Hawai'i* (Unpublished doctoral dissertation). University of Hawai'i, Manoa, Hawaii.

Liu, J. M., Ong, P. M., & Rosenstein, C. (1991). Dual chain migration: Post-1965 Filipino immigration to the United States. *International Migration Review, 25*(3), 487–513.

Maramba, D. C. (2008). Immigrant Families and the college experience: Perspectives of Filipina Americans. *Journal of College Student Development, 49*(4), 336–350.

Massey, D. S. (1981). Dimensions of the new immigration to the United States and the prospects for assimilation. *Annual Review of Sociology, 7,* 57–85.

Mizokawa, D. T., & Ryckman, D. B. (1990). Attributions of academic success and failure: A comparison of six Asian-American ethnic groups. *Journal of Cross-Cultural Psychology, 21*(4), 434–451.

Mumper, M. (1996). *Removing college price barriers: What government has done and why it hasn't worked.* Albany, NY: State University of New York Press.

Museus, S. D. (2009). A critical analysis of the exclusion of Asian American from higher education research and discourse. In L. Zhan (Ed.), *Asian American voices: Engaging, empowering, enabling* (pp. 59–76). New York, NY: National League for Nursing.

Museus, S. D., & Chang, M. J. (2009). Rising to the challenge of conducting research on Asian Americans in higher education. *New Directions for Institutional Research, 142,* 95–105. doi: 10.1002/ir.299

Museus, S. D., & Kiang, P. N. (2009). Deconstructing the model minority myth and how it contributes to the invisible minority reality in higher education research. *New Directions for Institutional Research, 142,* 5–15. doi: 10.1002/ir.292

Neidert, L. J., & Farley, R. (1985). Assimilation in the United States: An analysis of ethnic and generation differences in status and achievement. *American Sociological Review, 50*(6), 840–850.

Ngo, B., & Lee, S. J. (2007). Complicating the image of model minority success: A review of Southeast Asian American education. *Review of Educational Research, 77*(4), 415–453.

Nordyke, E. C. (1989). *The peopling of Hawai'i* (2nd ed.). Honolulu, HI: University of Hawaii.

Okamura, J. (1998). *Imagining the Filipino American diaspora: Transnational relations, identities, and communities.* New York, NY: Garland.

Okamura, J. (2008). *Ethnicity and inequality in Hawai'i.* Philadelphia, PA: Temple University Press.

Pascarella, E. T., & Terenzini, P. T. (1991). *How college affects students: Finding and insights from twenty years of research.* San Francisco, CA: Jossey-Bass.

Paulsen, M. B., & St. John, E. P. (2002). Social class and college costs: Examining the financial nexus between college choice and persistence. *The Journal of Higher Education, 73*(2), 189–236.

Reimers, D. (1985). *Still the golden door: The Third World comes to America.* New York, NY: Columbia University.

Tierney, W. G., & Venegas, K. (2009). Finding money on the table: Information, financial aid, and access to college. *The Journal of Higher Education, 80*(4), 363–388.

United States Census Bureau. (2003a). Income in 2002 by educational attainment of population 18 years and over, by age, sex, race alone, and Hispanic origin. Washington, D.C.: U.S. Census Bureau.

United States Census Bureau. (2003b). U.S. census of population and housing: Census 2000 summary file 2. Washington, D.C.: U.S. Census Bureau.

United States Census Bureau. (2010a). Hawaii, Filipino alone or in combination. *American community survey.* Washington, D.C.: U.S. Census Bureau.

United States Census Bureau. (2010b). Asian population by detailed group: 2000–2010. *Census Special Tabulation.* Washington, D.C.: U.S. Census Bureau.

United States Census Bureau. (2010c). Ranking of selected races for the state of Hawaii: 2010. *American Community Survey.* Washington, D.C.: U.S. Census Bureau.

United States Census Bureau. (2013). Table 2A: Earnings by selected characteristics: Fourth quarter (October, November, December) 2011. *Survey of income and program participation (SIPP), 2008 panel.* Washington, D.C.: U.S. Census Bureau.

Vernez, G., & Abrahamse, A. (1996). *How immigrants fare in U.S. education.* Santa Monica, CA: Rand.

White, M. J., Biddlecom, A. E., & Guo, S. (1993). Immigration, naturalization and residential assimilation among Asian Americans in 1980. *Social Forces, 72*(1), 93–117.

Wolf, D. L. (1997). Family secrets: Transnational struggles among children of Filipino immigrants. *Sociological Perspectives, 40*(3), 457–482.

PART III

VOICES AT THE MARGINS OF THE COMMUNITY

CHAPTER 11

QUESTIONS OF LEGITIMACY AND RIGHT TO CLAIM HAWAI'IAN IDENTITY

Moving Native Hawai'ian Identity Conversations From the Margins to Center

V. Leilani Kupo

"What are you?" This common question may be asked of people to describe their ethnic and cultural identities. When engaging in an introspective conversation with Native Hawai'ian people, "What are you?" can be a particularly complicated and, at times, painful discussion. This complex conversation is often informed by societal and cultural norms, community expectations, and, at times, political definitions, and location. This interaction and the nuances of identity politics and belonging may cause individuals to question their "right" to claim certain aspects of their identities because they may or may not meet the "requirements" needed to "prove" legitimacy.

Focusing on the Underserved, pages 195–208
Copyright © 2017 by Information Age Publishing
195

Claiming identity is complicated; it is not automatic. Rather, some individuals may have to defend and justify why they belong to a particular community (or hold a particular identity). Specifically, college students who identify as Native Hawai'ian may experience similar encounters regarding their Native Hawai'ian identities that cause them to question their legitimacy and belonging. They may grapple with whether they are allowed to claim Native Hawai'ian identity and membership with the Native Hawai'ian community. These experiences can have both positive and negative impacts on self-concept and identity development and can help construct a foundation that may lead to deeper understanding of one's identity as well as legitimize their place in a community.

The college experience provides opportunities that support and promote college student identity development, and theorists (e.g., Chickering & Reisser, 1993; McEwen, 2003) have acknowledged identity development as a central developmental task for college students. Within the college context, cognitive developmental theorists have advocated "introducing dissonance through challenging students' ways of making meaning" (Torres & Baxter Magolda, 2004, p. 335) and have emphasized the importance of providing support that helps them make sense of the dissonance (Kegan, 1994), or "welcomes students, as they are" (Torres & Baxter Magolda, 2004, p. 335), and encourages them to "become something more." These intentional developmental experiences are "critical to the mission of higher education" (p. 335) and assist college students' identity development processes. Understanding identity will better assist university officials in creating an environment that supports Native Hawai'ian students and innovative services and programs that assist students in developing a more complex understanding of their identities. The exploration of Native Hawai'ian experiences in college will help university officials identify and understand larger issues that impact the community members.

The purpose of this chapter is to explore the complex ways Native Hawai'ian undergraduate women conceptualize their identity. Specifically, the women's understandings of identity, legitimacy, and what it means to be Native Hawai'ian will be outlined. The information shared in this chapter is based on a narrative inquiry study utilizing tribal critical race theory (Brayboy, 2005) of the experiences of eight self-identified Native Hawai'ian undergraduate women enrolled at a large research university in the Pacific (Kupo, 2010). The participants all identified as Native Hawai'ian or Hawai'ian as their most salient identity. The eight women represented diverse ethnic backgrounds; seven identified being multi-ethnic, and one participant reported being only Native Hawai'ian. However, all participants identified having Native Hawai'ian ancestry and claimed a close identification with their Native Hawai'ian identity.

The following discusses the complex ways these Native Hawai'ian undergraduate women conceptualized their identity. First, I will outline how social and political notions frame understandings of what it means to be Native Hawai'ian. Using a series of vignettes, I will then discuss how the women negotiated their identities as Native Hawai'ians. These vignettes will be used to contextualize the themes, which include: the importance of blood, being "not enough" and "too much," tensions between Hawai'ian and American identities, and identity performance. Finally, I recommend how colleges can better support Native Hawai'ian women students.

LANGUAGE

Language is a powerful method used for inclusion, exclusion, and definition of what it means to be Native Hawai'ian/*Kānaka Maoli*. Kauanui (2008) addressed the issue of language and labels:

> I use "native Hawaiian" (with a lower case "n") referring to the 50% definition in any given legal context, whereas I use "Native Hawaiian" (with a capital "N") when referring to its legal context where it is defined as anyone of Hawaiian ancestry without regard for the blood quantum rule. When not referring to a specific legal definition, "Kanaka Maoli" and "Hawaiian" are used interchangeably to describe those indigenous to Hawai'i. I do so in order to underscore the shift between the two and remind the reader that the term "Hawaiian" does not work as a residency marker in the way "Californian" does. (p. xii)

Kauanui's clarification of terms illuminates a complex and important need to clarify labels when discussing Hawai'ian identity and concerns. Though *Kānaka Maoli*—the label for those who are descended from the original settlers of the Hawai'ian Islands—is used throughout much of the contemporary literature, the participants in this study referred to themselves as Hawai'ian or Native Hawai'ian. Thus, to honor their personal identification, the terms *Native Hawai'ian* or *Hawai'ian* will be used as labels unless specific language such as *Kānaka Maoli* is used.

SOCIETAL AND POLITICAL NOTIONS
FRAMING NATIVE HAWAI'IAN

When some people think about Native Hawai'ians, the typical construct that comes to mind is the images they encounter on television, in print ads, through stories told by friends and family about the people and the 'āina (land), and/or what they saw and experienced on vacation (Halualani,

2002; Kauanui, 2007; Osorio, 2001). Images of dark-haired women in grass skirts dancing in firelight, brown-bodied men in loin cloths twirling fire poles or carrying food from the *imu* (in-ground oven), and depictions of the luau are associated with and convey the archetypes of indigenous people of Hawai'i. Descriptions such as exotic, welcoming, hospitable, and entertaining are used to depict Native Hawai'ians (Halualani, 2002; Kauanui, 2000; Osorio, 2001). Yet opposing images—full of great mystery, savagery, brutality, and ambiguity—have also been intentionally passed on from generation to generation (Halualani, 2002) and shape the ways in which U.S. society describes Native Hawai'ian people and culture:

> Deep within the historical imagination, there lies the image of a Western explorer surrounded by dark and strange natives. A gold-embossed frame presents the intricately painted figure of James Cook, rifle in hand, who faced the native from the ever-famous Pacific story of Western contact. The naked natives, each indistinguishable from one another, sneak up behind an unsuspecting Cook, with spears in hand, ready to strike at any moment. (p. 1)

This description of the first Western contact with Native Hawai'ians has influenced and shaped what it means to be Native Hawai'ian in the twenty-first century. Powerful portrayals such as the example above have created an image of a population that is mysterious, faceless, brown-bodied, and in need of civilization; civilization that only Westerners can bring to their beings and to their communities. Brown-bodied people are portrayed as savage and unpredictable, heathen, and diseased (Halualani, 2002). All of these images and beliefs shape the concept of what it means to be a Native Hawai'ian person and create a framework imposed on the community which, in turn, impacts identity development, cultural awareness, and cultural practices.

The definition of Native Hawai'ian identity (also referred to as *Kānaka Maoli*, or true people) has been contested, defined, and redefined throughout history. Ever since the first contact with Western society and the enforcement of colonial and imperialistic practices, the ruling Hawai'ian *ali'i*[1] (i.e., chiefs) have increasingly encroached upon the rights and privileges of the indigenous people of the Hawai'ian islands. In turn, this encroachment has influenced understandings and conceptions of Native Hawai'ian identity. Hawai'ian identity is shaped not only by the Native Hawai'ian community, but also by those who conquered and settled the islands for the countries of Russia, England, and the United States (Mykkanen, 2003). In particular, the origins and transformations of a U.S. national identity for Hawai'ians is fraught with conflict given the history of an illegal armed invasion—a *coup d'état*—of the Hawai'ian Kingdom on January 17, 1893 by a group of White businessmen from the United States (Kauanui, 1999). The impact of outsiders on the identity formation and definition of Native

Hawai'ians is long-standing and shaped by oppression, assimilation, violence, and colonization.

Keeping this in mind, when one asks the questions, "What does it mean to be Native Hawai'ian?" "What does it mean to be *Kānaka Maoli?*" and "Who are the Native Hawai'ians?" the answers will depend on who is asking the questions and the context in which the questions are raised. Ultimately, Hawai'ian identity is part of a narrative, and "is always in part a narrative, always in part a kind of representation. It is always within representation. Identity is not something that is formed outside and then we tell stories about it. It is that which is narrated in one's own self" (Hall, 2000, p. 148). Essentially, the answer to the question is, "It depends." Yet to reach a genetic and scientific determination of race, the U.S. government requires proof of blood quantum (Hall, 2005; Halualani, 2002; Kauanui, 1999, 2000, 2007; Osorio, 2001), or a specific amount of Native Hawai'ian blood in one's body. In this instance, biology determines one's Hawai'ian identity and signifies a quantifiable measure of Hawai'ianness. In contrast, within the Native Hawai'ian/*Kānaka Maoli* community, Native Hawai'ian/*Kānaka Maoli* must be able to trace genealogical roots back to the ancient Polynesian settlers. In addition, genealogical connection are traced to **ʻāina** (land) in order to demonstrate knowledge and proof of parentage through, again, genealogy (Hall, 2005; Halualani, 2002; Kame'eleihiwa, 1992; Kauanui, 1999, 2000, 2007; Osorio, 2001). While these two definitions are both utilized to determine Native Hawai'ianness, they are in dialectical conflict with each other. Essentially, the long-standing question is, "What does it mean to be Native Hawai'ian/*Kānaka Maoli* and who can lay claim to this identity?" It is precisely here that many can see how the external (government) and internal (community) definitions of what it means to be Native Hawai'ians are often defined yet rarely explored in higher education.

Among the many aspects of Hawai'ian identity that conflict, two are most prevalent within identity politics discussions. First, indigenous conceptions of Hawai'ian identity are very different from non-indigenous conceptions (Hall, 2005). Hawai'ian identity lies in a genealogical relationship to the *ʻaumākua* (ancestral spirit), *ʻāina* (the land), and *kānaka* (other Hawai'ians). Hawai'ians are linked through *ʻaumākua* (ancestral spirits) and through *mākua* (adults/parents). As Hawai'ians have a responsibility to *mālama* the *ʻāina* (care for the land), the *ʻāina* (land) thus cares for us. Genealogies explain relationships to other Hawai'ians and, most importantly, where they came from, where they trace their roots, and how they are connected to each other and to the *ʻāina* (land). "Though these elements may be interpreted differently, with them we are Hawai'ian no matter what else we might be" (Hall, 2005, p. 405). Without these elements, however, there are no Hawai'ians. Concepts such as "part," "full," "50% or more," and "less than 50%" are colonial constructions that threaten to divide Hawai'ians from each other (Hall, 2005). This conception is a significant departure from the U.S. government's definition of Native Hawai'ian—those "descendants with at least one-half blood quantum of individuals inhabiting the Hawai'ian Islands prior to 1778" (HHCA, 1921).

Second, the U.S. government does not consider an individual with less than 50% Hawai'ian blood Native Hawai'ian, whereas the community definition allows for one who is genealogically connected and may have less than 50% blood quantum to still identify as Native Hawai'ian or *Kānaka Maoli*. These divergent conceptions of Native Hawai'ian identity lead to significant implications regarding access to government resources and cultural and community resources. Indeed, the access to these resources then influences how one defines "Native Hawai'ian."

DEFINING HAWAI'IAN

Conversations about legitimacy and belonging often begin with reflections on what it means to be Hawai'ian, essentially defining Native Hawai'ian identity. Asking one to define what it means to be Native Hawai'ian is a complicated and complex conversation. Ancestry, connection to the 'āina (land), and cultural practices are important aspects of Hawai'ian identity. As beliefs about Hawai'ians emerge from a mixture of personal experiences and reflection, they illustrate broader sociohistorical and political contexts. Although many of these views are reflections of past interpretations of what it means to be Hawai'ian and are both negative and positive, these views continued to surface and play a role in the understandings of contemporary Hawai'ianness in its present context. In a sense, they represent the sometimes basic, yet painful, understandings and interpretations to begin to think about and understand being Hawai'ian. When asked to discuss how they define and understand what it means to be Native Hawai'ian, the women participants talked about their Native Hawai'ianness in ways that incorporated values, biology, culture, location, and beliefs and honor both their multi-ethnic and multicultural backgrounds. Crucial for these participants were their perceptions of Hawai'ianness through self and family.

A Bloody, Bloody Mess: The Importance of Blood

Two students were discussing Native Hawaiian identity. U'i was talking about feeling connected to her ancestors, to her roots and the importance of knowing her history. To U'i, blood was important, and it was more than DNA, it was a connection to her ancestors, "Being Hawaiian is always remembering that you come from a lineage—something powerful." Rose responded with a different thought. Her Hawaiian blood did not have greater meaning, it was not symbolic. Blood did not have a greater value. To Rose, "It's just blood."

Blood is an important component of identity. As illustrated above, it is both biological and symbolic. It is essential in many ways and holds significant value in different contexts. The markers of identity can be based on components such as biology (DNA or blood), ancestry, cultural practice, values, and language. Discussions regarding definitions of Hawai'ian identify particular aspects essential to claiming a Hawai'ian identity. This conversation can be contentious and confusing. Conversations about blood may not always be explicit. Individuals may not specifically name "blood" as a connection to their Hawai'ian identity, or identify a specific blood quantum as a means to legitimize their Hawai'ianness. Yet, it is a way in which genealogical ties and acknowledgement of descent are recognized with notable significance. The value of blood is clear, as it is an important component in capturing and claiming Native Hawai'ian identity; however, its importance varies depending on how it is valued. In a biological sense, the quantity of "blood" Hawai'ians possessed, or blood quantum, may or may not be an issue, though it has become a concern in the context of U.S. policies regarding recognition and access to reparation resources. Rather, blood is a marker that allows individuals the "right" to claim a genealogical lineage. The vignette above—where Rose shared that her Hawai'ian blood was "just blood"—was biological in nature, and seemingly had no deeper meaning to Rose, others such as U'i have viewed blood quantum as an essential component to being able to claim Native Hawai'ian identity. To the college women in this study, blood was a tie to genealogical descent and connection to ancient Native Hawai'ians representing more than DNA.

Not Enough and Too Much

Matilda and Lisa were asked to talk about times when they felt they were "too Hawaiian" and "not Hawaiian enough." Thinking back, Matilda shared, "I've just been in the Hawaiian classes, and I've just felt like I'm not Hawaiian enough . . . " as she did not have all of the knowledge that she thought she should know about Hawaiian culture and did not have adequate Hawaiian language skills. Lisa was aware of being "too Hawaiian." "[J]ust talking to someone new who is not from here [Hawai'i] . . . I don't want them to think different of me . . . like [they question] the way I'm speaking and 'She doesn't know how to speak proper English . . . '" because she is Hawaiian.

Feelings of "not enough" or "too much" Hawai'ianness can arise after encounters with individuals or environments in which individuals are made to question whether one belongs and one's legitimacy. Often these experiences include feelings of not having cultural knowledge or looking or acting how individuals *expected* Native Hawai'ians to act. Themes of feeling not "Hawai'ian enough" and "too Hawai'ian" emerged and were part of understanding how one can make meaning of Native Hawai'ian identity. These moments were times when individuals were made to think about their behaviors and become overly aware of how they are perceived by others. During these moments they are forced to think about how they can legitimize their justification to claim Native Hawai'ian identity. As Matilda shared above, there are times when she felt as if she was "not Hawai'ian enough" because she did not have cultural competency and knowledge. Mediating these feelings can be difficult and impact the ways in which individuals express themselves. Feelings of being "too much," as Lisa discussed above, can cause individuals to perform their identity in a manner that is more socially acceptable. These behaviors can include changing language and speech patterns from *pidgin* (Hawai'ian Creole) to "proper English," being aware of how they were expressing emotions and how others may interpret and value the interactions, and performing their behaviors and actions in accordance with a more Westernized manner.

These behaviors were performed as such to avoid standing out and being considered different from those in their environment. Conversely, feelings of "not enough" can include behaviors of overcompensation of perceived Hawai'ian behaviors, seeking out education about culture and language, and feelings of shame. Interestingly, these feelings can change based on environment, others' expectations, and location. To address the struggle with feeling "too much" or "not enough" Hawai'ian—due in part to how they perceived external/environmental expectations—participants described how they each reframed their conception and definition of what it means to be Hawai'ian and further understood their personal identities.

Forced Choice: Native Hawai'ian and American Identities in Conflict

> Discussing issues of belonging, Mokihana talked about having to choose between American and Hawaiian identities. "I feel like I have been implanted. Like I don't belong..." in the United States. Mokihana did not feel like an American, even though she was born in the United States. "It's like I have to choose..." between being Native Hawaiian and American.

Issues of belonging, or having the right to claim Native Hawai'ian identity, can be contentious. As many Native Hawai'ians are multi-ethnic, balancing Native Hawai'ian identities with other cultural and ethnic identities is difficult. Underlying these discussions are concerns regarding feelings that individuals need to choose between a Native Hawai'ian identity and an American identity. A common theme included experiences with assimilation and being forced to adopt dominant culture and more American ways of being, rather than allowing them to celebrate individual cultures and differences. This process of assimilation eliminates aspects of identity and causes people to conform so they can be accepted. It forces people to create an identity that is more accepted by American culture. Notions of being "American" and "Hawai'ian" often conflict directly with each other. At times, this conflict resembles Hawai'i's own history, including the colonization and illegal occupation by the United States for more than 100 years, spanning the status of a U.S. territory to celebrating 50 years of statehood in 2009. Seeing Hawai'i as a place of cultural heritage, rather than an entity of the United States, has influenced the way one experiences identity. This can cause individuals to learn two, or more, sets of rules and to acknowledge and navigate two different worldviews. This navigation included knowing the "correct" behaviors associated with each culture and how to properly express them in the appropriate context and environment.

Being American can be in conflict with being Native Hawai'ian. This conflict can cause dissonance in how persons understand their identity and whether they believe they can claim to be Native Hawai'ian and/or American. In these instances, there is an inability to claim both; one *cannot* claim both. The straddling of two worlds—American and Native Hawai'ian—can be a source of concern for many. Accepting and rejecting certain parts of their identity in order to lay claim to being either "Hawai'ian enough" or American is not simple. While this struggle can deny individuals the opportunity to claim both identities and fully express all facets of their identity, this crisis can also prompt an exaggeration of behaviors to "prove" Hawai'ianness or Americanness.

Phenotype and Identity Performance

"What does a Hawaiian look like?" Pōmai asked this powerful question. She discussed that Hawaiians are multiracial and have been impacted by diaspora and colonization. There is "not one way" for a Hawaiian to look. She shared that she had had arguments with others about her identity, "I have had arguments with people who have told me that I don't look Hawaiian...and a person told me I must be full blooded." This was a source of frustration and constant stress. And yet, there is value in looking Hawaiian. For Pōmai, it is part of her legitimacy to claim Native Hawaiian identity.

The notion of "Hawai'ian enough" was based not only on acting, or the performance of Hawai'ian, but based on whether one physically "looked"

Hawai'ian. With this in mind, interview participants referenced phenotype, or the expression of specific physical traits based on genetic and environmental influences. Experiences with being treated differently and encountering different types of reactions due to how they physically appear (e.g., skin color, facial features, hair color) were powerful and surfaced throughout interviews. Questions regarding an individual's right to claim Hawai'ian identity were guided by whether they "look" and/or "act" Hawai'ian. Being misidentified or facing questions regarding cultural heritage because they do not "look" like a typical Hawai'ian caused participants to question the right to claim their Hawai'ian identity and/or become frustrated and angry because they had to define and defend their identity. To be sure, there is no defined way for a Hawai'ian to act or look. Rather, definitions seem to be based on societal notions of what Hawai'ian is or is not. These definitions are typically based on stereotypes and notions of Hawai'ianness put forth by the dominant society. As described earlier in the chapter, images of Native Hawai'ians include brown-bodied people dancing in the firelight. People who do not fit this image can encounter resistance because they do not "look" Hawai'ian, even though they trace their ancestry to the original settlers of the Hawai'ian archipelago and/or demonstrate that they possess Hawai'ian blood.

On a very basic level, society continues to describe Hawai'ians in terms of particular actions. Dancing *hula*, playing music, eating particular foods (e.g., "Hawai'ian foods" such as *poi*, raw fish, and roasted pig), engaging in particular activities (e.g., ocean sports like fishing or diving), and speaking Hawai'ian are all different kinds of performances of Hawai'ianness. Some of these activities were described by participants as necessary components that contribute to the formation of Hawai'ian identity. However, their descriptions also diverged from popular and societal notions of Hawai'ian and extended beyond the activities listed above. There was a significance associated with participating in Native Hawai'ian cultural protocols and activities. It included a calling to the ancestors and honoring of the values and peoples who came before. They valued being connected to and understanding the importance of honoring and understanding the cultural values, protocols, and history associated with each practice.

NATIVE HAWAI'IAN IDENTITY: NOT SO SIMPLE

Understanding and meeting expectations surrounding what it means to be Hawai'ian is a complicated process. In particular, the collegiate experience was a critical time to reflect and learn about Native Hawai'ian identity because it provided time to interact with cultural practitioners, faculty, and individuals who encouraged self-reflection, exploration, and intentional interaction with Native Hawai'ian cultural protocols and practices. For some of the participants, their collegiate experience was the first time they were encouraged to think about their Hawai'ian identities from multiple perspectives and have a better understanding of the numerous influences on how they understand and make meaning of who they are as individuals and community members. There are unwritten rules that govern behavior as well as definitions based on biology and cultural understanding. Having the ability to "qualify" as Native Hawai'ian was critical to many participants' understanding of identities. In addition, understanding the impact of racism and oppression on the way one was treated was important to navigating how one "proved" one's Hawai'ianness. Possessing the ability to exaggerate "acceptable" behaviors (as determined by the environment) was critical to being seen as legitimate, such as acting professional to disprove the stereotype of Hawai'ians being uneducated and lazy, or changes in speech pattern to be perceived as educated or Hawai'ian. These processes are exhausting and required the women to have cultural capital associated with "knowing" rules and expectations that governed what it meant to be Hawai'ian, as well as what it meant not to be Hawai'ian.

Feelings of mattering and belonging are critical to understanding one's self. These feelings are informed by how one defines one's self as well as by societal and community expectations and norms. In a society where it is important to be able to categorize and label communities and individuals, understanding the rules and having the ability to navigate multiple—and often conflicting and competing—expectations is essential. The questions, "What are you?" and "Who are you?" are not so simple, as evidenced above. As practitioners and scholars continue to explore notions of identity, they must understand: (a) the multiple factors that inform the ways in which persons understand themselves; (b) the critical space in which environment, performance, government, and society influence how individuals see themselves; and (c) how navigating multiple cultural contexts can influence their beliefs about belonging and claiming Native Hawai'ian identity.

SUGGESTIONS FOR PRACTICE

Recommendations for practice may not be evident within the text of this chapter. Better understanding of how to support Native Hawai'ian college student identity development can provide opportunities to develop programs that support student success and retention as they are related to helping students feel as if they belong on campus and matter. As conversations regarding identity occur, it is important to understand the complexity of identity and the ways in which identity definitions can change due to environment, political bodies, and comfort levels with engaging in conversations involving identity politics. Nonetheless, university administrators working with Native Hawai'ian college students, indigenous students, and other college students whose identities are politicized and complicated by government, community, societal, and other influences can benefit from keeping the following in mind:

1. *Self-Definition:* Providing opportunities for Native Hawai'ian college students to participate in identity development exercises that encourage self-definition are critical. With many different messages framing Hawai'ian identity, engaging Native Hawai'ian college students with the question, "What does it mean to be Native Hawai'ian" may be powerful.
2. *Opportunities for reflection about identity:* Reflection can and ought to occur in a variety of contexts in order to meet the needs of a diverse group of Native Hawai'ian students. Not all students are interested in or comfortable participating in Native Hawai'ian programs, and reflection opportunities should be varied and appropriate for a diverse student population.
3. *Cultural competency:* Administrators and program planners need to have cultural competency and understand the complexities of Native Hawai'ian history, culture, the impact of colonization and immigration, and the importance of location, land, culture, people, and the particularly complicated relationship with the U.S. government. Note: It is important not to rely on collegians to teach cultural competencies to professional staff. The responsibility to develop cultural competency is with the professional staff members and it should be acquired in a manner that is not exploitive or damaging.
4. *Formalized spaces:* There is a need for gathering places in which Native Hawai'ian students, faculty, and staff can meet and interact with one another and have access to a space and/or social structures and activities that connect students with adult role-models, and promote Hawai'ian culture, provide social support structures, and promote integration (Gloria, Kurpius, Hamilton, & Wilson, 1999).
5. *Community specific programs:* Administrators and program planners should consider ways to incorporate culturally relevant programs that honor Hawai'ian culture, address current Hawai'ian issues and concerns, and encourage professional skill building.

These recommendations are not to suggest that only Native Hawai'ian-identified individuals can provide services for Native Hawai'ian college students that will assist with identity development. However, it is critical to understand the socio- and geopolitical influences impacting understandings of these identities and the ways in which higher education administrators can promote Native Hawai'ian college student success and retention through a better understanding of the factors that influence identity development.

MORE WORK TO BE DONE

The exploration of Native Hawai'ian identity is a complicated and contradictory process. The complexity is created by the multilayered cultural, political, and historical contexts, practices, and beliefs that have converged and intersected with one another to create the contemporary lived Hawai'ian experience. The exploration is further complicated as negative and exotic notions of Hawai'ianness are perpetuated and maintained by the dominant culture. Inherent to Hawai'ian identity is the need for and value of self-definition. As a community, having the agency to define for themselves Hawai'ian identity, rather than having external organizations and non-Hawai'ian philosophies imposing identity definitions on Hawai'ians, is essential.

Understanding the relationship between education and identity is invaluable on both an academic and personal level. Academically, scholarship on identity development speaks directly to understanding social power— through education—and its effects on colonized communities. In turn, it also speaks of the empowerment of students who participate in an educational experience that has components of a Native-centered setting.

Currently, Native Hawai'ians struggle for survival in Hawai'i and across the United States. In spite of the tremendous challenges and struggles, Hawai'ians continue to persist and forge ahead, and not just merely survive. Hawai'ians look for answers to reverse the devastating effects of colonization, especially as they are perpetuated in the Western educational system. There is still much work to do, yet we continue to move forward to better our communities and futures of our children. *I mua!*

NOTE

1. Hawaiian language was translated using Pukui and Elbert's (1986) *Hawaiian Dictionary.*

REFERENCES

Brayboy, B. M. (2005). Toward a tribal critical race theory in education. *The Urban Review, 37*(5), 425–446.

Chickering, A. W., & Reisser, L. (1993). *Education and identity* (2nd ed.). San Francisco, CA: Jossey-Bass.

Gloria, A. M., Kurpius, S. E. R., Hamilton, K. D., & Willson, M. S. (1999). African American students' persistence at a predominantly White university: Influences of social support, university comfort, and selfbeliefs. *Journal of College Student Development, 40*(3), 257–268.

Hall, L. K. (2005). "Hawaiian at heart" and other fictions. *The Contemporary Pacific, 17*(2), 404–413.

Hall, S. (2000). Old and new identities, old and new ethnicities. In L. Back & J. Solomos (Eds.), *Theories of race and racism: A reader* (pp. 144–153). New York, NY: Routledge.

Halualani, R. T. (2002). *In the name of Hawaiians: Native identities and cultural politics.* Minneapolis, MN: University of Minnesota Press.

Hawaiian Homes Commission Act (HHCA). 1921. Title IA.

Kame'eleihiwa, L. (1992). *Native land and foreign desires.* Honolulu, HI: Bishop Museum.

Kauanui, J. K. (1999). "For Get" Hawaiian entitlement: Configurations of land, "blood," and Americanization in the Hawaiian Homes Commission Act of 1921. *Social Text, 59,* 123–144.

Kauanui, J. K. (2000). *Rehabilitating the Native: Hawaiian blood quantum and the politics of race, citizenship, and entitlement* (Unpublished doctoral dissertation). University of California, Santa Cruz, CA.

Kauanui, J. K. (2007). Diasporic deracination and "off-island" Hawaiians. *The Contemporary Pacific, 19*(1), 138–160.

Kauanui, J. K. (2008). *Hawaiian blood: Colonialism and the politics of sovereignty and indigeneity.* Durham, NC: Duke University Press.

Kegan, R. (1994). *In over our heads: The mental demands of modern life.* Cambridge, MA: Harvard University Press.

Kupo, V. L. (2010). *What is Hawaiian? Explorations and understandings of Native Hawaiian college women's identities* (Unpublished doctoral dissertation). Bowling Green State University, Bowling Green, OH. Retrieved from https://etd.ohiolink.edu/ap/0?0:APPLICATION_PROCESS%3DDOWNLOAD_ETD_SUB_DOC_ACCNUM:::F1501_ID:bgsu1273603294%2Cinline

McEwen, M. K. (2003). The nature and uses of theory. In S. R. Komives, D. B. Woodard, Jr., & Associates (Eds.), *Student services: A handbook for the profession* (4th ed., pp. 153–178). San Francisco, CA: Jossey-Bass.

Mykkanen, J. (2003). *Inventing politics: A new political anthropology of the Hawaiian Kingdom.* Honolulu, HI: University of Hawai'i Press.

Osorio, J. K. (2001). "What kine Hawaiian are you?" A *mo'olelo* about nationhood, race, history, and the contemporary sovereignty movement in Hawai'i. *The Contemporary Pacific, 13*(2), 359–379.

Pukui, M. K., & Elbert, S. H. (1986). *Hawaiian dictionary.* Honolulu, HI: University of Hawai'i Press.

Torres, V., & Baxter Magolda, M. B. (2004). Reconstructing Latino identity: The influence of cognitive development on the ethnic identity process of Latino students. *Journal of College Student Development, 45*(3), 333–347.

CHAPTER 12

UNDERSERVED AND UNSEEN

Southeast Asian Americans
in Higher Education

Phitsamay Sychitkokhong Uy

To date, Southeast Asian Americans (SEAAs) from Cambodia, Laos, and Vietnam are among the largest group of refugees to resettle in the United States (Office of Refugee Resettlement, 2005). Coming from Laos, where approximately 90% of people who were employed worked as subsistence farmers, many Laotian villagers had only the compulsory five years of education.[1] Indeed, few Laotian citizens completed a secondary education, which took an additional three years. These realities are partially due to the fact that, during the U.S. Secret War on Laos, those living in northern Laos had their education interrupted by the U.S. Air Force's constant bombing. Likewise, the majority of the Cambodians who fled the Killing Fields and the Khmer Rouge were similarly from farming backgrounds and had interrupted educational experiences.

Laotian and Cambodian Americans have found more educational opportunities in the United States. However, few Laotians and Cambodians progress to higher education. According to U.S. Census figures, only 13%

Focusing on the Underserved, pages 209–226
Copyright © 2017 by Information Age Publishing

of Laotian and 16% of Cambodian adults hold a bachelor's degree or higher, compared to 28% of the national population (Museus, 2013, 2014; SEARAC, 2010).

Scholars have noted the paucity of research focused on Asian American Pacific Islanders (AAPIs) in higher education (Ching & Agbayani, 2012; Museus, 2014; Museus, Maramba, & Teranishi, 2013), especially AAPIs from refugee backgrounds. Although current dominant discourse within Asian American Studies focuses primarily on East Asians (e.g., Chinese, Japanese, and Korean Americans), the experiences of SEAAs (e.g., Cambodian, Hmong, Laotian, and Vietnamese Americans) and South Asian Americans (e.g., Bangladeshi, Asian Indian, Pakistani, and Sri Lankan Americans) have been persistently marginalized (Museus, 2013, 2014).

In this chapter, I discuss the challenges and barriers faced by many SEAAs, in particular Lao and Khmer,[2] as they pursue higher education. To examine SEAA high school students' experiences with overcoming educational barriers in order to pursue higher education, I begin by discussing the utility of Bourdieu (1986) and Coleman's (1988) work on social capital theory. Then, I provide an overview of the theoretical framework, methods, and cultural contexts that guided my study. A discussion then features my analysis of the three major networks to which SEAA youth have access. Three critical findings arose from the analysis: (a) parents are seminal sources of motivation, (b) role of teacher support is vital, and (c) peer networks have immense power. I then conclude with policy and practice recommendations that may increase the number of SEAA students who succeed on their journey to higher education.

THEORETICAL FRAMEWORK

Social capital has become a widely used framework with which to understand the variation in achievement levels between ethnic groups (Bankston, 2004; Noguera, 2004). Pierre Bourdieu (1986) discusses the importance of the transference of different types of capital—economic, cultural, and social—from one generation to the next. Bourdieu argues that key members of society hold valuable knowledge, monetary currency, and resources that ensure their children's social mobility in a hierarchal culture. Bourdieu defined social capital as the "aggregate of actual or potential resources" which are linked to a group of members in an institutionalized network (e.g., a family lineage, a class, a tribe, or a political party, etc.). It is developed when people form relationships or networks and exchange resources with one another, whether as members of a dyad or a network.

Social capital is a useful framework to examine achievement within ethnic groups, as members within or between specific ethnic groups may have access to different resources. James Coleman (1988) broadened the discussion of social capital to the education system by analyzing the role that social capital plays in the probability of dropping out of school. He argues that social capital manifests in many forms, including information channels and social norms. Coleman also asserts that social capital is predicated on obligations, expectations, and the trustworthiness of social structures. In a network of people, social norms govern behavior by sanctioning members whose behavior strays from what is deemed acceptable. Similarly, social norms can be seen as a resource when a group's norms benefit the individuals who belong to that group. For example, it might be the norm for students in an advanced class to always do their homework, participate in class, and earn A's on tests. Since all students will work to do well in class, these pro-school norms benefit each member of the group.

Role of Parents

Since children are born into families that have pre-established relationships and networks, it is logical to first examine familial networks within the SEAA community. Both the popular press and scholarly research have underscored the important role of SEAA parents in shaping their children's educational trajectories (Museus, 2013, 2014), and the majority of the SEAA parents see education as a means to improve their children's lives (Goyette & Xie, 1999; Suárez-Orozco & Suárez-Orozco, 2001). SEAA parents viewed their role as providing moral support and encouragement at home. In this way, the SEAA parents in this study resembled some Latino parents (Auerbach, 2006). In her 2006 study on parent involvement, Auerbach found that Chicano mothers provided their children with "noninterventionist" moral support and "indirect guidance" on education. Although low-income Chicano parents could not provide concrete information about what educational pathways to follow, some Chicano mothers were found to be involved in school-based parental programs. Currently, the voices of Southeast Asian American parents have been nominal in parental involvement literature, but Musues (2013) found that SEAA students felt that their parents placed a high value on education as a means to an end. In fact, their parents believed that "education is the key to getting anywhere in life" (Museus, 2013, p. 724).

Most Southeast Asian parents who respected their children's teachers did not want to interfere with the educators' work and often deferred to their children's teachers (Te, 1997; Yan & Lin, 2005). As these parents thought that it was the teachers' responsibility to educate their children, they assumed that the teachers had more education and a better understanding of their children's academic needs (Saito, 2002; Smith-Hefner, 1990, 1993).

One possible explanation for this perception was that their limited educational backgrounds led to a perceived minimal role in their children's education (Smith-Hefner, 1990).

Some SEAA parents have stressful life circumstances that limit their ability, and their availability, to help their children (Nou, 2006; Sack, Kinzie, Angell, Clarke, & Ben, 1986). For example, many of the Khmer parents who experienced the Killing Fields and the Lao parents who experienced the Secret Bombings of Laos may have post-traumatic stress disorder, which can seriously affect their—and their children's—daily lives (Kinzie, Sack, Angell, Clarke, & Ben, 1989; Sack et al., 1986). Adult Khmer refugees reported having stress that manifests in various ways: feelings of helplessness, being unable to cope with simple life tasks, becoming socially withdrawn, having low self-esteem and loss of identity, feeling indifferent to regular life activities, feelings of constant worry and frustration, lack of organization in the household, and neglecting family duties and obligations (Nou, 2006).

Louie's (2004) study on immigrant students from working-class backgrounds found that immigrant students had to fend for themselves because the parents' low socioeconomic status and lack of social and cultural capital limited their ability to advocate for their children at school. Similarly, SEAA parents are limited by their working-class networks and lack of social capital, which then inhibited their ability to provide academic and career support to their children (Museus, 2013, 2014). In response to this context, many of these students turn to their teachers and friends for concrete help.

Role of Institutional Agents

For refugee and immigrant students, interacting with people who understand their experiences helps reduce their sense of alienation and loneliness, which lead many students to disengage from school (Fine, 1991; Rumberger, 1983). Since racial minority students are more likely to experience discrimination and social exclusion (Stanton-Salazar & Dornsbusch, 1995), it is important for educators to establish trust and rapport with them early in their academic careers.

Accessing institutional agents who can provide support is not a skill taught to all youth, nor do all young people acquire it easily. And, it is even more difficult for minority or immigrant youth, who often are challenged by social distance and a mistrust of institutional agents. They face structural barriers in asking for help, including teachers' low expectations, stereotyping, discrimination, and racism (Stanton-Salazar & Dornsbusch, 1995). Scholars have found that having a caring relationship with an institutional agent or an adult advocate can help minority and immigrant youth overcome barriers to developing trust and overcoming social mistrust (Gibson & Hidalgo, 2009; Stanton-Salazar & Dornsbusch, 1995; Valenzuela, 1999).

Students need caring adults or mentors who show what Valenzuela (1999) deems "authentic caring." These influential adults motivate students to work harder (Conchas, 2006). Valenzuela argues that students need far more of this kind of caring in their classrooms to foster their success. Scholars such as Noddings (1992) and Valenzuela (1999) argue that teachers are the active agents who should initiate relations with students and work to develop caring relationships that involve reciprocity—teachers must both demonstrate a willingness to reveal their true selves, and take the time to get to know their students' culture, families, and background.

Similarly, Stanton-Salazar (1997, 2001, 2011) has carefully established that institutional agents have a significant impact on the academic achievement of racial minority students. He argued that high school teachers and guidance counselors, in their role as institutional agents and gatekeepers, have access to and knowledge of information that could bridge the gap for minority students who lack the resources, privileges, and support systems to advance to higher education (Tovar, 2015). In other words, Stanton-Salazar (2011) posits that these institutional agents have a "determining role in either reproducing or *interfering with the reproduction of* class, racial, and gendered inequality" (p. 161, emphasis in original).

Role of Peers

Although relationships with parents and educators have proven to be important, as children grow into adolescents, they devote an increasing amount of time and energy to peers their own age, who soon replace parents as the primary source of companionship and intimacy (Berkel et al., 2009; Laursen, 1998; Lehman, 2012; Li & Wright, 2014). Peers can provide social capital (Koyama, 2007). Through peer relationships, students can develop social skills, obtain information about the world, and learn how to behave (Berndt, 1999; Hartup, 1993; Ryan, 2001).

Peer friendships have been found to influence a host of school-related behaviors in the lives of adolescents (Bulkowski, Newcomb, & Hartup, 1998; Heaven, Ciarrochi, & Vialle, 2008). For example, peers have been found to impact high school students' choices regarding whether to engage in academic or social activities and their college aspirations and enrollment (Berndt, Laychak, & Park, 1990; Choy, Horn, Nuñez, & Chen, 2000; Fuligni, Eccles, Barber, & Clements, 2001; Hallinan & Williams, 1990; Hamm, Lambert, Agger, & Farmer, 2013; Jones, Irvin, & Kibe, 2012; Lynch, Lerner, & Leventhal, 2013; Somers, Owens, & Piliawsky, 2008). Furthermore, educational researchers have found that peer expectations can lead to higher interest in academics and higher GPAs (Butler-Barnes, Estrada-Martinez, Colin, & Jones, 2015; Wentzel, Battle, Russell, & Looney, 2010).

THE SOUTHEAST ASIAN CONTEXT

In this section, I describe the historical and community contexts in which SEAAs are embedded. Scholars have noted that such context is important for refugee and immigrant populations, and underscored the long-term effects of their families' migration on their children (Kinzie et al., 1989; Rumbaut & Portes, 2001; Suárez-Orozco & Suárez-Orozco, 2001). In the next section, I provide an overview of SEAA refugees' political, social, and economic journeys to the United States. I also discuss the community and familial characteristics most relevant to the SEAAs schooling (e.g., role of language and linguistic isolation).

Refugee Resettlement

Large-scale immigration to the United States from Southeast Asia dates back to the Vietnam War (Takaki, 1989). After the U.S. government pulled out of Vietnam in the mid-1970s, a mass exodus of refugees from Vietnam, Cambodia, and Laos flooded the shores of the United States. These people fled political persecution, "re-education camps," famine, torture, and displacement. In attempting to escape, many families were split up, and some family members died along the way. The "boat people" often fell victim to Thai pirates, who attacked and abused the men and raped the women. Some children died of malnutrition (Rumbaut, 1996, 2006).

Southeast Asian refugees came in three waves. The first wave migrated from 1972 to 1974, and included refugees who were the upper class, elite Southeast Asians with high levels of education and exposure to the Western world. The second wave of refugee resettlement took place in 1974–1978. This group of SEAA refugees was of the middle-class, mainly professionals and military personnel. My family came in 1979 at the beginning of the third wave of refugees—working-class villagers and farmers. The majority of refugees spent some time in refugee camps in Thailand, Hong Kong, and the Philippines before being resettled in the United States. Some spent as little as a few months, others as long as three years, waiting to be resettled.

In 1980, the U.S. Congress passed the Refugee Act, which standardized the refugee resettlement process and established the Office of Refugee Resettlement (ORR). ORR was responsible for providing federal assistance to states and municipalities that accepted refugees into their states and cities. The reception Southeast Asians received from U.S. citizens varied considerably, depending on the geographic location. The states that accepted the most Southeast Asians were California, Minnesota, Wisconsin, and Massachusetts. New refugees were given resettlement money ($300–$500 depending on the state) and connected to social service agencies (Pho, Gerson, & Cowan, 2007). Employment, housing, and language assistance were the top SEAA refugee issues, and refugees who settled in large urban areas like Los Angeles, Minneapolis, and New York City had more resources available than their counterparts who settled in rural areas of Vermont, Kansas, and Montana. ORR also helped establish mutual assistance associations, which are social service agencies operated by Southeast Asian personnel and other people familiar with the Southeast Asian populations. Other agencies such as Catholic Charities, the American Friends Service Committee, and the Mennonite Central Committee also assisted in the resettlement process (Pho et al., 2007).

Now totaling more than 2 million and increasing, Southeast Asian Americans can be found in all 50 U.S. states. Due to the combined efforts of U.S. refugee policy and voluntary secondary migration,[3] the seven states where the most Southeast Asians reside are California, Texas, Washington, Pennsylvania, Wisconsin, Minnesota, and Massachusetts (SEARAC, 2010).

METHODS

This qualitative study explored the schooling experience of 40 SEAA high school students (i.e., 13 Laotian and 27 Khmer). Sixteen SEAA participants were men and 24 were women. The participants came from low socio-economic backgrounds, identified as 1.5- and second-generation immigrants, and had parents born in Southeast Asia. Eleven students were in the higher-tracked classes (i.e., honors, high honors, and advanced placement courses) and 39 students were in lower tracks (i.e., not enrolled in honors, high honors, and advanced placement).

Data Collection and Analysis

Data were collected from three sources: interviews, observations, and documents. Over the course of one academic year, I conducted two semi-structured interviews with each participant. I also conducted participant observations and collected documents, such as student handbooks, course schedules, classroom assignments, and public high school records found on the Department of Education and school websites.

The interviews consisted primarily of open-ended questions about the students' experiences in high school, particularly accessing support. Each semi-structured interview took approximately 50 minutes to complete, and all of them were audiotaped and transcribed. Once the interviews were transcribed, they were organized and coded using Atlas.ti qualitative analysis software. First, I used open coding to identify thematic categories around academic and moral support from teachers, families, and friends, and then axial coding was used to further investigate issues that arose during the open-coding process (Strauss & Corbin, 1998). I conducted cross-section analysis by grade level, gender, and majors declared.

Researcher Subjectivity, Reflexivity, and Trustworthiness

While some scholars posit that there is a need to underplay the impact of researcher subjectivity (Strauss & Corbin, 1998), I support Charmaz's (2005) argument about the importance of researcher reflexivity and the need to acknowledge personal bias and assumptions that influence how the researcher looks at, makes decisions about, and interprets the data. As a Lao American scholar, I share many traits with the SEAA students in the study, such as similar phenotype, linguistic challenges, and cultural and religious background. I firmly believe that my unique position as a 1.5-generation Lao refugee—I spent two years in a Thai refugee camp—facilitated my connection with participants and helped me build trust and rapport with the SEAA students. I was cognizant of my role as insider–outsider (i.e., SEAA refugee–academic researcher). I acknowledge that, as an individual who has knowledge about refugee experience and Southeast Asian community, my experiences influence my biases. My biases include the belief that more attention needs to focus on first-generation SEAA college students. Likewise, I believe that institutions of higher education need to provide systemic support to faculty and staff in order for them to properly advise and support SEAA students.

FINDINGS

Three findings emerged from the analysis of what support SEAA students access during their academic careers in high school. First, SEAA parents play a significant role as motivators in SEAA student lives. Second, the majority of SEAA students lacked support from their teachers. Third, SEAA peer networks can have powerful influences on academic and social behaviors.

Parents as Motivators

All of the participants' parents valued education and spoke about the benefits of high school graduation. While the SEAA parents saw education as a means to improve their own and their children's lives, they believed that schools are primarily responsible for their children's education. They saw their role as providing moral support and encouragement at home. Channapha, a Lao freshman, describes her parents' influence:

> My parents have always just taught me that school is very important and it helps you out in life. And I've kind of like built it into me that school is very important. And I'd like to get into a good school so I can have a better life.

Channapha's parents stressed to her the importance of school and it has become ingrained in her thinking. Parents often spoke to their children about the importance of education and used their own lives as examples of how hard life could be without a high school education. Sareoun, a Khmer freshman further elaborated:

> I don't want to drop out. I really want to get a good job because I see the way my mom, she's struggling because she don't have a diploma. I don't want to be like her because that's really hard. And she has five kids and works two jobs and she keeps telling me to do well in school so I don't have to work as hard as she does in life.

For students like Sareoun, seeing how hard their parents worked to provide for their children was a source of motivation. This finding suggests that when immigrant and refugee families are working hard to make ends meet, they do not have the time to help their children navigate the school system. Nor do they have the knowledge. Chanvon, a Khmer senior, expounds:

> My parents were born in Cambodia. They did go to school in Cambodia, but they had to drop out when they were in middle school, so they can help out their family because my dad is the third oldest in the family and my mom is the oldest in her family. So they basically had to quit school and helped out because of Khmer Rouge and stuff... So when they came to the U.S., [it was] really hard to find jobs because they don't speak English and they never went to school in U.S.; so they don't know what we do here and can't really help us. My parents tell me to ask my teachers.

Chanvon understands through her parents' life stories that they were not afforded the same educational opportunities as she has. Since the majority of the SEAA students could not turn to their parents for concrete help with schooling, they had to rely on the other networks in their lives, namely: teachers and peers. Scholars have found that peers and teachers provided encouragement, support, supervision and information to the youth (Goyette & Conchas, 2002). This pattern was echoed in my findings amongst the high-achieving SEAA students.

Role of Teacher Support

One key difference between the high-achieving (i.e., students with GPAs of 3.0 or higher) and low-achieving students is that the former were able to get concrete help with school work from teachers, but the latter did not seek help or get the same level of support. Trust and care were the two factors that enabled participants to ask for help. Students who were higher achieving developed caring and trusting relationships with teachers at their schools. Teachers showed their care and investment in these students' lives by extending themselves beyond the classroom. For example, Bopha, a Khmer junior, illustrated this point as she described her teacher:

> They [friends and teachers] both give me good advice ... my advisory teacher, he just recently gave me his number to help me with whatever or anything. And he's one of my references to put on my job applications.

Bopha can rely on her teacher for academic support as well as a job reference. The fact that her advisory teacher knew her well enough to provide a character reference reflects his investment in her as a student. Further, by giving her his phone number, he is signifying his commitment to being available to her at any time for anything.

A minority of the SEAA students in this study had teachers who provided them with noteworthy encouragement, support, and information. These teachers helped the students with homework assignments, provided guidance about what courses to take and with whom, and gave advice about college and careers. The combination of having parents who motivated them and teachers who provided concrete help fostered their academic success.

Unfortunately, the majority of the students had negative experiences with teachers, who had low expectations of them. For some of the lower-achieving SEAA students, the negative experiences with their teachers in the past made it difficult for them to establish relationships with new teachers. Sonny, a lower-achieving Khmer student, confided:

> I can't turn to teachers because they're not [trustworthy]. I don't want them in my business and telling [my parents], the school authorities and stuff especially without my permission. That happened once. I don't want that much involvement. I just talk to my other friends who understand what I'm going through.

Students, like Sonny, did not trust teachers, so they would not turn to them for help.

The lower-tracked SEAA students in this study do not have many positive relationships with their teachers, or solid connections with any adults in the school building. Mike, a Khmer junior illuminated this reality when he shared that he thinks that students should be able to turn to teachers for help but sometimes the teachers do not seem dependable:

> Well, I think that in school teachers are there to support you, but sometimes some teachers you really can't openly depend on them that much. It just depends on what the communication you have with them. I mean, some people don't like to be open.

Since Mike is a shy student, he depends on his teachers to be open with their students but he also does not necessarily experience this open communication with his current teachers.

The majority of his teachers are white middle-aged women. The teachers were focused on covering the material for the day and there was no exchange of personal chitchat or pleasantries with the exception of Ms. Moriarty, who bade the class "good bye" and wished them "a good night." While the majority of the teachers stuck to their lesson plans and curriculum, some felt comfortable expressing their anger with the students. Sombath, a Lao sophomore described an experience with an irate teacher:

> Sometimes, when they're mad, they just put out the anger and say stupid stuff. I had one teacher. He was grouchy, really grouchy. And all of a sudden he was just ranting on about, "I don't know what you guys want to do. You guys will never be successful. I'm going to see you guys working at [McDonalds]. You won't be able to make it. But if you do make it, I want to know. I want to know how you make it." And I was really offended by that because ... Why would you say that to your students?

Sombath felt that he did not deserve to be disrespected. He was offended by his teacher's tirade and lack of caring for the students and their feelings. Negative experiences like the one described above go a long way in increasing the students' distrust of teachers. In addition, SEAA students are turned off by teachers' perpetuation of stereotypes. Jason, a Khmer senior, recounted this stereotyping:

> Sometimes when I look at a teacher [and] when I see them look at the Khmer kids [and] the people that I know even though they don't look like gang bangers and sometimes it seems like the teacher don't give them a chance just 'cause of the way they look. Sometimes they see kids dress like gang bangers but they're not.

Because Jason knows that not all Khmer students are "gang bangers" (i.e., gang members), despite their looks, he sees his teacher's action as unfair. These remarks illustrate how teachers misperceived SEAA participants as holding an oppositional stance and being "thugs" or gangbangers because of their urban, hip-hop style and dress. These misperceptions are a disservice because they fail to move beyond media images and stereotypes.

Powerful Effects of Peer Networks

In the school context, it would seem logical for students to ask for help from educators. However, the majority of the students in this study (77%) reported turning to their friends for help before asking adults. Steve, a successful Lao senior, explained how he and his friends identify people who can help:

> We would all try to see who's available, and see who can help each other. And if they can't, they'll probably call a friend that they know who's probably like in college … or older, that can help us. Basically, our network, it's just my friends and their close relatives, or anyone that they can find in the community.

Steve knows that, when a need arises, he can trust his peers to provide assistance. His systematic process of identifying people who can help him is sophisticated. The majority of the low-income SEAA participants in this study benefited from such networks. Khone, a Lao freshman, emphasized the importance of having networks of motivated peers and the ways that it can influence his behavior in the following comments:

> Cause if like they were lazy, or like off like doing something else in class, then it would distract you. You probably might want to go do what they're doing, or you'll probably lose focus in your work. So that's why if you see that, I would like just try to convince them to do what you're doing so you don't lose focus. Usually I would lose focus, and like they would get me back in focus, and it'll be like back and forth.

Khone's quotation underscores how friends can influence his behavior—if they are focused, so is he—but it also demonstrates the importance of who you choose as friends.

However, among the low-income students in the study, about one-quarter did not have access to middle-class peer networks. Those who lived in a poorer neighborhood and took the lower-track classes were limited in their opportunities at home and in school to interact or engage with friends of more affluent social classes. Lower-achieving SEAA students also tended to have more friends within their race and also talked more about the racial tensions between racial groups. Johnny, a Khmer junior described this phenomenon:

I do hang out with the Asian kids but they're not just Khmer. Like they all speak Laos, Vietnamese, everything. Because in the high school, I guess the Asians hang out and there's the whites but then we get along though. Unless sometimes. I don't see an ethnic problem in school unless there's a serious [issue], because there's different, a lot of kids, probably like a million different groups in high school. There are certain Spanish people that don't get along with certain Asians and certain white people but then there are the Asians and whites and blacks and green and yellow that do get along.

These lower-tracked SEAA students talked more about having friends cover "their backs" as an element of their friendships and less about them providing academic support. They also talked about "skipping school" to hang out in the mall or going to the movies in the middle of the day.

IMPLICATIONS FOR RESEARCH AND PRACTICE

The findings of the current study have important implications for higher education practitioners and researchers. First, this study underscored the importance of institutional agents who understand SEAA students. Current higher education faculty and staff need to undergo professional development training to better understand the SEAA student experiences. Culturally relevant training for faculty and staff would ensure that anyone working with SEAA students would have a working knowledge of SEAA cultures and communities, the refugee background, and the challenges and demands they face at home and in school. I echo Museus' (2013) call for faculty and staff to "take into account the ways in which [SEAA] students' lives are shaped by their parents, families, and communities and incorporate that understanding into their work" (p. 733). Training to effectively design such culturally relevant curriculum and pedagogical practices should be part of orientations for all new faculty and staff working with SEAAs.

In addition, a mentor program is needed to ensure that SEAA students do not fall in between the cracks and matriculate to a career. The study's findings emphasized the powerful role of peer networks in SEAA students' academic and social lives. Therefore, it would be proactive to ensure that each incoming first-year student has an upper-class mentor whom can share sage advice about college life. Matching the upperclassman and freshman by majors would ideally support the career development process as well.

Regarding research, one limitation of this study is that it took place in high school. While the challenges that prevent SEAA students from reaching higher education are important, it is equally important to understand the challenges encountered by SEAA students who successfully enter higher education. And, while participants in this study indicated that these were the challenges and barriers to their academic experience in high school, their experiences cannot be generalized to SEAA students in colleges. Although some research has been conducted on SEAAs in college (e.g., Chhuon & Hudley, 2008; Kiang, 2002, 2009; Museus, 2013, 2014; Museus, Shiroma, Dizon, & Nguyen, 2013), empirical studies on this population are sparse.

Finally, it is essential for researchers to share effective evidence-based practices with faculty, staff, and student development officers in order to enhance their capacities to better support SEAA students more effectively. For example, colleges and universities should consider hosting a symposium with scholars and practitioners together focusing specifically on serving SEAA students. Scholars and practitioners usually attend their professional organizational meetings (i.e., American Educational Research Aassocation, Association for the Study of Higher Education, NASPA—Student Affairs Professionals, American College Personnel Association, etc.) and SEAA issues are often marginalized within these spaces. Having one event that brings together the researchers, practitioners, SEAA students in K–12 and higher education, and SEAA communities around issues that are most relevant to this population could help educators understand how to increase college access and success for SEAA students.

NOTES

1. Laotian is used to refer to all ethnic tribes from Laos including but not limited to Lowland Lao, Hmong, Iu Mien, Khmuu, and Thaidem. The Lao government acknowledges 167 different ethnic tribes.
2. I use Southeast Asians, SEA, and Lao and Khmer interchangeably in this chapter.
3. Voluntary second migration occurs when refugees relocate to another city/town after their initial settlement in the United States.

REFERENCES

Auerbach, S. (2006). "If the student is good, let him fly": Moral support for college among Latino immigrant parents. *Journal of Latinos and Education, 5*(4), 275–292.

Bankston, C. L. (2004). Social capital, cultural values, immigration, and academic achievement: The host country context and contradictory consequences. *Sociology of Education, 77*(2), 176–179.

Berkel, C., Murry, V. M., Hurt, T. R., Chen, Y., Brody, G. H., Simons, R. L.,... Gibbons, F. X. (2009). It takes a village: Protecting rural African American youth in the context of racism. *Journal of Youth and Adolescence, 38*(2), 175–188.

Berndt, T. J. (1999). Friends' influence on students' adjustment to school. *Educational Psychologist, 34*(1), 15–28.

Berndt, T. J., Laychak A. E., & Park, K. (1990). Friends' influence on adolescents' academic achievement motivation: An experimental study. *Journal of Educational Psychology, 82*(4), 664–670.

Bourdieu, P. (1986). The forms of capital. In J. G. Richardson (Ed.), *Handbook of theory and research for the sociology of education* (pp. 241–258). New York, NY: Greenwood.

Bukowski, W. M., Newcomb, A. F., & Hartup, W. W. (1998). *The company they keep: Friendships in childhood and adolescence.* Cambridge, England: Cambrdge University Press.

Butler-Barnes, S. T., Estrada-Martinez, L., Colin, R. J., & Jones, B. D. (2015). School and peer influences on the academic outcomes of African American adolescents. *Journal of Adolescence, 44,* 168–181.

Charmaz, K. (2005). Grounded theory: Methods for the 21st century. *Handbook of Qualitative Research. Third Edition.* London, England: Sage.

Ching, D., & Agbayani, A. (2012). *Asian Americans and Pacific Islanders in higher education: Research and perspectives on identity, leadership, and success.* Washington, DC: National Association of Student Personnel Administrators.

Chhuon, V., & Hudley, C. (2008). Factors supporting Cambodian American students' successful adjustment into the university. *Journal of College Student Development, 49*(1), 15–30.

Choy, S. P., Horn, L. J., Nuñez, A.-M., & Chen, X. (2000). Transition to college: What helps at-risk students and students whose parents did not attend college. *New Directions for Institutional Research, 107,* 45–63.

Coleman, J. S. (1988). Social capital in the creation of human capital. *American Journal of Sociology, 94,* 95–120.

Conchas, G. Q. (2006). *The color of success: Race and high-achieving urban youth.* New York, NY: Teachers College Press.

Fine, M. (1991). *Framing dropouts: Notes on the politics of an urban high school.* Albany, NY: State University of New York Press.

Fuligni, A. J., Eccles, J. S., Barber, B. L., & Clements, P. (2001). Early adolescent peer orientation and adjustment during high school. *Developmental Psychology, 37*(1), 28–36.

Gibson, M. A., & Hidalgo, N. (2009). Bridges to success in high school for migrant youth. *Teachers College Record, 111*(3), 683–711.

Goyette, K. A., & Conchas, G. Q. (2002). Family and non-family roots of social capital among Vietnamese and Mexican American children. *Schooling and Social Capital in Diverse Cultures, 13,* 41–72.

Goyette, K., & Xie, Y. (1999). Educational expectations of Asian American youths: Determinants and ethnic differences. *Sociology of Education, 72*(1), 22–36.

Hallinan, M. T., & Williams, R. A. (1990). Students' characteristics and the peer-influence process. *Sociology of Education, 63*(2), 122–132.

Hamm, J. V., Lambert, K., Agger, C. A., & Farmer, T. W. (2013). Promotive peer contexts of academic and social adjustment among rural African American early adolescent boys. *American Journal of Orthopsychiatry, 83*(2–3), 278.

Hartup, W. W. (1993). Adolescents and their friends. In B. Laursen (Ed.), *Close friendships in adolescence* (pp. 3–22). San Francisco, CA: Jossey-Bass.

Heaven, P. C. L., Ciarrochi, J., & Vialle, W. (2008). Self-nominated peer crowds, school achievement, and psychological adjustment in adolescents: Longitudinal analysis. *Personality & Individual Differences, 44*(4), 977–988.

Jones, M. H., Irvin, M. J., & Kibe, G. W. (2012). Does geographic setting alter the roles of academically supportive factors? African American adolescents' friendships, math self-concept, and math performance. *The Journal of Negro Education, 81*(4), 319–337.

Kiang, P. N. (2002). Stories and structures of persistence: Ethnographic learning through research and practice in Asian American Studies. In Y. Zou & E. T. Trueba (Eds.), *Ethnography and schools: Qualitative approaches to the study of education* (pp. 223–255). Lanham, MD: Rowman & Littlefield.

Kiang, P. N. (2009). A thematic analysis of persistence and long-term educational engagement with Southeast Asian American college students. In L. Zhan (Ed.), *Asian American voices: Engaging, empowering, enabling* (pp. 21–58). New York, NY: NLN Press.

Kinzie, J. D., Sack, W., Angell, R., Clarke, G., & Ben, R. (1989). A three-year follow-up of Cambodian young people traumatized as children. *Journal of the American Academy of Child & Adolescent Psychiatry, 28*(4), 501–504.

Koyama, J. P. (2007). Approaching and attending college: Anthropological and ethnographic accounts. *Teachers College Record, 109*(10), 2301–2323.

Laursen, B. (1998). Closeness and conflict in adolescent peer relationships: Interdependence with friends and romantic partners. In W. M. Bukowski, A. F. Newcomb, & W. W. Hartup (Eds.), *The company they keep: Friendships in childhood and adolescence* (pp. 186–212). New York, NY: Cambridge University Press.

Lehman, B. (2012). The impacts of friendship groups' racial composition when perceptions of prejudice threaten students' academic self-concept. *Social Psychology of Education, 15*(3), 411–425.

Li, Y., & Wright, M. F. (2014). Adolescents' social status goals: Relationships to social status insecurity, aggression, and prosocial behavior. *Journal of Youth and Adolescence, 43*(1), 146–160.

Louie, V. (2004). *Compelled to excel: Immigration, education, and opportunity among Chinese Americans.* Stanford, CA: Stanford University Press.

Lynch, A. D., Lerner, R. M., & Leventhal, T. (2013). Adolescent academic achievement and school engagement: An examination of the role of school-wide peer culture. *Journal of Youth and Adolescence, 42*(1), 6–19.

Museus, S. D. (2013). Unpacking the complex and multifaceted nature of parental influences on Southeast Asian American college students' educational trajectories. *Journal of Higher Education, 84*(5), 708–738.

Museus, S. D. (2014). *Asian American students in higher education.* New York, NY: Routledge.

Museus, S. D., Maramba, D. C., & Teranishi, R. T. (2013). *The misrepresented minority: New insights on Asian Americans students and Pacific Islanders, and their implications for higher education.* Sterling, VA: Stylus.

Museus, S. D., Shiroma, K., Dizon, J. P., & Nguyen, P. C. (2013). *A Qualitative Examination of the Impact of Community Cultural Connections on Southeast Asian American College Student Success.* Paper presented at the 2013 Annual Meeting of the Association for the Study of Higher Education, St. Louis, MO.

Noddings, N. (1992). *The challenge to care in schools: An alternative approach to education.* New York, NY: Teachers College Press.

Noguera, P. A. (2004). Social capital and the education of immigrant students: Categories and generalizations. *Sociology of Education, 77*(2), 180–183.

Nou, L. (2006). A qualitative examination of psychosocial adjustment of Khmer refugees in three Massachusetts communities. *Journal of Southeast Asian American Education and Advancement, 1*(1), 1–31.

Office of Refugee Resettlement. (2005). *Annual Report to Congress.* Retrieved from http://www.acf.hhs.gov/programs/orr/resource/annual-orr-report-to -congress-2005

Pho, T.-L., Gerson, J. N., & Cowan, S. R. (Eds.). (2007). *Southeast Asian refugees and immigrants in the Mill City: Changing families, communities, institutions—Thirty years afterward.* Lebanon, NH: University Press of New England.

Rumbaut, R. G. (1996). A legacy of war: Refugees from Vietnam, Laos, and Cambodia. In S. Pedraza & R. Rumbaut (Eds.), *Origins and destinies: Immigration, race, and ethnicity in America* (pp. 315–333). Belmont, CA: Wadsworth.

Rumbaut, R. G. (2006). Vietnamese, Laotian and Cambodian Americans. In P. G. Min (Ed.), *Asian Americans: Contemporary trends and issues* (2nd ed., pp. 262–289). Thousand Oaks, CA: Sage.

Rumbaut, R. G., & Portes, A. (Eds.). (2001). *Ethnicities: Children of immigrants in America.* Berkeley, CA: University of California Press.

Rumberger, R. W. (1983). Dropping out of high school: The influence of race, sex, and family background. *American Educational Research Journal, 20*(2), 199–220.

Ryan, A. M. (2001). The peer group as a context for the development of young adolescent motivation and achievement. *Child Development, 72*(4), 1135–1150.

Sack, W., Kinzie, D., Angell, R., Clarke, G., & Ben, R. (1986). The psychiatric effects of massive trauma on Cambodian children I: The children. *Journal of American Academy of Child Psychiatry, 25*(3), 370–376.

Saito, L. (2002). *Ethnic identity and motivation: Socio-cultural factors in the educational achievement of Vietnamese American students.* New York, NY: LFB Scholarly.

SEARAC. (2010). Southeast Asian Americans at a glance: Statistics on Southeast Asians adapted from the American Community survey. Washington, DC: Southeast Asia Resource Action Center.

Smith-Hefner, N. J. (1990). Language and identity in the education of Boston-area Khmer. *Anthropology & Education Quarterly, 21*(3), 250–268.

Smith-Hefner, N. J. (1993). Education, gender, and generational conflict among Khmer refugees. *Anthropology & Education Quarterly, 24*(2), 135–158.

Somers, C. L., Owens, D., & Piliawsky, M. (2008). Individual and social factors related to urban African American adolescents' school performance. *High School Journal, 91*(3), 1–11.

Stanton-Salazar, R. D. (1997). A social capital framework for understanding the socialization of racial minority children and youths. *Harvard Educational Review, 67*(1), 1–40.

Stanton-Salazar, R. D. (2001). *Manufacturing hope and despair: The school and kin support networks of U.S.-Mexican youth.* New York, NY: Teachers College Press.

Stanton-Salazar, R. D. (2011). A social capital framework for the study of institutional agents and their role in the empowerment of low-status students and youth. *Youth & Society, 43*(3), 1066–1109.

Stanton-Salazar, R. D., & Dornbusch, S. M. (1995). Social capital and the reproduction of inequality: Information networks among Mexican-origin high school students. *Sociology of Education, 68*(2), 116–135.

Strauss, A., & Corbin, J. (1998). *Basics of qualitative research: Techniques and procedures for developing grounded theory.* Thousand Oaks, CA: Sage.

Suárez-Orozco, C., & Suárez-Orozco, M. M. (2001). *Children of immigration.* Cambridge, MA: Harvard University Press.

Te, B. (1997). *Unfamiliar partners: Asian parents and U.S. public schools.* Boston, MA: NCAS.

Takaki, R. (1989). *Strangers from a different shore: A history of Asian Americans.* Boston, MA: Little, Brown.

Tovar, E. (2015). The role of faculty, counselors, and support programs on Latino/a community college students' success and intent to persist. *Community College Review, 43*(1), 46–71.

Valenzuela, A. (1999). *Subtractive schooling: U.S.-Mexican youth and the politics of caring.* Albany, NY: State University of New York Press.

Wentzel, K. R., Battle, A., Russell, S. L., & Looney, L. B. (2010). Social supports from teachers and peers as predictors of academic and social motivation. *Contemporary Educational Psychology, 35*(3), 193–202.

Yan, W., & Lin, Q. (2005). Parent involvement and mathematics achievement: Contrast across racial and ethnic groups. *Journal of Educational Research, 99*(2), 116–127.

CHAPTER 13

THE HAI BÀ TRU'NG PROJECT

Engaging Undergraduates in Survey Research on Vietnamese (American) Women's Leadership Perspectives

Loan Dao and Linda Tran

In the area of leadership, Asian Americans face unique challenges. In terms of the historical biases that society holds against Asian Americans with regard to leadership, Ching and Agbayani (2012) explained:

> Many people mistakenly assume that AAPIs are either sufficiently represented or do not need representation. The issue of sufficient representation rests on whether issues of parity and equity should be applied to AAPIs. From an affirmative action viewpoint, some might argue that because AAPIs are over-represented in college student enrollment, there is no need to recruit them for visible leadership positions. As a result of this incorrect assumption, many institutions have purposely not established diversity agendas that embrace and target the hiring and advancement of AAPIs. (p. 176)

In reality, researchers have shown that AAPI in higher education are underrepresented in executive administrative positions and AAPI faculty

Focusing on the Underserved, pages 227–240
Copyright © 2017 by Information Age Publishing
227

members face a "glass ceiling" (Lee, 2005; Yan & Museus, 2013). Indeed, this scholarship shows that AAPI faculty members earn significantly lower salaries than their White peers and are less likely than White faculty to hold tenured appointments in U.S. colleges and universities. Thus, it is important for higher education researchers to advance knowledge of the challenges that AAPIs face in the area of leadership and how they might better support the development of more AAPI leaders.

The Hai Ba Trung, or the "Two Trung Sisters," are historic figures in Vietnamese anti-colonial history. As an allusion to these women leaders and our knowledge of anti-colonial histories from Southeast Asia, this project aims to contribute to current understandings of Asian American leadership through a survey of leadership development among Vietnamese and Vietnamese American female students at the University of Massachusetts Boston (UMB). The study introduces three main contributions to this area of research. First, the project targets an under-studied student population in the area of leadership development—those who self-identify as Vietnamese American or Vietnamese and as women. Second, the survey aims to provide spaces for students to reflect on and articulate their own definition and perceptions of leadership through their personal experiences. Third, the project sheds light on the linkages across student experiences at home, on campus, and in the classroom. We believe the cross-spatial experiences are particularly insightful in that the small body of research on Asian American students in higher education "clearly suggests that community and family influences do play a role in shaping Asian American students' educational trajectories... Indeed, evidence indicates that parental expectations of academic success, parental valuing of education and parental sacrifice and students' feelings of responsibility to repay their parents for these sacrifices are all associated with motivation and success among these students" (Museus, 2014, p. 116).

In the following sections, we describe our investigation of Vietnamese and Vietnamese American female student leadership. Initially, we provide an overview of the current project's methods. Then, we discuss the findings of the study. Finally, we propose implications for leadership educational programming and practice geared toward supporting the development of Vietnamese and Vietnamese American women college students.

METHODS

Site Setting

This study was implemented over a span of nine months during the 2012–2013 academic year at the University of Massachusetts, Boston (UMB). UMB is an urban public research university that has been a designated Asian American Native American Pacific Islander Serving Institution (AANAPISI) research university since 2008. In Fall 2014, 52% of enrolled undergraduate UMB students were U.S. students of color; Asian Americans comprised 13.6% of all full-time undergraduates (UMB Office of Institutional Research). As a commuter university that is adjacent to one of the largest Vietnamese enclaves in the country, UMB enrolls high-need Asian American students who typically come from local, low-income, immigrant families and under-resourced communities, and who face limited college access and low graduation rates. Two-thirds of Asian Americans living in the state are foreign-born, almost half are low-income, and less than half have obtained a Bachelor's degree (Lo, 2012). For these reasons, UMB served as a fertile site to access the targeted subject pool.

Leadership Development and Mentoring Through Research

I intentionally aimed to foster leadership development through engaging undergraduates in research by hiring two Research Assistants (RA) from the target population—first- and second-generation low-income Vietnamese women who grew up in the metropolitan Boston area. Because my topic focuses perspectives and opportunities for leadership at a site with a large, working-class population of Vietnamese and Vietnamese American undergraduate women, I felt it was both ethical and mutually beneficial to have RAs who were a part of this population. As a Vietnamese American female faculty member, I committed myself to guiding them through the research process as a means of offering exposure to social science research, building their repertoire of project design and management experience for their future goals, and mentoring them through regular meetings and conversations in relation to the research process. In our weekly meetings, we discussed our personal experiences as starting points to delve into research, and the process itself became an opportunity for the RAs to reflect on their own perceptions and experiences in addition to engaging in the scientific method. In turn, they offered invaluable insight to the design of the survey questions and outreach strategies. The team completed CITI training, literature reviews and was supervised through every stage of the research process. RA and co-author Linda Tran participated in the entire research process, and the second RA, Julie Tran, participated in survey design, outreach, and preliminary data analysis. At the end of her tenure as an RA, Julie also presented on her participation and a summary of our project at a campus-wide event in the presence of the university's provost. As the RAs went through the stages of the study, they were given increasing responsibilities as part of their leadership development, and through their outreach, they built self-confidence in public speaking and interaction such that they continued to assume leadership roles on campus after the study.

Study Design

The stages of the project included study and survey design and planning, outreach and recruitment of subjects, survey analysis and recommendations, and dissemination of results. We discussed each of these phases herein. The first stage of the current project involved meeting with scholars in the New England area who had conducted survey research on similar populations. These consultations revealed a need for basic demographic data of Vietnamese and Vietnamese American female college students because state agencies that would typically have the capacity to collect, organize, and disseminate this information either currently did not gather detailed disaggregated data on Southeast Asian American populations or these agencies did not currently have the capacity to organize and disseminate the information.

Two Vietnamese American female undergraduate RAs at the University of Massachusetts Boston, helped to design and pilot the survey, outreach and recruit to their peers as subjects, and assist in analyzing results. Because these students were included in the target population for the study, they were ideal candidates to assist with giving feedback about the survey design and recruitment. Throughout the study, the research team decided on major themes for the survey, helped brainstorm the areas of leadership that needed to be explored, co-constructed language, and assisted with interpretation of the survey questions.

Subject Sampling and Recruitment

University records approximately estimated that 1,200 students identified as Asian American, but this number was not disaggregated into specific ethnic groups. Although our personal knowledge of the student population evinces an overwhelming majority are of Vietnamese or Chinese descent, university privacy laws prohibited us from accessing lists of surnames or any other demographic data. Based on the office of enrollment's broader information about the university's ethnic and gender distribution, however, we confidently estimated that, at maximum, one-third of the students ($n = 400$) might identify as Vietnamese or Vietnamese American, and of that number, about half ($n = 200$) identified as female. From this estimate of student demographics, we concluded that a sampling of 132 surveys would give us an accurate view of student perceptions and experiences (95% confidence level with 5% margin of error).

The RAs created a plan to reach out to their peers, faculty, offices, and organizations on campus to recruit participants for the study. They devised an outreach and recruitment plan based on the snowball sampling method—"a technique for gathering research subjects through the identification of an initial subject who is used to provide the names of other actors" (Atkinson & Flint, 2004, p. 1044). Snowball sampling (Atkinson & Flint, 2001) is an accepted technique used by both qualitative and quantitative researchers to access difficult to reach target populations that are not readily accessible subject pools for studies or may be less willing to participate due to certain characteristics or behaviors in which they engage—drug use and prostitution are common examples of when snowball sampling would be useful (Biernacki & Waldorf, 1981). While this technique can only offer limited generalizations due the inherent sampling bias of the network of the subjects involved, the under-researched population of Vietnamese and Vietnamese American women qualify as a difficult to reach population in their reluctance and unfamiliarity with participation in studies such as this. The inability to access this population through university records or university-wide email or outreach methods also led us to use snowball sampling as our primary technique until we determined we reached saturation.

The RAs first solicited the participation of students in their own campus social networks, the clubs to which they belonged, and their classmates and personal friends. Next, the research team identified gaps in the subject pool, and the RAs conducted broad outreach via university list-serves offered through the office of student life, in the cafeteria and other popular campus sites where students congregated, computer labs, student union, and presentations in classrooms that the RAs determined had high enrollment of our target population.

The RAs created a tracking document of the individuals whom they had personally recruited. From that list, they were able to follow up periodically through the on-line survey system to remind the students to access or to complete the survey if they had not done so already. This method proved critical to ensuring the retention of subjects who had started the survey but did not complete it in one sitting. The research team met for 1–2 hours every week to reflect on our process, assure accountability of responsibilities, ensure adherence to Institutional Review Board (IRB) regulations, reinforce learning objectives, and develop the students' analytical skills. The RAs collected the response data, summarized the responses, and interpreted the responses. Through this process, the research team was able to conduct an ongoing analysis, triangulate our interpretations, and engage in additional mentoring and encouragement for the development of the RAs' undergraduate research skills.

DATA ANALYSIS

Our interpretation of the data focuses on descriptive analysis for several reasons. The small sample in our study and the inherent bias in snowball sampling technique limit our ability to make broad generalizations. Moreover, the target population is broadly understudied and rarely targeted in terms of (a) survey research and (b) topics of leadership. The dearth of previous scholarship compels this effort to gather and communicate this data as a baseline for future studies. Initially, we collected all responses through the on-line survey system, which removed any duplicate surveys based on open-ended responses and any surveys in which demographic responses did not meet subject criteria as Vietnamese or Vietnamese American, female, and enrolled student at UMB. To "clean" the data, we determined if there were surveys that demonstrated subject attrition (subjects dropped out) or surveys that had significant sections not completed. These responses were removed. We recruited a total of 136 study participants, of which 76 completed surveys were retained, giving us 9% margin of error with 95% confidence level. We used various methods to analyze data. First, we filtered for household income, year in school, and identification as Vietnamese or Vietnamese American, for which we found few differences. We then examined the data as frequency tables, and identified questions that were related in sequence to conduct cross-tabulations as a means of comparing responses. The demographic differences and comparative responses are outlined below, and the results discussed herein focus on the population of 76 who completed the survey.

FINDINGS

There were five main categories of questions in the survey. We began with demographic questions that included immigration history, socio-economic status (SES), household size and members, family educational background, and student profile information (e.g., year in school and major). The second category of questions asked students how they define leadership. We first asked them to recall a leader in their minds, describe attributes of the leader through open-ended and multiple-choice questions, and define the word "leader" in an open-ended question. The third category asked students to gauge their perceptions of leadership in society along ascribed identities of gender, race, and nationality. Ranking questions asked them about societal, faculty, and student perceptions of leadership based on the intersection of these three identities. The participants were also asked to rate how they believed other students, faculty, and staff on campus viewed them in terms of their leadership qualities and capabilities.

Fourth, participants were asked to identify leadership opportunities they have had on campus, in the classroom, and in the Vietnamese American communities in Greater Boston. Finally, the students were asked to offer their opinions about what was needed on campus and recommendations for improved leadership opportunities and development for Vietnamese and female students on campus.

Demographic Profile

The survey participants generally fit into the overall demographic profile of the university. The majority of participants were undergraduates in their second, third, or fourth year at UMass Boston and ranged from 19–25 years of age. Approximately 75% of students lived with four or more people in their household, with one or more persons 10 years older than the subject. Approximately 57% were second-generation immigrants. Thirty-five percent of first-generation respondents lived in Viet Nam between 1–7 years prior to migrating to the United States. These participants mostly arrived between the ages of 6–17 years, after 2001 (53.5%). However, 72% of all respondents stated that they were enrolled in an English as a Second Language (ESL) program at some point in their K–12 educational experience in the United States. The overwhelming majority (over 66%) reported that they were fluent in speaking, reading, and writing English. Thirty percent of participants reported that they were fluent in spoken Vietnamese, while 44% felt they had difficulty with reading and writing Vietnamese.

The majority of students estimated their household income to be between $10,000–$25,000 (36%) or $26,000–$40,000 (32%), which is consistent with the general demographic profile of UMB students. When asked about the educational levels of parents, just over 47% of students responded that their parents had a high school degree, and 22.5% reported that one or more parents had a bachelor's degree, with the remainder having less than a high school degree. When asked about the people in their household, 27.1% reported that household members held a high school degree, while 51% said someone in their household held a bachelor's degree. For both parents and household, very few students reported these primary relations having a professional or graduate degree (4% and 8%, respectively). The remainder had less than a high school degree. Given that the majority of students said they lived with immediate family members, the data suggest that the respondents have one or more siblings who have attended a university, offering them the potential of some college guidance and mentorship.

Defining Leadership

The second section of questions asked students to think about leadership. Our goal was for students to develop their own definition of leadership. Recognizing that leadership is a relatively abstract concept that students do not often consider in their daily lives, we first asked students to name someone they consider a "leader." The responses included popular, historical, and political leaders, such as musical artist Alicia Keys, politicians Hillary Clinton and Barack Obama, and Nguyen Van Thai, a political figure in early Vietnamese history. Surprisingly, a large percentage of people identified their mother or adult female relative (52%). About 52% of the responses identified a male and 47% identified a female leader, while 1% identified a public figure (politician or pop star). Among respondents, 56% identified a Vietnamese leader. Most leaders were still alive and living in the United States.

We created open-ended questions asking participants to define leadership qualities in their own words. The most frequently used adjectives by survey respondents to describe a leader were passionate, intelligent, brave, responsible, perseveres, compassionate, caring, independent, acts as a role model, good listener, hard-working, inspiring, good speaker, outspoken, charismatic. The list represents a description of what the students view leadership to encompass, and as we see in subsequent sections, these characteristics influence their gendered internal and social perceptions of "leadership" and their own perceptions of their leadership capacity.

Perceptions of Leadership

We wanted a better understanding of the perceptions and experiences of leadership of our participants. In discussing leadership development, leading scholars prioritized the need to incorporate the value and influence of one's cultural practices and beliefs:

> Cultural factors can influence the way Asian American students display leadership as well as how they are perceived as leaders. Redefining leadership and devising inclusive leadership development programs can help to empower Asian American students and encourage them to become more involved on campus... Cultural values can affect the way that Asian American express leadership as well as how Asian Americans are perceived as leaders... For example, assertiveness and decisiveness are generally viewed as positive traits for effective leadership, although Asian Americans have been found to be less assertive in comparison to whites. (Liang, Lee, & Ting, 2002, pp. 81–82)

We discerned that the Vietnamese and Vietnamese American female students at UMB tended to espouse socially conforming notions of leadership based on socially dominant perceptions of race, gender, and nationality.

The first question in this section asked students, "Who are better leaders?" to which 57% replied "men." Yet, the very next question asked who possessed the qualities of leadership they thought were important, which they reported in the previous section, and 53% replied "women." The next three questions were ranking questions whereby students were asked to rank leadership and studiousness based on gender, race, and nationality. The responses were calculated based on the averaged sum of numbers assigned to each identity by the respondents, with one ($n = 1$) being the highest ranking. The highest ranked answer received the lowest score, or rating average. The first ranking questions asked students how people in the United States would rank leadership, comparing Vietnamese to Vietnamese American and men to women. Vietnamese American men were seen to be most viable leaders in American society (1.77), followed by Vietnamese American women (2.13), with Vietnamese men third (2.81) and Vietnamese women ranking last (3.29). When students were asked the same question with more choices added to include Black and White options, White American men scored significantly higher (more than 1.0) than any other group (1.53), with White American women achieving the highest second-place ranking. From highest to lowest, students ranked-ordered African American men, African American women, Vietnamese American men, Vietnamese American women, Vietnamese men, and finally Vietnamese women.

Interestingly, the results were almost reverse for the next question, which asked students to rank the same groups based on who "teachers think are better students." While the margins between responses for this questions were much closer, Vietnamese American women ranked highest (2.81), with Vietnamese women ranking second (3.52), and White American women ranking third (3.73). Instead of following the gender differential, however, the respondents then ranked White American men (4.09), Vietnamese American men (4.27), and Vietnamese men (4.94) in that order. African American women (6.02) and African American men (6.63) were ranked lowest in how students thought teachers viewed students. The responses suggest that there is a perception of leadership as a male dominant social position compared to women, but among same-sex comparisons, race (White) and nationality (American) were seen as superior. However, it is important to note that it is unclear whether students were actually reflecting on their observations in the classroom or whether they were projecting their own biases onto teachers and their classroom experiences.

Experiences With Leadership

While students' perceptions of leadership might be contradictory in their understanding and internalization of dominant narratives of leadership, we also wanted to document how they actually experience leadership in their daily lives.

The questions in this sub-section asked students their experiences of leadership within their families. When asked who they thought the leader was in their family, 51% identified their mothers, 28% said their fathers, and 13% viewed themselves as head of the household. For a clearer understanding of how they came to this conclusion, we asked a multiple-response question about what responsibilities this "leader" had in the family. Exactly 93% said the person had financial responsibilities, 84% specifically identified employment as the defining responsibility, 79% said the person made "major decisions" in the family, and 67% reported childcare as the major responsibility of household leaders.

When participants were asked about their examples of household leadership, 78% said they included housecleaning, while employment and coordinating social activities both came in second at 46%. The results suggest that many of the subjects did not have opportunities or were not seen as leaders within their household to date, and yet they tended to be responsible for gendered roles within the kind of household responsibilities they have in addition to working and going to school. Moreover, the majority viewed their mothers as the head of household whose responsibilities included having a job, maintaining the financial responsibilities in the house (such as paying the bills), making major decisions, as well as caring for children.

In the classroom, the most common response was that they "sometimes" feel like other students (50%) and teachers (32.4%) view them as leaders. However, when asked the circumstances of the situations when they were seen as leaders or recognized as such by the faculty, by indicators such as calling on them to talk, or openly recognizing or designating them as leaders in class, 49.2% of these students reported this at a significantly higher rate in classes that (a) tend toward small group projects and activities or lab teams, and (b) had bearing on their major (health science or math courses) and Asian American Studies courses. In small group situations, 52.3% stated that they assumed leadership positions. Finally, students stated that developing leadership in the classroom positively affected their success in school (61.2%), motivation to stay in school (53%), potential career opportunities (71.6%), and their potential leadership opportunities within their communities (59.7%). These findings encourage a need for a conscious effort to integrate inclusive leadership pedagogies in the classroom, as research has found that when female leadership was institutionalized, female leaders had as much influence over participants as did male leaders with comparable ability when female leadership was not institutionalized (Lucas, 2003; Lucas & Baxter, 2012).

As discussed previously, students identify mentorship as a highly influential way in which their work is recognized and their leadership skills are developed beyond the space of the classroom. Yet, over 60% of respondents said they did not have a mentor on campus but desired one. Of the respondents who did identify a mentor, 37.5% identified the person as a faculty member, while 25% said the mentor was a campus staff person. Only 8% sought mentorship from a peer, and 12.5% saw a more advanced level student as a mentor. The data suggest that students tend to have less interaction and support from peers, and particularly more advanced peers. This result may very well be correlated with the commuter-based culture of the student population at UMB. Finally, respondents perceived mentorship as individualized guidance from a faculty or staff member, and the majority desire it but do not have access to such mentorship.

Students who reported receiving mentorship were asked what they felt could be improved in the mentoring relationship. The vast majority (57%) desired more time with their mentors, while an almost equal number wanted more career guidance. Many respondents felt that one way in which these challenges could be addressed is for them to have opportunities to work for faculty and staff on campus. Twenty-two percent reported having employment on campus, and 77% reported having no access to research opportunities. Being involved in a faculty member's research project tends to be the most common way for students to gain individualized mentorship and guidance from faculty members. Students report that they feel leadership opportunities on campus significantly raise their desire to be involved in their community and their retention at school. We asked the question, "What do you feel the university needs to do to create more leadership opportunities for you or other Vietnamese and Vietnamese American students on this campus?" and responses show how students felt they were perceived racially or ethnically:

- *Respondent 1:* Open courses for cultural sensitivity, section for racism, mediation, be understanding and listening to individual idea and circumstances, offer job opportunities on campus, raise Vietnamese culture month, connect Vietnamese and Vietnamese American with local community organizations.
- *Respondent 2:* Have frequent group meeting among Vietnamese student where we can discuss about above issues and develop coping strategy. I think that will help us to overcome the self-conscious[ness] of being minority and ESL status.
- *Respondent 3:* It's not that there are not enough leadership opportunities for Vietnamese/Vietnamese American students on campus,

but rather there is not a cohesive/collective vision for the Vietnamese community among the Vietnamese student body. There are also not enough examples of role models/leadership to draw from.

- *Respondent 4:* Vietnamese and Vietnamese American students often feel like those who are in leadership positions are those that are inclined to work in the management or in politics. However, the definition of leadership can be based on qualities that an individual has, but they do not realize they can be a leader themselves.

The emphasis of the racial and ethnic prioritization in these responses—the analysis of the situation based on self and public perceptions, and recommendations—directly contradict previous questions where respondents were asked if their race, ethnicity, or gender affected their leadership opportunities and potential on and off campus. In all responses, over 70% replied these identifying factors had "no effect." The contradiction here, as well as in the previous ranking questions about perceptions of leadership, demonstrate the potential that students do experience and comprehend racial, ethnic, and gender differences, during their educational tenure, but are possibly under-reporting their perceived effects and instead engage in "coping" strategies that leave them to seek support and opportunities through non-institutional channels. Significantly, these data also show a major shortcoming in institutional opportunities that potentially provide reciprocal benefits for the students' ethnic communities and their perceived capacity at work.

RECOMMENDATIONS

This study suggests some major opportunities for our commuter-based, working class institution that has a large population of first generation immigrant and first generation college students. We offer the following recommendations, with the emphasis that "while a focus on leadership training may have a significant impact on individual success, it will have a limited impact on organizational change unless non-AAPI leaders, policymakers, institution, and national associations help establish and promote inclusive policies and attitudes" (Ching & Agbayani, 2012, p. 174).

- Universities can support student leadership by offering continuing pedagogical training and education to faculty on ways to create curricula that encourage critical thinking and leadership for Vietnamese American women and other diverse student populations.
- Individualized faculty mentoring is one important and impactful vehicle for fostering leadership development among Vietnamese

American women on campus. One effective way to encourage these relationships is undergraduate research assistants for faculty, so that they can advance their research agenda while mentoring students. Moreover, the extent to which faculty can identify research projects that privilege the skills and knowledge of their students about their local or ethnic communities potentially serve an additional benefit for these communities in both the short and long term.

- Cascading mentorship programs that connect more senior students with incoming students are recommended. Such programs serve the dualistic goal of offering leadership opportunities and on-campus employment to senior students and providing role models and peer-to-peer guidance to their younger peers. The bonds that come from cascading mentorship models allow for an increased sense of belonging and community on campus, which is often missing on commuter campuses.

- These kinds of leadership and mentoring models can also be replicated at the departmental level to meet specific career goals, such as STEM-oriented recruitment that highlights the specific contribution of women and minorities in these fields. As students have indicated in responses above, the desire to create a sense of community through support, encouragement, and opportunity offer them invaluable experiences that potentially lead to retention, higher achievement, and long-term community engagement.

REFERENCES

Atkinson, R., & Flint, J. (2001). Accessing hidden and hard-to-reach populations: Snowball research strategies. *Social Research Update, 33*(1), 1–4.

Atkinson, R., & Flint, J. (2004). Snowball sampling. In M. S. Lewis-Beck, A. Bryman, & T. Futing Liao (Eds.), The SAGE *encyclopedia of social science research methods* (Vol. 3, pp. 1043–1044). Thousand Oaks, CA: SAGE.

Biernacki, P., & Waldorf, D. (1981). Snowball sampling: Problems and techniques of chain referral sampling. *Sociological Methods & Research, 10*(2), 141–163.

Ching, D., & Agbayani, A. (2012). *Asian Americans and Pacific Islanders in higher education: Research and perspectives on identity, leadership, and success.* Washington, DC: National Association of Student Personnel Administrators.

Lee, S. (2005). *Up against whiteness: Race, school and immigrant youth.* New York: Teachers College Press.

Liang, C. T. H., Lee, S., & Ting, M. P. (2002). Developing Asian American leaders. *New Directions for Student Services, 97,* 81–90.

Lo, S. (2012). *Asian Americans in Massachusetts: A Census Profile.* Boston, MA: Institute for Asian American Studies.

Lucas, J. W. (2003). Status processes and the institutionalization of women as leaders. *American Sociological Review, 68*(3), 464–480.

Lucas, J. W., & Baxter, A. R. (2012). Power, influence, and diversity in organizations. *The ANNALS of the American Academy of Political and Social Science, 639*(1), 49–70.

Museus, S. D. (2014). *Asian American students in higher education.* New York, NY: Routledge.

Yan, W. & Museus, S.D. (2013). Asian American and Pacific Islander faculty and the glass ceiling in higher education. In S. D. Museus, D. C. Maramba, & R. T. Teranishi (Eds.), *The misrepresented minority: New insights on Asian Americans and Pacific Islanders, and the implications for higher education.* Sterling, VA: Stylus.

CHAPTER 14

CONCLUSION

Scholarship, Policy, and Praxis Recommendations for Institutional Change

Amefil Agbayani and Doris Ching

In 1993, more than two decades ago, we presented results of our survey of Asian American and Pacific Islander (AAPI) student affairs professionals at the National Association for Student Personnel Administrators (NASPA) Conference in Boston. The presentation, *Asian and Pacific Americans in Higher Education*, included problems and recommendations identified by Asian Pacific Americans[1] (APA) student affairs professionals in doctoral degree granting institutions (Agbayani & Ching, 1993). The survey respondents were predominantly U.S.-born Chinese American and Japanese American women in mid-level student affairs positions who cited lack of resources, role models, mentors, and support, resulting in *glass ceiling* and limited career mobility. A majority of respondents viewed AAPIs as non-assertive and not politically well organized, which inhibited a strong unified voice and capacity to effect change and challenge stereotypes such as the model minority myth or assumption that all AAPIs achieve universal and unparalleled success.

Focusing on the Underserved, pages 241–254
Copyright © 2017 by Information Age Publishing
All rights of reproduction in any form reserved.

The respondents also reported that the major campus adversities AAPI students faced were prejudice and stereotypes, lack of organization and visibility, low levels of campus involvement, and lack of representation in the curriculum despite the growing AAPI student population. APA participants believed institutions were more attentive to issues of other groups of color. The actions suggested by the respondents to improve campus climate and diversity included training and programs on cultural sensitivity and diverse cultures, building coalitions among minority and other diversity groups, making the curriculum more inclusive of diverse groups and perspectives, hiring faculty and staff who reflect students' ethnic backgrounds, and demanding resources and leadership at all levels of the institution to support diversity efforts.

While the topic and participants of the 1993 study differed from the current issues and student populations presented in this book, the concerns identified in 1993 are similar and overlap with the issues currently faced by AAPIs. On one hand, it is problematic that the issues identified in 1993 continue to persist and challenge AAPI students, staff, and faculty in 2016. On the other hand, there is a sign of hope for improved campus support of AAPI students. In 1993, there were 98 APA members within NASPA, the largest student affairs professional association across the nation, compared to 831 AAPI members today. The significant gain in AAPI members of NASPA is a positive indication of the substantial growth of AAPI student affairs professionals in higher education on U.S. campuses over two decades, and a clear signal that AAPI staff resources on college campuses have increased. It is this hope upon which the authors of chapters in this book present their recommendations for change in higher education policy and practice.

NEW CONTEXT AND UNCHANGED STATUS OF ASIAN AMERICANS AND PACIFIC ISLANDERS

We began this chapter with a reference to our 1993 research on AAPI in higher education. In this section, we offer data and recommendations that have changed or remained the same over two decades since our 1993 research and proffer actions for developing and implementing policies and programs to transform the culture of campuses toward greater awareness and support of AAPIs.

In the last two decades, major worldwide changes and significant national developments have occurred, including the rapid expansion of the use of technology, shifting global power relations with notable stronger roles of China and India, growing concerns for environmental sustainability, an aging and increasingly non-White domestic population, challenges to civil rights laws, and growing and alarming income inequalities. During this period, intentional changes were made in the collection of U.S. census racial and ethnic data, including the inclusion of the option to choose more than one race or ethnicity, substantially more choices of ethnic groups and categories, and the separation of Native Hawaiʻians and Pacific Islanders from Asian Americans as two distinct racial groups. As a result, the nation now has the capacity to identify, analyze, and better understand individuals from mixed heritage, undocumented status, and previously invisible AAPI communities (e.g., Micronesian and Burmese Americans).

Despite these unprecedented global and national changes, it is striking that important AAPI concerns that we identified decades ago persist today. Even after more than two decades of debate, issues of data aggregation and disaggregation, affirmative action policies, and the relative focus of accountability on individuals and the environment continue to be contentious.

The following points from our 1993 study on AAPIs in higher education continue to be relevant in 2015 and provide evidence that AAPI data and status remain relatively unchanged (Agbayani & Ching, 1993):

- The fastest growing minority group in the United States today is Asian and Pacific Americans.
- Asian and Pacific American immigrants form a sizeable population of low-wage workers. Southeast Asian refugees, originally from Cambodia, Laos, and Vietnam and minority populations such as the Hmong from Laos, comprise the majority of Asians living below the poverty level in the United States.
- The struggles by the majority of Asian and Pacific Americans seeking access to basic general education are not widely reported.
- The majority of APA students are not enrolled in four-year institutions but are in two-year community colleges.
- Asian and Pacific Americans continue to have the lowest tenure rate of all populations.
- Gains of Asian and Pacific Americans, whose principal activity is administrative and who hold titles of academic department chairperson or the equivalent and above in higher education administration, constitute only 1% of the executive and managerial positions in the nation's colleges and universities.

ONGOING DISCUSSION ON ASIAN AMERICAN AND PACIFIC ISLANDER PANETHNIC CATEGORIES AND DISAGGREGATED DATA

A continuing debate involves the appropriate use of pan-ethnic categories and specific disaggregated ethnic categories in research, policy, and practice. In 2012, we wrote:

244 A. AGBAYANI and D. CHING

Although there are good reasons to use a pan-ethnic category (e.g., AAPI), it is inaccurate to consider this category as homogeneous.... The AAPI category raises two competing challenges for the AAPI community, researchers, media, and policymakers. Some see the need for a visible and effective single group in a multiethnic and multiracial community and nation, while others identify with only one ethnic group or country of origin. Some individuals and groups resent being part of a larger group that includes historical enemies or groups that are considered privileged. Others see the need to disaggregate information for more accuracy and to understand and respond to the many differences of the subgroups.... The heterogeneity of groups compels disaggregating the AAPI data while simultaneously retaining a pan-Asian category (e.g., AAPI). (Ching & Agbayani, 2012, xxiv–xxvi)

Although most researchers who use aggregated and disaggregated data acknowledge and recommend nuanced and specific programs and policies to address complex issues, this issue persistently creates challenges in the development and implementation of recommendations to serve the fastest growing and highly diverse AAPI community.

The extreme range of diversity in economic and educational status among AAPIs makes it difficult to develop, advocate, and implement policies. Asian Indians, Chinese, Japanese, and Filipinos are significantly better off financially than the general U.S. population. Yet, most AAPI groups, including the Hmong, Native Hawai'ians, Micronesians, Laotians, and Cambodians, are significantly worse off than the U.S. population and other AAPI groups. The three largest Asian American groups combined—Chinese (22%), Filipino (19%), and Asian Indian (16%) Americans—represent 57% of the Asian American community. These three populations are the largest groups with higher incomes and educational status that drive the average AAPI status significantly above the total U.S. population. The following indicators show the wide disparity among Asian American groups in comparison with the total U.S. population (White House Initiative on Asian Americans and Pacific Islanders, 2012).

- Living in poverty: Total U.S. (13.2%); AAPI (11.8%); Hmong (27.4%); Filipino (7.1%).
- Unemployed: Total U.S. (4.2%); AAPI (3.5%); Micronesians (10.0%); Chinese (3.9%).
- Did not graduate from high school: Total U.S. (15.0%); AAPI (14.4%); Cambodian (35.2%); Japanese (4.8%).
- High school degree only: Total U.S. (28.5%); AAPI (16.3%); Native Hawai'ians (40.0%); Asian Indian (8.8%).
- Graduate or professional degree: Total U.S. (10.2%); AAPI (19.5%); Asian Indian (39.7%); Laotian (3.0%).

Although this book intentionally focuses on AAPI groups that are underserved, disadvantaged, and generally not included in any significant way by educational researchers, we cannot ignore the data and impact of the large advantaged AAPI subgroups. In fact, more research may be needed on the power and educational success of Chinese Americans and Asian Indians and the role of their powerful home countries and prominent leaders—who are among the most influential world leaders—and their role in policy debates on affirmative action and other profound issues. The range of socio-economic and educational status within the AAPI category makes it difficult, but not impossible, to make national or institutional policy recommendations on issues such as college affirmative action.

CONTINUING DEBATE ON AFFIRMATIVE ACTION

There is a continuing and contentious debate on the need for a national policy on affirmative action and its impact on some AAPI subgroups in higher education and employment. AAPIs are clearly divided on the matter of affirmative action. In the case of *Fisher v. University of Texas at Austin*, the Supreme Court in 2013 reaffirmed a compelling interest in higher education diversity. We joined California State Polytechnic University President Emeritus Dr. Bob Suzuki and other academic leaders supporting the amicus brief filed by the Asian American Legal Defense and Education Fund (ALDEF) before the Supreme Court supporting the University of Texas–Austin. ALDEF provided reasons and evidence that effectively countered Fisher and the claims of the National Education Foundation "80–20" that Asian Americans are harmed by affirmative action and that the majority of Asian Americans oppose affirmative action (Asian American Legal Defense and Education, 2014). In 2015, sixty Asian American groups filed a discrimination claim that Harvard University discriminated against a high performing Asian American applicant. In response, more than 135 AAPI groups reaffirmed their support of affirmative action:

> Affirmative Action...does not constitute quotas, discrimination, or bias against Asian Americans. Currently, Affirmative Action at universities consists of race-sensitive holistic admissions policies. These policies promote equal opportunity in a society where racism still exists and racial barriers continue to limit educational opportunities unfairly for students of color. (Asian American Civil Rights, 2015, May)

RESEARCH HAS POTENTIAL TO INFLUENCE CHANGE IN HIGHER EDUCATION FOR ASIAN AMERICAN AND PACIFIC ISLANDERS

In our 1993 study, the comments of the AAPI student affairs professionals who responded to the study continue to persist in 2015. Their counteractive feelings and attitudes—of both alienation and sense of community with other minorities, a call to action yet resignation that little positive change can be expected, a feeling that issues facing APAs cannot be ignored yet recognition that APA issues are not seen as primary on their campus—remain relevant today. One respondent expressed frustration that it is difficult to make changes or that much can be done: "Ignorance is a hard thing to get rid of." Another wrote, "quit talking about it and just do it" (Agbayani & Ching, 1993, p. 13).

In 2012, we wrote:

> We . . . call for higher visibility and a stronger voice for AAPIs, encouraging more research and increasing AAPI representation and leadership in higher education . . . But, the changes will only be accomplished as a result of efforts to make the characteristics, status, and aspirations of AAPIs and the AAPI subgroups visible by developing more AAPI leaders and disseminating more research that will enable our voices to be heard. (Ching & Agbayani, 2012, pp. 343–344)

We are grateful to the chapter authors in this book for their passionate and thoughtful views on policy and program development and implementation. Their perspectives, research findings and recommendations reinforce our own experiences and reinforce the importance of research and leadership for effecting institutional transformation.

As AAPI executives, researchers, and student advocates in higher education, we have intentionally sought changes over the decades, primarily in our home state of Hawai'i and our home institution of the University of Hawai'i (UH). In retrospect, however, we reflect that we have neither systematically analyzed our successes or failures nor shared recommendations on strategies to influence policy development and implementation, impact institutional practice, and actively engage in action research that focus on the nexus of policy, research, and practice. We are mindful that we now have the opportunity to provide practical suggestions on how to implement recommendations to improve the status of AAPIs in higher education that were omitted in our 1993 study and the chapter in our edited book published in 2012.

*We recommend increasing research productivity on AAPIs and more
AAPI researchers.*

A review of a decade of articles published by five of the major journals
in higher education showed only 1% included Asian Americans and fewer
included Pacific Islanders (Museus, 2009). Recently, one of us declined an
invitation to endorse a newly-updated *handbook for student affairs* that had
neither representation nor mention of AAPI authors, issues, or research,
noting that a handbook for student affairs with no recognition that AAPIs
are a major part of higher education, is both incomplete and outdated. We
are not advocating that research on AAPI topics be conducted only by AAPI
researchers, but we are advocating for more AAPI graduate students and
faculty be trained and hired at universities and research institutes. We believe that more AAPI researchers engaged in research on AAPIs in higher
education is a positive contribution to scholarship and policy because their
perspectives are valuable.

*We recommend that research reports are disseminated for use
by non-academic audiences, such as AAPI community groups; blogs
and videos; public media in English and non-English languages;
testimonies and briefs; grant proposals.*

While academicians are trained and rewarded for scholarly articles,
books, and conference presentations to advance knowledge and address
critical issues in methodology and theory, information derived from the research must be translated to concepts that are understood by policymakers
and practitioners who influence changes on university campuses. Through
brief summaries of their research findings for the media, state legislator,
amicus briefs in court cases, academicians can affect institutional policies
and budget decisions. As an example, while research on undocumented
students contributes to knowledge, it is of true value when it convinces policy makers, administrators, and university professionals to develop policies
and programs that address the needs and concerns of undocumented AAPI
students. In 2013, the University of Hawai'i Board of Regents approved a
policy to waive the non-resident tuition rate for undocumented students,
enabling undocumented students to attend UH at more affordable resident tuition rates. The Regents' decision was influenced by our data that
they could understand and were interested in—mainly the projection that
such an action would result in far fewer undocumented students and significantly lower loss of tuition revenue than they had previously estimated. The
data presented to the Regents were reinforced by local and national studies
of other campuses and interviews with undocumented students, which we
arranged, who articulated their needs and aspirations. Through strategic
data presentation, such as a brief FAQ and interviews with undocumented

students, the Regents gained fuller understanding of the issues resulting in their approval of a policy to support undocumented students' access to UH.

Without sufficient research on AAPI students, grant writers are unable to vie successfully in competitive grants that would benefit AAPI students. Many private and government grants require proposals to include evidence of funding need and a strong evaluation component. An example of a grant that requires such evidence is the Fund for the Improvement of Postsecondary Education (FIPSE) First in the World (FITW) Program. FITW awards multimillion dollar grants

> to support the development, replication, and dissemination of innovative solutions and evidence for what works in addressing persistent and widespread challenges in postsecondary education for students who are at risk for not persisting in and completing postsecondary programs...The focus of the FITW program is to build evidence for what works in postsecondary education by testing effectiveness of these strategies in improving student persistence and completion outcomes. (Department of Education, 2015, p. 27057)

We recommend institutional and other data be reviewed and revised periodically for accuracy and relevance.

We illustrate this recommendation with our experience adding a new item to the University of Hawai'i (UH) student application form. In collaboration with institutional researchers and the Native Hawai'ian faculty and students at UH, we added one question to the collection of institutional data that resulted in highly positive outcomes. The National Center for Education Statistics (NCES), the primary source for collecting and analyzing Integrated Postsecondary Education Data System (IPEDS) used by government and higher education institutions, including UH, had one category for Hawai'ians (and no options for part-Hawai'ians). This omission consistently resulted in an under-count of Native Hawai'ian students, differed from local understanding of the definition of Hawai'ian/part Hawai'ian, and placed UH–Mānoa at a disadvantage from applying for grants, such as the Title III Native Hawai'ian Higher Education grant. With consent of the UH institutional research office and support from Native Hawai'ian faculty and students, we recommended a creative solution by asserting two questions on the application: (a) no change in the IPEDS question, and (b) addition of a new question, "Are any of your ancestors Native Hawai'ians?" The responses to this new question dramatically increased the number of Native Hawai'ian students at UH–Mānoa, which enabled the campus to attain an accurate account of our student population and meet the minimum percentage to qualify for millions of dollars to support educational programs for Native Hawai'ians. The IPEDS ethnic and racial categories were also used for other information requests and national comparisons. Data and research on the status of Native Hawai'ians also contributed to our testimonies in support of legislation to provide tuition waivers worth millions of scholarship dollars for Hawai'i-resident Native Hawai'ian students.

We recommend increasing communication among researchers, policy makers, and practitioners.

Chapter 1 of this book listed more than a dozen "national networks of advocacy, representation, and support based on visions of AAPI educational equity since the 1970s." Among those listed are the National Commission on Asian American and Pacific Islander Research in Education (CARE) founded in 2008 and Asian Pacific Islander American Association of Colleges and Universities (APIACU) founded in 2011—both of which explicitly seek to close the gap among researchers, policy makers, and practitioners. As AAPI educators, we have been directly associated with one of the earliest AAPI research and advocacy association—the National Association for Asian Pacific American Educators (NAAPE) founded in 1977—and one of the newest associations, the Asian American and Pacific Islander Research Coalition (ARC) founded in 2012. A concerted effort to bridge this communication gap was made by the Association for the Study of Higher Education (ASHE), which held its 2015 annual meeting in Washington, DC with a conference theme, *Weaving Scholarship and Policy Making.* Our panel on *Advancing the College Completion Agenda Through Policy-Relevant Research on Asian Americans and Pacific Islanders* included an AAPI policy maker, higher education administrator, researcher, and faculty member. This conference encouraged discussions on "how current scholarship may inform today's policy making and practice and, on the other hand, how policy making may inform scholarship and practice" (Association for the Study of Higher Education, 2014, p. 4). In addition, we actively supported faculty to offer a new undergraduate course *Diversity in Higher Education* through the Ethnic Studies department at UH–Mānoa that brought together student affairs professionals, community leaders, and researchers.

We recommend more research on higher education AAPI talent, leadership styles, and environmental context.

The lack of research and information on AAPIs in the general literature on higher education is a disservice to AAPI groups. A recent 200-page book on leadership, published in 2013 by a large major national association, featured chapters on various topics on leadership and leadership styles by an array of higher education administrators. Yet, not one chapter included diversity issues or AAPI students, and not one author was AAPI. Leadership studies and training often focus on characteristics and behaviors of leaders and demand that individuals change and adapt, rather than on how the environment needs to change for greater productivity and results. Having served successfully as educational administrators, we believe that research on AAPI leadership styles and environmental factors can add to a deeper understanding of leadership, talent development, and institutional effectiveness. There is a growing literature on multicultural mentoring that may be relevant to AAPI researchers and emerging leaders (Turner and Gonzales, 2014).

We recommend higher recognition of effective AAPI talent and diversify higher education leadership with more AAPIs at top executive posts.

There has been no significant change in the number of AAPI University presidents in two decades, despite increases in AAPI college graduates and faculty. AAPIs are also underrepresented in other sectors of society, even in areas with large numbers of AAPI professionals. A recent study of five Silicon Valley companies—Google, Yahoo, Intel, Hewlett-Packard, and LinkedIn—showed a huge imbalance between Asian American managerial positions (14%) and Asian American professional staff (27%), compared to White management (80%) and White professional staff (62%). Asian American women leaders in these companies were even more underrepresented. The unfortunate explanation for the imbalance by a Chinese American blamed the victim,

> Many Asians are taught to be deferential and cling to and believe that doing a good job will automatically be rewarded . . . There are cultural norms and attitudes that help get Asians to a certain level of success, but then work against them and hold them back from reaching a higher rank. (Liedtke, 2015)

In a 2005 book, *Breaking the Bamboo Ceiling*, trainer and author Jane Hyun urged Asian Americans to adapt and change their behavior in order to be promoted to a leadership position. Hyun later acknowledged that she "put a lot of the onus" on Asian Americans to manage differences between cultural styles and became later convinced that the onus should also be on managers and corporations to understand that there is more than one way to be an effective leader (Mundy, 2014). In a later co-authored book, *Flex: The New Playbook for Managing Across Differences*, Hyun discusses the need to develop *fluent leaders* who are comfortable working with different genders and cultures.

We recommend that AAPI researchers and faculty employ valuable leadership training.

Most leadership and management seminars lack AAPI expertise and participants. A notable exception is the Leadership Development Program in Higher Education (LDPHE) training, offered by Leadership Education for Asian Pacifics, Inc. (LEAP) designed "to prepare and motivate more AAPIs to aspire to leadership positions in higher education."

Since 1995, hundreds of AAPI faculty and higher education faculty and administrators have participated in these workshops. Over the past two decades, we have actively supported LEAP and LDPHE as board members, faculty, and sponsors of our UH mid-level and senior AAPI faculty and staff to participate in the training. While the appointments of AAPI to executive offices in higher education continues to be low, scores of LDPHE graduates have been tenured and successfully appointed to president, vice president, dean, and other college and university executive positions (Yamagata-Noji & Gee, 2012).

We recommend that AAPI researchers interact with and conduct research on relationships among AAPI communities and non-AAPI communities.

AAPI researchers and students can increase their effectiveness as leaders by working with individuals and groups who share similar goals to provide additional and mutually beneficial resources and perspectives. Forming alliances and working with policymakers from diverse ethnic or racial backgrounds can benefit all groups. As noted above, affirmative action is one issue opposed by a minority of AAPI communities that increases distrust of AAPIs among communities of color. As two of the few AAPI executives at the University of Hawai'i, our very first appointments to administrative positions were made by White male executives and policymakers, who continued to mentor and nurture us. Recently, non-Filipino administrators responded immediately to Filipino students and staff to offer an Ilokano language course for the first time at the University of Hawai'i–West Oahu, with a 20% Filipino student population. There are numerous anecdotal stories of multicultural relations, cooperation, and competition among AAPI groups and with other groups and more research on the topic is welcomed.

We recommend more collaboration and focus on scholarship–policy–practice nexus.

The introductory chapter of this book, *The State of Scholarship on AAPI in Education: Anti-Essentialism, Inequality, Context, and Relevance* identifies the crucial joint scholarship–policy–practice nexus as a critical collaboration in future research on AAPIs. The authors, citing crucial collaboration, "as we envision it, is a dialogical process of policymaking and program development undertaken by researchers, policymakers, educators, and activists working together," emphasize the importance of collaborative discussion, development, preparation, and pursuit of goals for research and policy recommendations to be implemented effectively and with relevance to AAPIs and institutions of higher education. We strongly urge more researchers to engage in critical collaborative research.

We recommend that more AAPI community leaders, faculty, staff, and students engage in governance and politics to influence policy.

Implementing recommendations to improve higher education and the status of AAPIs can be hampered or supported by community politics, appointed and elected government officials, and voters. Although there is increasing awareness of the importance of the AAPI community, AAPI faculty, researchers, and students are still underrepresented among voters, campaign workers, candidates, and elected officials. Asian American voters "will double to about 12 million in 2040, making them one of the fastest growing electorates over the next quarter century. This could be a game changer" (Ong & Ong, 2015). The AAPI community can become politically influential in select areas and future presidential elections. The report notes that Asian American voters will not only grow but will change, with increasing native born and multiracial Asian Americans.

In 2015, AAPIs are adequately represented at 6% among state governors—two Asian Indian Americans and one Japanese American. However, AAPIs are underrepresented in Congress—only 1% of the Senate and 2.3% of the House of Representatives. U.S. Senator Mazie Hirono, born in Japan and raised in Hawai'i, is the only AAPI in the 100-member U.S. Senate. Senator Hirono is seen not only as a senator from the state of Hawai'i, but a national leader and voice for AAPIs. She worked closely with AAPI leaders on a comprehensive immigration reform including amendments supporting undocumented persons, family reunification, and Filipino World War II veterans. Senator Hirono and other Hawai'i Congressional delegates advocate for Pacific Island migrants who are excluded from many governmental benefits because of their status.

There are positive outcomes for those who are politically active and participate in community projects and electoral politics. As private citizens, we have encouraged and supported our former AAPI and non-AAPI students and community leaders to seek political office by contributing to their campaigns, volunteering in campaigns, and sharing—even initiating—our views on issues. Over the years, as AAPI university administrators and private citizens, we have been supported by public leaders and contacted by leaders, including the late Congresswoman Patsy T. Mink (co-author of Title IX of the Higher Education Act) and scores of other public policymakers who sought our views on higher education, civil rights, and other issues. We continue to work on AAPI matters with U.S. Senator Hirono, who has from time-to-time contacted our offices to seek our views regarding AAPI undocumented students and educational grants. More recently, a former Asian American UH student leader was elected to the U.S. House of Representatives, and we look forward to our work with Congressman K. Mark Takai, who has a strong interest in AAPI and higher education policies at the national level.

We have been involved in getting AAPI faculty, students, and community leaders appointed to key decision-making positions such as the Hawai'i state board of education, University of Hawai'i board of regents, Hawai'i Civil Rights Commission, and Western Interstate Commission on Higher Education. These AAPI researchers and community leaders have been strong advocates for policies in multi-language policy, civil rights and immigrant rights, and other issues facing AAPI and other underrepresented groups.

We also note that campus governance structures can support or hamper institutional change. On most campuses, AAPI trustees, faculty, administrators, and students are part of a campus environment where they are a small minority and where their concerns are not a priority. We have no specific recommendations in this area other than to state the obvious need to build alliances, provide more support, and conduct research on AAPI leadership in campus politics and governance.

CONCLUSION

We express our appreciation to the readers for your interest, and our deep gratitude to the chapter authors for advancing scholarship and recommendations supporting the inclusion and success of underserved Asian Americans and Pacific Islanders in higher education. We appreciate and continue to learn from research studies that do not include recommendations on policy and practice. However, we urge more researchers to work with decision makers to make recommendations for programs and policies for quality and equity for all students, including AAPIs in higher education. Access to quality education is an American imperative, but gaps in income and education are widening. Some groups, including specific AAPI communities have the least access to higher education. We hope this book contributes to scholarship and actions to improve the status of AAPIs in higher education.

NOTE

1. Asian Pacific Americans (APA) was the term commonly used in the 1990s, and Asian Americans and Pacific Islanders (AAPI) is the more current term. These terms are used interchangeably in this chapter.

REFERENCES

Agbayani, A., & Ching, D. M. (1993, March). *Asian and Pacific Americans in higher education.* Paper presented at the National Association for Student Personnel Administrators (NASPA) Conference, Boston, MA.

Asian American Civil Rights. (2015, May). *135+ AAPI community organizations stand up for equal opportunity in higher education.* Retrieved from http://asianameri-cancivilrights.org/letter-equal-opportunity-higher-education

Asian American Legal Defense and Education. (2014, July). *AALDEF applauds appeals court's reaffirmation of UT-Austin's affirmative action program.* Retrieved from http://aaldef.org/press-releases/press-release/aaldef-applauds-appeals-courts-reaffirmation-of-ut-austins-action-program.html

Association for the Study of Higher Education. (2014). *Annual conference program.* Washington, DC: Association for the Study of Higher Education.

Ching, D. M., & Agbayani, A. (2012). *Asian Americans and Pacific Islanders in higher education: Research and perspectives on identity, leadership, and success.* Washington, DC: National Association of Student Personnel Administrators.

Department of Education. (2015, May 11). Applications for new awards: First in the world program-development grants. *Federal register: The daily journal of the United States government.* Retrieved from https://www.federalregister.gov/articles/2015/05/11/2015-11336/applications-for-new-awards-first-in-the-world-program-development-grants

Liedtke, M. (2015, May 6). Study: Top tech firms bypassing Asian workers for exec jobs. *The San Francisco Chronicle.* Retrieved from https://www.yahoo.com/tech/study-top-tech-firms-bypassing-asian-workers-exec-070345919.html

Mundy, L. (2014, November). Cracking the bamboo ceiling: Can Asian American men learn from *Lean In? The Atlantic.* Retrieved from http://www.theatlantic.com/magazine/archive/2014/11/cracking-the-bamboo-ceiling/380800/

Museus, S. D. (2009). A critical analysis of the exclusion of Asian American from higher education research and discourse. In L. Zhan (Ed.), *Asian American voices: Engaging, empowering, enabling* (pp. 59–76). New York, NY: National League for Nursing.

Ong, P., & Ong, E. (2015, May 7). *The future of Asian America in 2040.* Los Angeles, CA: UCLA Center for the Study of Inequality and Asian Pacific American Institute for Congressional Studies. Retrieved from http://luskin.ucla.edu/sites/default/files/AA2040_report.pdf

Turner, C. S. V., & Gonzales, J. C. (Eds.). (2014). *Modeling mentoring across race/ethnicity and gender.* Sterling, VA: Stylus.

White House Initiative on Asian Americans and Pacific Islanders. (2012). *Key facts and figures on Asian Americans and Pacific Islanders.* Retrieved from https://www.whitehouse.gov/administration/eop/aapi/data/facts-and-figures

Yamagata-Noji, A. & Gee, H. (2012). Asian American and Pacific Islanders in leadership: Pipeline or pipe dream? In D. M. Ching & A. Agbayani (Eds.), *Asian Americans and Pacific Islanders in higher education: Research and perspectives on identity, leadership, and success* (pp. 173–192). Washington, DC: National Association of Student Personnel Administrators.

ABOUT THE EDITORS

Sam Museus, PhD, is an associate professor of higher education and student affairs and serves as Founding Director of the Culturally Engaging Campus Environments (CECE) Project at Indiana University Bloomington. He has produced over 200 publications and conference presentations focused on understanding the racial, cultural, and structural factors that affect the educational experiences and outcomes of diverse populations education. These include 10 books, including *Asian American Students in Higher Education, Conducting Research on Asian Americans in Higher Education*, and *The Misrepresented Minority: New Insights on Asian Americans and Pacific Islanders, and the Implications for Higher Education.* He has also published several peer-reviewed academic journal articles in venues, such as the *Harvard Educational Review, Journal of College Student Development, Journal of Diversity in Higher Education, Journal of Higher Education, Review of Higher Education*, and *Teachers College Record.* Museus has received several national awards for his scholarship, including the Association for the Study of Higher Education's (ASHE) Early Career Award and the NASPA George D. Kuh Outstanding Contribution to Research and Literature Award.

Amefil "Amy" Agbayani, PhD, is a faculty member, former Assistant Vice Chancellor for Student Diversity and founding Director of Student Equity, Excellence, and Diversity at the University of Hawai'i at Mānoa. She has been a student affairs administrator for projects serving students from under-served groups, including Native Hawai'ians, underrepresented ethnic groups, women, students with disabilities, lesbian, gay, bisexual, and

Focusing on the Underserved, pages 255–256
Copyright © 2017 by Information Age Publishing
255

transgender individuals. She has been chair of the Hawai'i Commission on Civil Rights, Hawai'i Judicial Selection Commission, and the Filipino Community Center. Honpa Hongwanji Mission of Hawai'i honored her as a Living Treasure for preserving the spirit and values of Hawai'i and she has been recognized as one of the 100 Most Influential Filipina Women in the United States. Her research is in the area of diversity and inclusion in higher education and Filipinos in Hawai'i. She is co-editor of *Asian Americans and Pacific Islanders in Higher Education Research and Perspectives in Identity, Leadership, and Success* (2012). She received her bachelor's degree from the University of the Philippines, an East–West Center grant, and a PhD in political science from the University of Hawai'i at Mānoa.

Doris Ching, EdD, is Interim Chancellor of the University of Hawai'i (UH) West O'ahu and Emeritus Vice President for Student Affairs of the (UH) System. Her previous positions include Vice President for Student Affairs at the UH at Mānoa, assistant to the UH President, associate professor and Associate Dean of Education, Chair of International and Education of the Pacific International Center for High Technology Research, and others. Her EdD in Educational Administration and Supervision is from Arizona State University, and her BEd and MEd in secondary education are from UH–Mānoa. She was the first woman of color and first Asian Pacific Islander to be elected president of the National Association of Student Personnel Administrators (NASPA). She has served on numerous local and national boards, commissions, and accreditation teams, and has consulted in various states, Asia, and the Pacific Islands. She led the development and expansion of many UH programs to increase success and equal rights for all students. She is mentor to numerous student affairs and academic professionals of diverse ethnicities and racial backgrounds across the nation. She is recipient of the 2013 Asian and Pacific Islander American Scholarship Fund (APIASF) Higher Education Award, 2013 NASPA Region VI Mentoring Award, 2013 Hawai'i United Okinawa Association Legacy Award, 2012 NASPA Foundation Distinguished Achievement Award, 2011 NAAAP 100 Award, 2011 NASPA Legacy Award, 2004 Alpha Gamma Delta Distinguished Citizen Award, and numerous other recognitions. She is co-editor of Asian Americans and Pacific Islanders in Higher Education Research and Perspectives in Identity, Leadership, and Success (2012), and has served as chair of the Hawai'i Judicial Selection Commission and member of the Judicial Conduct Commission.

ABOUT THE CONTRIBUTORS

Jeffrey Tangonan Acido, PhD, is an educator in the field of popular education and critical pedagogy. He has taught Philippine courses and Nakem Theory and Pedagogy at the University of Hawai'i at Mānoa. He received his Doctorates in Education at the University of Hawai'i at Mānoa. A son of immigrant parents, he was born and raised in the Philippines and grew up in the working class and indigenous neighborhood of Kalihi. He is a Regent Emeritus on the University of Hawai'i Board of Regents and a program director for the Civic Engagement and Community Education department at Kokua Kalihi Valley. He serves in leadership roles on various local, national, and international community boards and organizations. He is co-editor of *Kabambannuagan: Our Voices, Our Lives. Hawai'i, 2010: Writings of Young Ilokanos in Hawai'i,* and author of *Barok, My Son: Rekuerdo Memento: Estrangement and Homing in Ilokano Poetics, 2009.* He received his BA in religion at UHM and was a 2005 Freeman Foundation Scholar. He received the MA degree in Theology from the Pacific School of Religion in Berkeley, California and studied at Kyungbook National University, Korea.

Sefa Aina is Director of the Asian American Resource Center (AARC) at Pomona College, California. His prior position was as a counselor, organizational advisor, and instructor at the University of California Los Angeles (UCLA) Asian American Studies Center. He is a founding member of Pacific Islander Education and Retention (PIER) program, which provides tutoring and mentoring for Pacific Islander youth in the Carson, Long Beach, and Inglewood areas of Los Angeles, California. He is a founding member

Focusing on the Underserved, pages 257–266
Copyright © 2017 by Information Age Publishing
257

of the National Pacific Islander Educators Network (NPIEN) and Empowering Pacific Islander Communities (EPIC). Mr. Aina graduated from UCLA with a BA in History and is currently in the Masters program in Asian American Studies at UCLA.

anthony lising antonio, PhD, is Associate Professor of Education, Associate Director of the Stanford Institute for Higher Education Research, and Director of the Asian American Studies Program at Stanford University. His research focuses on stratification and postsecondary access, impact of racial diversity on students and institutions, student friendship networks, and student development. His work is widely cited, and in 2004 he received the Early Career Award from the Association for the Study of Higher Education. In 2003, with collaborators Michael Kirst and Andrea Venezia, he published the policy report and brief, *Betraying the College Dream: How Disconnected K–12 and Postsecondary Education Systems Undermine Student Aspirations*, one of the most widely cited reports on college access and K–16 education policy. His work has been published in *Journal of Higher Education, Research in Higher Education, Psychological Science, Review of Higher Education*, and *Anthropology and Education Quarterly*. His research projects include extensive student survey work, multi-site longitudinal case studies, and randomized control trials of college counseling interventions. He has received grant support from Hewlett, Carnegie, Ford, Spencer, and Irvine Foundations.

Tracy Lachica Buenavista is an associate professor in the Department of Asian American Studies at California State University, Northridge (CSUN) and a Research Fellow with the Asian American and Pacific Islander Research Coalition (ARC). She is also co-principal investigator for the CSUN Dreamers, Resources, Empowerment, Advocacy, and Mentorship (DREAM) Center, one of the first undocumented student resource projects in the California State University system. She has published articles on U.S. Pilipina/o college access and retention, undocumented Asian student experiences, and the militarization of immigration reform in various journals including *AAPI Nexus, Amerasia, Asian American Policy Review*, and *Race Ethnicity and Education*. She has also contributed to several book projects focused on Asian American and Pilipina/o American educational experiences, and co-edited with her colleagues, *"White" Washing American Education: The New Culture Wars in Ethnic Studies* and *Navigating the Great Recession: Immigrant Families' Stories of Resilience*. Dr. Buenavista received her PhD in Education at the University of California, Los Angeles and MA in Asian American Studies at San Francisco State University.

Mitchell J Chang is Professor of Higher Education and Organizational Change and Asian American Studies (by courtesy) at UCLA. Chang's research focuses on diversity-related issues and initiatives on college campuses. He has written over ninety publications, some of which have been cited in U.S. Supreme Court rulings concerning the use of race conscious admissions practices. Chang received a National Academy of Education/ Spencer Fellowship in 2001 and was recognized for outstanding research in both 2000 and 2008 by the American College Personnel Association. In 2006, *Diverse: Issues in Higher Education* profiled him as one of the nation's top ten scholars. Chang has also served in elected positions for both the American Educational Research Association, which inducted him as a Fellow in 2016, and the Association for the Study of Higher Education, which awarded him the Founder's Service Award in 2014.

Anna Chiang, received her MA degree in Higher Education at the University of Michigan and her BA degree in Ethnic Studies at the University of California, Berkeley. Broadly, she is interested in college access, educational equity, and institutional diversity in higher education. Currently, she is a research assistant at the Detroit Schools–Higher Education Consortium, working on a project that documents and examines university outreach partnerships in Detroit, MI.

William (Nick) Collins, PhD, is Executive Director of the Center for Educational Outreach at the University of Michigan (UM). He previously served as director of the Comprehensive Studies Program and adjunct associate professor of Psychology at UM, director of the Learning Skills Center at Cornell University, and staff psychologist and assistant professor of Psychology at the University of Wisconsin–Stevens Point. He earned the bachelor's degree and doctorate in psychology from the University of Michigan and is a member of the Association for Psychological Science, Society for Personality and Social Psychology, and Society for the Psychological Study of Social Issues.

Jennifer Custodio, MEd, is a program developer in the College of Professional and Global Education at California State University, Los Angeles. She earned her MA in American Studies and MEd in Educational Administration in Higher Education from the University of Hawai'i at Mānoa and her BA in History from California State University, Long Beach. Her research interest focuses on the academic advising experiences of first-generation college-goers and the recruitment and retention of under-represented students of color in higher education. Previously, she served as an educational specialist and academic advisor at the University of Hawai'i at Mānoa.

Loan Thi Dao, PhD, is an assistant professor of Asian American Studies at the University of Massachusetts Boston. She is a graduate of the Comparative

Ethnic Studies doctoral program at the University of California Berkeley and completed her undergraduate degree at the University of Texas Austin in Pre-Law with a major in Psychology and a minor in Mass Communications. Her fields of specialty include Southeast Asian refugee migration and community development, immigrant and refugee youth, and social movements.

Christin DePouw, PhD, is an assistant professor in the Professional Program in Education at the University of Wisconsin–Green Bay. She has worked with Hmong American communities around issues of race and education for over 15 years, focusing on the impact of institutional and cultural racism on the educational experiences of Hmong American youth. Her areas of interest include critical race theory in education, critical Whiteness studies, Hmong American studies, and educational policy. She received her PhD from the University of Illinois, and MEPD and BA degrees from the University of Wisconsin–La Crosse.

Joshua Fisher has a MA in higher education with a concentration in diversity and social justice from the University of Michigan. His degree concentration aligns closely with his personal and professional experience. For the past seven years Joshua has worked for various non-profit organizations coordinating youth leadership programming with underrepresented students in California, Michigan, and New York.

Peter Nien-chu Kiang (江念祖), PhD, is Professor and Director of the Asian American Studies Program and professor of curriculum and instruction in the College of Education and Human Development at the University of Massachusetts Boston where he has taught since 1987. Peter's research focuses on the impact of education in the development of Asian American studies programs, the connection between veterans and Asian American studies, and continuing education with the refugee and immigrant populations. His research, teaching, and advocacy in both K-12 and higher education with Asian American immigrant and refugee students and communities have been supported by the National Academy of Education, National Endowment for the Humanities, Massachusetts Teachers Association, Massachusetts Association for Bilingual Education, and others. He received the Lifetime Achievement Award from the National Association for Asian American Studies in 2014.

Simon Kim, PhD, is a professor of Educational Psychology and serves as Associate Vice President for Research and Sponsored Programs at California State University, Long Beach (CSULB). His research agenda includes educational partnerships and accountability, culturally and linguistically diverse students, and conceptualization and practice of evaluation of educational programs. He has authored many refereed journal articles, book chapters, and technical reports; served on the Leadership Council of the Long Beach College Promise; and is former chair of the California K–16 Partnerships and Student Success Conference for educators and policymakers. He has played a leadership role in developing and implementing student success initiatives at CSULB, including learning communities, regional collaborative education partnerships, and programs to support students from underrepresented Asian American and Pacific Islander communities. Kim received his BA in mathematics from Westminster College, MS in operations research from the University of Kentucky, and PhD in educational psychology from the University of Southern California.

Angela W. Kong, PhD, is a coordinator in the Office of Academic Support and Instructional Services at University of California, San Diego and adjunct instructor at Miramar Community College. She is a daughter of immigrant parents and a product of San Francisco public schools. She has worked with Summer Bridge Programs, and TRiO's Student Support Services and McNair Scholars Programs supporting low-income and first-generation college students to successfully transition to and graduate from college. She uses an interdisciplinary lens in higher education and ethnic studies with the goal of challenging students, faculty, and administrators to understand Asian Pacific Islander American student experiences in relation to achieving social and educational equity for diverse communities. She is a founding member of Outrigger Hoe Wana'ao, a non-profit organization in San Diego, California. She earned a doctorate in Ethnic studies from UC San Diego, bachelor's degree in Psychology, and master's degree in Counseling and Student Personnel from San Jose State University.

Keali'i Troy Kukahiko founded PISA's Carson High School Tutoring & Mentorship Program in 1998, now called Pacific Islander Education and Retention program (PIER) at the University of California Los Angeles (UCLA). He has supported various nonprofit organizations such as the AIGA Foundation (www.AIGAfoundation.com). He has trained and mentored student-athletes for the last 15 years, and his mission is to create opportunities for higher education through athletics. His company, *Prodigy Athletes*, provides customized sports training programs, expert coaching, and exclusive exposure, in a concentrated, high energy, focused environment. He is pursuing a doctoral degree from UCLA's Higher Education & Organizational Change (HEOC) program, and his research is on student-athletes and the experience of Pacific Islanders in college sports.

V. Leilani Kupo, PhD, a Native Hawai'ian raised away from her ancestral land of Maui, Hawai'i, grew up in the continental United States and often questioned her right to claim her Native Hawai'ian ancestry. She depended on her 'ohana (family) to guide and teach her cultural practices from a distance. She is the Director for the Calvin E. Bright Success Center at University of California–Merced. Her research interests include educational access, identity intersectionality, gender equity, and indigenous knowledge, which she explores from national and international perspectives. Her dissertation topic, *What is Hawai'ian?: Exploring Native Hawai'ian College Women's Understandings and Conception of Identity* focused on issues of culturally relevant education, indigenous knowledge systems, bicultural/multicultural identity, and the impact the collegiate environment has on cultural and gender identity development.

Gordon Lee, PhD, JD, MPH, was born on the island of O'ahu. He is the great grandson of immigrants and grandson of farmers from Kalihi Valley, Hawai'i. He is an educator and theorist of Asian Diasporic Psychology and History. He studied psychology at Pacifica Graduate Institute and taught Asian American Studies at San Francisco State University. Presently, he is a lecturer at University of Hawai'i at Manoa (UHM) where he teaches Community and Liberation Psychology.

Niki Libarios, PhD, is Director of the Office of Student Academic Services in the College of Education at the University of Hawai'i at Mānoa. Niki previously served as an academic advisor in the same office, as a counselor for Honolulu Community College, and as an elementary education teacher for the Hawai'i Department of Education. His research interest centers on Filipinos in higher education with a focus on recruitment, persistence, and transfer. Niki has been active in several Filipino organizations and is co-chair of the *TINALAK Filipino Advisory Council* in the College of Education which he helped co-found in 2012. Niki earned his PhD in Education with a Specialization in Educational Administration from the University of Hawai'i at Mānoa where he also obtained a BEd in Elementary Education. He also received an MS in Counseling Psychology from Chaminade University and an AA in Liberal Arts from Leeward Community College.

Karen Nakai, EdD, is Chief of Staff to the President at California State University, Long Beach. She previously served as Assistant Chair, Department of Advanced Studies in Education and Counseling and Director of Field Programs in the Department of Teacher Education. As a Professor of Educational Leadership, Karen has provided professional development for pre-service and practicing PreK–16 teachers and administrators. She has partnered with local school districts and educational institutions to facilitate and support reciprocal learning experiences. Her research interests include pre-service, induction, and professional development for teachers and administrators; educational leadership and school renewal; and school-university partnerships. She is a former public school teacher and principal and has worked collaboratively with educators and community members to enhance educational opportunities, experiences, and learning for all students. She serves on the Asian American Pacific Islander (AAPI) Steering Committee for the California State University.

Sumun L. Pendakur, EdD, is Associate Dean for Institutional Diversity at Harvey Mudd College. Sumi is a member of the president's cabinet and serves as the co-Chief Diversity Officer, partnering with Academic Affairs, to focus on campus-wide efforts related to access, equity, campus climate, and inclusion. She also directs HMC's social justice education center, the Office of Institutional Diversity (OID). Sumi serves as a consultant, speaker, and facilitator regionally and nationally, helping campuses, non-profits, and other organizations build capacity for cultural competence, social justice, and equitable practices. Prior to Harvey Mudd College, Sumi spent 7.5 years at the University of Southern California, where she served as the director for Asian Pacific American Student Services. She is a scholar-practitioner, whose research interests include critical race theory, Asian American and Pacific Islander students, and institutional transformation. Pendakur is a graduate of Northwestern University with a double major in Women's Studies and History and a Minor in Spanish. She holds an MA in Higher Education Administration from the University of Michigan. She received her doctorate in Higher Education Leadership from the USC Rossier School of Education.

Vijay Pendakur, EdD, is an associate vice president in the Division of Student Affairs at California State University–Fullerton. He holds a BA in History and East Asian Studies from the University of Wisconsin–Madison and an MA in U.S. History from the University of California–San Diego. He completed a doctoral degree in education from DePaul University with a dissertation titled, *Asian American College Students: Making Racial Meaning in an Era of Color-Blind Racism*. He is the editor of the new book, *Closing the Opportunity Gap: Identity-Conscious Strategies for Retention and Student Success* and is the author of several chapters on Asian American race consciousness and color-blind racism. His primary research interests are Asian American college students, critical race theory, and college student retention and student success interventions.

Karen Quintiliani, PhD, is a professor and the chair of the Department of Anthropology at California State University, Long Beach. She has conducted ethnographic and applied research in the Long Beach Cambodian community since 1988. She has worked as an applied anthropologist for community based organizations, specializing in developing and implementing programs focused on community health and education for Southeast Asians and their children. Her areas of research include: cultural history of the Cambodian immigrant experience; social welfare policy; gender and sexuality; refugee and immigrant health; youth cultures; and program development and evaluation. She is the co-founder and director with Dr. Susan Needham of the Cambodian Community History & Archive Project (www.camchap.org). She has served on the Advisory Council and the Board of Directors of Cambodia Town, Inc. and is also the associate editor for the journal *Collaborative Anthropologies.*

Natasha Saelua is a research project associate at Indiana University's Center for Postsecondary Research. Prior to pursuing her doctoral degree in higher education, Natasha served as associate director at the University of California Los Angeles (UCLA) Community Programs Office. She is a founding member of the UCLA Pacific Islander Education and Retention (PIER) project, an outreach effort by Pacific Islander undergraduates to support high school students and youth in Southern California. She received both her Master of Arts degree in Asian American Studies (2013), and Bachelor of Arts degree in History (2001), from UCLA. Born and raised a military brat, her homeland is Tutuila, American Samoa.

Mary Ann Takemoto, PhD, is the associate vice president for Student Affairs, and director of Student Health Services at California State University, Long Beach (CSULB). She previously served as Director for Counseling and Psychological Services at CSULB. She was also a lecturer in Asian American Studies and Psychology at University of California Irvine (UCI) and associate director and training director of the UCI Counseling Center. She is a licensed psychologist who has been involved in administration, consultation, training, and private practice. Her interests include Asian American mental health, multicultural counseling, women's issues, and wellness. She received her BA from Barnard College, Columbia University and her PhD in Clinical Psychology from Indiana University. Her internship was completed in the department of Psychiatry at Yale University.

Meg Malpaya Thornton is coordinator for Student and Community Engagement with the University of California Los Angeles (UCLA) Asian American Studies Center. She is a Pilipina Islander who navigates the changing currents of the higher education institution working with first generation/working class/emerging majority student–scholar–activists. She is on the working committee for the Native and Pacific Islander Summer Intensive Transfer Experience with the UCLA Center for Community College Partnerships.

Marie Ting, PhD, is the associate director at the National Center for Institutional Diversity (NCID) at the University of Michigan. The mission of the NCID is to strengthen and integrate research about diversity, equity, and inclusion in education and society, and to promote its effective use in addressing contemporary issues. She joined the NCID after serving as a program manager at the University of Michigan's Center for Educational Outreach (CEO), which is designed to promote pathways and access to higher education for underserved communities. Marie has also served as university director of student affairs and special programs at the City University of New York (CUNY), one of the nation's leading public urban universities. Marie earned her bachelor's degree in psychology and a master's degree in higher education from the University of Michigan, and her doctorate in higher education policy and leadership from the University of Maryland.

Linda Tran is currently a senior pursuing a bachelor degree in Biology at the University of Massachusetts, Boston. She is a second generation Vietnamese American born and raised in Dorchester, Massachusetts. She is currently a supporting member of the Vietnamese Student Association (VSA) and the creative director of the Asian Student Center (ASC) at the University of Massachusetts.

Phitsamay Sychitkokhong Uy, PhD, is assistant professor in Leadership in Schooling at University of Massachusetts–Lowell. Her research focuses on Southeast Asian immigrant students' educational experiences and family/community engagement. Her K–16 experience includes teacher, literacy specialist, youth development coordinator, and Asian American Studies instructor. She has developed planning strategies for community-based organizations, professional development for schools, and research and evaluation projects for school districts, including examining immigrants' dropouts and achievement gaps and minority students' STEM pipeline. Her BS in Human Resource Management and MEd in Curriculum and Instruction are from Boston College. Her MEd and EdD in Administration, Planning, Social Policy are from Harvard University—the first Lao American to receive the EdD from Harvard. She is former Solicitation editor of *Harvard Educational Review* and current associate editor of *Journal of Southeast Asian American Education and Advancement.* She has served on the board of directors of Southeast Asia Resource Action Center (SEARAC), Asian American Resource Workshop (AARW), UMass Boston Institute for Asian American Studies, and others.

Erin Kahunawaika'ala Wright, PhD, is Kanaka 'Ōiwi Hawai'i (Native Hawai'ian) from Kalihi, O'ahu raised on the land that has fostered her mother's family for the last five generations. Currently, she serves as an assistant professor for the Educational Administration department in the College of Education at the University of Hawaiʻi at Mānoa. Previously, Kahunawai served as the Director of Native Hawaiʻian Student Services at the University of Hawaiʻi at Mānoa in Hawaiʻinuiākea School of Hawaiʻian Knowledge, an award-winning culturally-grounded, community-minded program designed to support all Native Hawaiʻians interested in pursuing higher education. Her scholarly work focuses on understanding the intersections of Native Hawaiʻian and Pacific Islander identities and higher education and the ways these insights inform educational environments and kuleana lāhui. She prioritizes collaborative research and writing and has utilized and disseminated her research in a variety of ways including successful grant proposals, book chapters, technical reports, and journal articles. Among her most recent publications are two books, *A Nation Rising: Hawaiʻian Movements for Life, Land, and Sovereignty* (co-edited with Noelani Goodyear-Kaʻōpua and Ikaika Hussey, 2014, Duke University Press) and *Kanaka ʻŌiwi Methodologies: Moʻolelo and Metaphor* (co-edited with KapKapā Oliveira Oliveira, 2016, University of Hawaiʻi Press).

CPSIA information can be obtained
at www.ICGtesting.com
Printed in the USA
BVHW040216090319

542226BV00004B/5/P